ESSENTIAL
TURKISH
CUISINE

ENGIN AKIN

PHOTOGRAPHY BY HELEN CATHCART

STEWART, TABORI & CHANG | NEW YORK

Published in 2015 by Stewart, Tabori & Chang
An imprint of ABRAMS

Text copyright © 2015 Engin Akin
Photographs copyright © 2015 Helen Cathcart
Additional photographs by Bekir İşcen (pages 8, 9, 60, 99, 141,
166, 173, 199, 248, 253, 256) copyright © 2015 by Bekir İşcen
Styled by Helen Cathcart

Library of Congress Control Number: 2014959137

ISBN: 978-1-61769-172-0

Editor: Camaren Subhiyah
Designer: Kimberly Glyder
Production Manager: True Sims

The text of this book was composed in
ITC Galliard Pro, Exquise FY, and Neutra Text
Printed and bound in China

10 9 8 7 6 5 4 3 2 1

Stewart, Tabori & Chang books are available at special discounts
when purchased in quantity for premiums and promotions as
well as fundraising or educational use. Special editions can also
be created to specification. For details, contact specialsales@
abramsbooks.com or the address below.

115 West 18th Street
New York, NY 10011
www.abramsbooks.com

CONTENTS

Foreword

The first time I saw Istanbul was as a student in the mid-1980s. Back then, donkey carts still trundled across the old iron Galata Bridge and the *dolmuş* (shared taxis; same etymology as the word *dolma*, or "stuffed") were hoary 1950s Plymouths and Chevrolets. And from the very first day I was smitten. I couldn't get enough of the magical skyline with its domes and rocket-like minarets; I kept riding the hulking white public ferries at dusk as the skies flared up cinematically over the sixth-century silhouette of the Hagia Sophia. But mainly I was hooked on the food. With its succulent kebabs and simple grilled fish, its healthful vegetable stews, bright salads, *böreks* (shaggy savory pastries), and sun-ripened vegetables, Turkish cuisine seemed to me like the last undiscovered frontier of Mediterranean cooking. I got addicted to the tulip-shaped glasses of strong, sweet tea drunk in shady tea gardens. I loved the dollhouse-like baklava shops and the scent of grilled mackerel sandwiches along the docks. I spent my evenings at *meyhane*, atmospheric dens serving raki (an anisey spirit) and all manner of meze (small plates), from creamy garlicky dips to stuffed mussels. Even the slender cucumbers sold by street vendors as a refresher seemed somehow ambrosial. And the meals often came framed by views so breathtakingly beautiful, I couldn't shake off the feeling that the city was a mirage.

More than a decade later, as a newly minted food writer, I returned to report a magazine article on Istanbul's foodscape and had the blessed luck of having Engin Akin as my guide to the city's clamorous bazaars, smoky kebab joints, and genteel fish restaurants on the Bosphorus shores where white-jacketed waiters ceremoniously mosaicked the table with meze. Though previously we'd met only briefly at a food conference in Greece, Engin tended to me with unflagging zeal—Turkish hospitality personified. Going around with Engin was thrilling, and a little intimidating. A walking textbook on Ottoman food mores and vernacular street snacks, she examined spices like a sultan inspecting troops, haggled fishmongers and butchers into submission, imperiously waved away any morsel of food she considered imperfect. Together we searched for the ultimate *lahmacun* (wafer-thin, lamb-topped flatbreads baked in a wood-burning oven), the most pistachio-intensive baklava, and the plumpest *mantı* (thimble-size dumplings) served under a tart cloak of yogurt.

I kept returning to Istanbul again and again, until finally, besotted with the city and inspired by Engin, I ended up buying an apartment there—a little place with a Bosphorus view. Now I own my own set of tulip-shape glasses for sipping tea while gazing at the boat traffic outside my window. Istanbul's restaurant food is more delicious than ever, but it's nothing compared to the flavors in people's homes—especially Engin's home, where dinner could involve an Ottoman-era stuffed melon, an epic lamb shank with burnished, caramelized quince, and homemade halva for dessert.

Over some two decades of friendship, Engin and I have cooked together at many different places. Or rather she's cooked and I've watched—and tried to keep up and take notes. "Turkish cuisine marries palace finesse with rugged nomadic traditions," Engin will expound while fashioning an addictive *börek* from thin sheets of *yufka* pastry and a meat filling sweetened with masses of onions, or while putting a fragrant finishing flourish of mastic on an Ottoman pilaf. On Engin's boat during an indolent Aegean voyage, instead of the usual boat fare—*makarna*, or pasta—she'll concoct a sophisticated warm salad of bulgur studded with walnuts and pomegranate seeds.

At the cooking school Engin operates in her stately ancestral home in the traditional hamlet of Ula, I've learned my all-time favorite eggplant preparation: charred over live fire, briefly sautéed in olive oil with sun-dried tomatoes, then presented on a bed of garlicky yogurt with a finish of sizzled brown butter. That, and a majestic clay pot–baked chicken stuffed with spiced rice. At Engin's Istanbul house, I've watched her throw an impromptu meze party for ten on her lush grassy lawn overlooking the Bosphorus. From that bash, I picked up her recipe for dainty herbed *köfte* (meatballs) laced with pistachios, which I make all the time, and braised fresh pinto beans scented with cinnamon.

Back in New York, craving more "Engin food," I've urged her many times to write a Turkish cookbook in English. Finally, that book is here. It's the product of Engin's skills as a cooking teacher, her flair in the kitchen, and her deep love and knowledge of her country's cuisine, culture, and history. The recipes you'll find in it are both classic and fresh. As the title suggests, the book is indeed "essential" thanks to primers on Turkey's garlicky dips, smoky grilled meats, plump stuffed vegetables, earthy meat-and-legume stews, and syrup-drenched pastries. But there are also surprises aplenty. You will be introduced to *zeytinyağlı* (zey-thin-yah-lih), a wondrous silken veggie confit in which beans or artichokes or leeks are braised for an eternity in olive oil with a secret pinch of sugar that teases out their natural sweetness. You will discover fresh, surprising flavor combinations such as lentils with quince and mint from the town of Bolu, bulgur with chestnuts and tangerines (Engin's invention), and every iteration of eggplant. And if, like me, you regard cuisine as a window onto culture and history, Engin's texts on everything from the grand kitchens of the Ottoman palaces to the evolution of Turkish meze rituals will keep you up all night reading. Welcome to the wondrous world of Turkish cuisine.

— Anya von Bremzen

Introduction

When you think of Turkish food, you may envision the sumptuous array of small plates known as meze—delectable savory pastries filled with meat and vegetables, hummus and smoky-eggplant dips served with grilled flatbread, refreshing cucumber salads, and briny olives, all shared communally alongside drinks. Or perhaps you've purchased shish kebabs, succulent char-grilled meat on a stick, from a street vendor. If you have a sweet tooth, you may also conjure up images of the pastel candies called Turkish delight, or flaky pastries dripping with honey, served alongside a small, dark and frothy cup of Turkish coffee. Turkish cooking is all of this and so much more.

The Roots of Turkish Cooking

This venerable cuisine has its origins in pastoral times, when Turks lived in what is now called Mongolia, north of China. The history of these Turkish tribes can be traced back to 3000 BCE. Descended from the Huns, the Hsiung-Nu, as the Chinese called them, were said to be the best archers and horsemen on the Asian steppes, and legend has it that the Chinese built the Great Wall to guard against their invasions.

Over the centuries, as these nomadic tribes moved westward to the sea, Turkish cuisine came to encompass a fusion of food cultures inspired by not only the diverse inhabitants and landscapes of Turkey's expanding borders, but also through trade with countries near and far, from China to India, Persia, Arabia, Eastern Europe, and the entire coastline of the Mediterranean and almost the entire northern half of Africa.

(ABOVE) LEFT TO RIGHT: WHOLE CLOVES, DRIED BLACK PEPPERS, AND CUMIN SEEDS.

We can assume these Asian tribes grazed their animals in highland pastures in the summer and wintered in their valley settlements, but their diet would have been limited and dependent for their sustenance primarily on sheep and goats and the products made from their milk. Yogurt was a critical component of this early Turkish diet, and one of the most significant Turkish culinary contributions to the world. It was—and still is—drained in muslin bags and either kept that way or, when solid enough, made into balls and dried. The dried *keş*, as it is called, can be kept "forever" and is either diluted or, if mixed with herbs, grated to be used in different dishes.

Another dairy dish that dates back to the Turks' earliest nomadic days is *kaymak* (literally "cream"), which is the cream retrieved from warmed milk (similar to clotted cream). The Chinese called it *su* and their Turkish neighbors provided it to them. The dumplings the Chinese offered in trade are said to have been an inspiration for the popular Turkish pasta dish *mantı* (page 219), which takes its name from Chinese *mantou*. The dumpling inspiration is very likely, but the traditional garlic and yogurt sauce served with *mantı* makes the dish very Turkish.

As the range of the Turkish tribes expanded, new tastes were integrated into their gastronomy. In the mid-500s, the Göktürks (the first Turkish tribe to officially call themselves Turks) consolidated power in their traditional tribal lands and established the Göktürk Empire.

The Oguz Turks, consisting of twenty-four clans not wanting to be ruled by the Göktürks, crossed Central Asia from east to west, first settling near the middle course of the Syr Darya river and along the eastern coast of the Aral Sea, next to what is now the western Kazakhstan steppes. They eventually united politically and founded the Oguz Yabgu state in year 750 CE.

This migration provided new opportunities for the Oguz, as those who did not own large herds were able to farm and fish. Thus, during the Middle Ages, Turks became so well established in Central Asia, it was inevitably "Turkified" so much that the area was named *Oguzeli*, meaning "the land of the Oguz." When the Turkish state Karakhanids conquered Transoxania (between the Syr Darya and Amu Darya, bordering Oğuzeli) and ruled it from 999 to 1211, their arrival signaled a definitive shift from Persian to Turkish predominance in Central Asia. With Arab immigration during the seventh and eighth centuries, the population of the territory became mixed. Turkish-speaking people were in the majority, but the administrative language was Arabic, and Persian was the intellectual language.

The eleventh-century dictionary *Divanü Lügat-it Türk* by Mahmut from Kaşgar, which translates Turkish to Arabic, is an invaluable resource for studying the culinary world of the Turks during this time. It depicts a more varied Turkish food scene that reflects the change from a nomadic to a semi-nomadic culture. Now with states of their own, by farming, fishing, and hunting, the Turks could and did widen the borders of their gastronomy. By this time they were already seasoning their dishes with saffron, pepper, and garlic. Their affinity to make use of the aromatic greens found in the flora of wherever they settled is a continued legacy today that gives unique character to the regional cuisine.

From the wide range of terms for vineyards and winemaking found in this dictionary, we know that they were involved extensively in making wine along with other fermented alcoholic drinks. Prohibition of making and drinking wine during the Ottoman era due to Islamic orders had put an end to it. By order of Mustafa Kemal Atatürk, founder of the Turkish Republic in 1923, many

research centers for wine were established all around Turkey, leading the way for a number of wine producers. Today Turkey produces excellent wines.

A description of banquets like *yoğ* (banquets in honor of the dead) shows that food was the center of Turkish life, much as it is today. Women of the time were expert in making thin breads called *yuwka* (see *yufka*, as it is now called, page 50). Their legacy now lies in the expert hands of Turkish men who provide us with these thin sheets of dough, which is easily shaped at home into savory *böreks*, desserts, and other preparations.

Kavurma, small cubes of meat cooked in the animal's tail fat then salted, was stored in large earthenware containers for later consumption. Thinly sliced beef was also salted, spiced, and dried in an airy, shaded area to make *pastırma*. Both preparations remain popular today. In fact, *kavurma* is one of the favored ingredients of *pide*, an essential bread filled with a variety of fillings (page 196).

And although the drying of all kinds of foods, including in-season vegetables and fruits, was a matter of survival in those times, today almost every village household continues the tradition, making ingredients like tomato paste (page 21), vinegar (page 102), the ubiquitous soup mix *tarhana* (page 118), and bulgur.

THE ESSENCE OF ANATOLIAN CUISINE

When the Turks came to the Anatolian Peninsula, the roots of Turkish cuisine were already formed. To this medley of food they now added all the unique flavors of this varied region with its diversity of flora and climates. Eastern Anatolian cuisine (like that of its neighboring nations, Syria, Iraq, and Iran) is known for its variety of spices. Cumin, coriander, and herbs such as mint, dill, tarragon, purple basil, and green fenugreek infused traditional dishes with new flavors and aromas. Western Anatolian cuisine shows a Mediterranean and Aegean influence with its liberal use of olive oil and fresh, easy-to-make condiments. Almost every preparation is finished with a sprinkling of fresh herbs, giving each dish a freshness and vitality.

The last people to settle in Anatolia, Turks discovered that Anatolia's fertile soil could grow quality wheat to sustain them. Their farming heritage, acquired along the banks of Syr Darya river, has become a legacy in Anatolia. Wheat products like bread, bulgur, and *yufka* (used both as thin bread and as the dough for *böreks* and pastry desserts like baklava) thus became an integral part of Turkish culture and a unifying factor among all the regional cuisines. Special *firik* wheat, previously called *suruş,* produced by smoking the young milky kernels and then pounding them into a type of bulgur, is one of the unique assets of the famous gastronomy of the southeastern city of Gaziantep.

Arabic, Persian, and Islamic Influences

By the tenth century, the Turkish tribes of Central Asia gained political strength in lands far and near, including India, all of Arabia, and a large part of Persia. Arabic cuisine, which most likely was influenced by the Persian use of spices and elaborate way of cooking, made an impact, especially on the Turks' elite and ruling class. In time, however, these sophisticated cuisines intertwined with the simplicity of nomadic foods to create a unique Turkish character.

THE ASTOUNDING REACH OF THE OTTOMAN EMPIRE

The Ottoman Empire, named after its founder Osman (of the Oguz Turks), was one of the most extensive and enduring empires in history. By the end of the fifteenth century, the Ottomans established themselves as a world power in Europe, and at its zenith in the sixteenth century, the empire encompassed a coastline of 3,200 miles along the Black Sea, the Mediterranean, the Red Sea, and the Persian Gulf, the longest coastline of any single state in history. As undisputed masters of the Eastern Mediterranean, Turks traveled from the imperial capital of Constantinople (now Istanbul) overland to the Balkans and by sea to the Arab world, returning with new flavors that eventually altered and refined the existing Mediterranean food culture.

They easily adopted ingredients used by other cultures and modified these cuisines to suit their own tastes. A good example is the world-famous *Imam Bayıldı* (page 127). The dish integrates eggplants from India, the garlic known to the Turks' nomadic ancestors, and the New World's tomato with olive oil from the Mediterranean, cooked slowly in the style of Arabic and Persian cuisines. The unique and original dishes the Turks created were a fusion of styles and food cultures that resulted in the creation of one of the world's leading cuisines.

Turks also exported Turkish cuisine to other parts of the globe, and many international foods today still reflect that heritage. For example, Turks quickly accepted the large, broad-breasted poultry imported by the Spanish from North America into their own cuisine. When these dishes were in turn exported to Europe, the birds became knows as turkeys, and that name was brought *back* to the Americas by the first English settlers there.

Peppers were another imported ingredient introduced to other lands through the Ottomans. Hungarians for a long while called peppers "Turkish eggplants," while Italians referred to corn as *grano turco,* also thinking it came from Turkey.

The New World's products were more than welcomed. Tomatoes gave a new face and taste to Turkish dishes and became the indispensable ingredient, simmering in olive oil with meat and other vegetables of worlds both old and new, like peppers, potatoes, zucchinis, green beans, corn, and pumpkins. To these regional fresh herbs and other traditionally nomadic ingredients would be

(OPPOSITE PAGE) OTTOMAN-ERA CUTLERY.

added, giving preparations a unique Turkish taste and character. *Böreks* now had a great variety of vegetable fillings; fried dishes like eggplant, potatoes, and zucchini would benefit from the tangy taste of yogurt sauce; legumes like dried beans and chickpeas were now cooked with tomatoes and became tasty and nutritional enough to be served on their own.

The Turks' love for fish flourished in the coastal areas of Anatolia, a peninsula with three sides surrounded by seas. The fish of the Black, Aegean, and Mediterranean seas are still eaten with the simplest of preparations.

The influence of the Turks on many towns that were either built or expanded during the Ottoman era—Sarajevo and Mostar in Bosnia and Herzegovina, Kavala, and Salonika in Greece, Chania in Crete, Skopje in Macedonia, Elbasan in Albania, Budapest in Hungary, and many others in the Balkans or Eastern Europe—is reflected in magnificent Ottoman architectural elements like mosques, bridges, khans (small country inns), hamams (baths), and other relics from the Turkish Ottoman culture once present in these places.

Sarma, *turli göveç (tave)*, baklava, *kadayıf*, *çörek*, and *börek* (page 200) have become part of the traditional cuisines of all these countries, just as they are in Turkey. Ultimately, Turks left imprints of their culture in both Asia and the West, and they transformed the Ottoman heartland into a melting pot of several distinct cultures.

The Imperial Palace and Its Kitchens

In 1453, more than 150 years after the Empire was founded, its seventh Sultan, Mehmed II, conquered Istanbul and brought an end to the Eastern Roman (Byzantine) Empire. The dream to rule over both Asia and Europe had become a reality, and the twenty-three-year-old sultan would be known as Mehmed the Conqueror.

After Sultan Mehmed captured Constantinople, one of his first acts was to build Topkapı Palace, which would be a home for the sultans until 1856. At its peak, the palace was home to almost 4,000 people, while the kitchen staff numbered more than 1,200. This was the first step toward the development of the palace cuisine, which would become a lifestyle model for Turkish subjects, even more so for people of social or governmental importance within the borders of the Empire. This is why you will find dishes that can be traced back to the palace kitchen in all areas of Turkey in addition to regional cuisines.

THE CUISINE OF THE IMPERIAL PALACE

In Turkish palace cuisine, appearance and innovation were secondary to the flavor of the food, which was absolutely paramount, and chefs were expected to attain perfection. The palace kitchens always emphasized flavorful ingredients, prepared simply but flawlessly to best showcase any virtues or faults in the ingredients themselves, a philosophy that is strikingly in line with many of today's most revered chefs internationally. Even haute Turkish cuisine has always possessed an elegant simplicity. This is why the culinary ties between the palace and the public were never severed. The same simple styles are still followed today, and even people who have Turkish food for the first time usually do not find the taste exotic.

SUPPLYING THE PALACE KITCHENS: SUPERB QUALITY, ENORMOUS QUANTITIES

The splendid ceremonies, lavish banquets, and large population of the palace meant that it was an astoundingly huge institution that consumed five hundred sheep per day. Ultimately, the palace created an immense kitchen that placed no limits on the quality or quantity of ingredients. A monthly list from the palace archives in 1526, during the Ottoman Empire's golden age, includes 544 chickens, 61 geese, 11 pounds of saffron, 116 mussels, 87 lobsters, 400 fish, 5 ounces of musk, 6 pounds of black pepper, 6½ pounds of olive oil, 7 gallons of molasses, 49 pounds of Wallachia salt, 7½ pounds of starch, 51 jars of *boza* (a fermented millet drink), the heads and trotters of 616 sheep, 180 tripe, and 649 eggs.

These ingredients and many others were assembled by virtue of an unbounded geography. As the capital city of the empire, Constantinople was supplied with rare gastronomical delights from all over the world: rice, sugar, spices, dates, and plums from Eygpt; fragrant apples from Crete; cheese from Milan; white amber (for sherbet) from the coasts of Japan and Madagascar; and mastic from Chios (Sakız) Island, a Greek island just off the Turkish Aegean coast. Merging the rainbow of colors and flavors of these ingredients from around the world created a cuisine hundreds of years ago that today would be fashionably known as "fusion food." Bread with mastic and cinnamon, desserts scented with distilled flower essences, halva fragrant with amber, ice cream scented with musk, and saffron rice are just a few examples of this rich mélange.

In fact, many of the dishes eaten at the palace were fundamentally no different from the food eaten by Ottoman subjects in ordinary homes. This similarity is plainly seen in the palace kitchen account books of the mid-sixteenth century, which lists such standard dishes as *aşure* (page 243), cheese *pide* (similar to pie but made with softer bread dough), pilaf with chickpeas, spinach *borani*, tripe soup, stuffed grape leaves, and stuffed chicken. All of these dishes are still very much a part of ordinary household cooking in modern Turkey.

Turkish Cuisine Today

Turks today still favor the simple food of their nomadic heritage. *Böreks* (savory filled pastries, pages 200–204) are the product of nomadic tribes' *yufka* dough, a cornerstone of Turkish cuisine. *Mantı* (dumplings, page 219) is another all-time favorite dish. Dried vegetable dolma are another example of contemporary cuisine with roots in nomadic times, as are the yogurt soups and sauces that delectably dress most Turkish dishes.

But by the end of the Ottoman Empire, the nomadic, Mediterranean, and Islamic cuisines had blended so completely that a unique cuisine was created, bearing the best gastronomical elements of each: healthy, sustainable, flavorful, filled with variety, and easy to cook.

When the English author Julia Pardoe visited Constantinople in the nineteenth century, she wrote: "There is no such thing as overeating. The Ottomans eat to live, but they don't live to eat. Also the reason for having so many different dishes served at one time is so that each one can find something he or she likes."

The aim of Turkish cuisine is to satisfy the diner, and a great deal of care is given to achieving the best flavor in even the simplest dish. Seasonal cooking with local ingredients is a hallmark of Turkish food, and it's interesting that this contemporary culinary trend can be traced back to nomadic times. Those tribes cooked with what was available in the best and most economical way possible, and as a result, Turkish dishes are created in harmony with nature and are not concerned with being ostentatious. There are more herbs used than spices, which gives Turkish cuisine a freshness that is reflective of the way we eat today. Turkish food is honest in its simplicity, yet it is at its utmost, delicious and pleasing to even the most discerning of palates.

Spices and Ingredients

Turkish cuisine is not, as most people think, spicy; however, it has its own unique aromas that are not always derived from spices. The heavenly aroma of browned butter, used especially in pilafs and *börek* (savory pastries), and the smoky fragrance of grilled eggplant are two delectable examples. The refreshing smell of mint or dill that's sprinkled on most summer dishes and salads also characterizes Turkish cuisine. In contrast to these fresh fragrances, whole and ground aromatic spices are used sparingly, which is much in line with today's almost universal precept of using spices judiciously so as not to overpower the natural flavors of the other ingredients. This approach is especially apparent in Turkish dishes that originated in the kitchens of the Ottoman palace. Some regional dishes, however, are more powerfully spiced, making them attractive to those who like more robust tastes.

This careful use of spices derived first from the simple cooking of the nomadic cuisine and also the palace's view that spices should be used strictly for medicinal purposes. Some spice concoctions are still produced today for their health benefits in honor of this traditional view. Occasionally, the palace showed its opposition to using spices in cooking by forbidding them. Nevertheless, the consumption of spices remained high in the palace because they were used extensively for purposes other than cooking.

Until the sixteenth century, the spice used most often in the palace was black pepper, followed by cumin, saffron, ginger, mustard seed, and mastic. As the borders of the empire expanded, new spices entered the palace, including nutmeg, anise, cardamom, celery seed, basil, cassia, and coriander. Recipes of the time suggest that these spices were most likely used in food preparation.

OLD AND NEW WORLD SPICES MINGLE

Today's dishes that use an abundance of a variety of spices are kofta (balls or patties made from lamb, beef, or a mixture of the two) and, in some cases, dolma (stuffed or wrapped vegetables)—especially those made in the cities of Urfa and Gaziantep in southeastern Turkey. The Egyptian Bazaar in Istanbul, thus named because the spices of the Far East used to come by ship from the port of Alexandria in Egypt, was assembled in this covered area, with spices to be sold to local dealers and also transferred to European markets. At the Egyptian Bazaar, also known as the Spice Market, one can find special mixtures of spices for dolma and kofta: combinations of black pepper, hot red pepper flakes, coriander, cumin, thyme, and mint. These Old World spices are supplemented by New World spices such as allspice and ground red pepper that hold an established position in Turkish cuisine—so much so that in some areas allspice is literally called "dolma spice." Cumin, used both in food preparation and as a condiment on tables where grilled meat is served, is favored as much for its digestive qualities as for its aroma and taste.

REGIONAL AROMATICS

In Turkish cuisine, the flora specific to particular geographical regions play an important role in how dishes are spiced or flavored. In eastern and southeastern Turkey, hot red pepper flakes, cumin, dried mint, sumac, and tarragon form the spice backbone of the regions' cuisines. In these

(OPPOSITE PAGE) CONDIMENTS, CLOCKWISE FROM LEFT: HOT PEPPER FLAKES,
ONION AND PARSLEY SPRINKLED WITH SUMAC (SEE PAGE 81), CUMIN, AND DRIED HOT PEPPERS.

SPICES AND INGREDIENTS • 15

regions, a soup is never served without browned butter and dried mint or tarragon to give it a final twist. In eastern Turkey, fresh coriander is brined—creating a spice found nowhere else—so that it can be used in the region's famous yogurt soups. In southeastern Turkey, this aromatic herb is replaced by *haspir* (false saffron) and is used in yogurt soups as well. (*Haspir* is not related to saffron but, as it looks like saffron and also gives a yellow color to foods, it has been called so by American cooks.) Central Anatolia competes with these regions with a special spice mixture called *çemen*. A paste made from ground fenugreek, cloves, cumin, allspice, cinnamon, garlic, hot red pepper flakes, and pepper, *çemen* makes any dish delicious. For locals, it makes an appetizing spread that is perfect on a slice of bread. *Çemen* is the spice that gives *pastırma* its unique taste and which helps preserve this spicy dried meat.

INDISPENSABLE SPICES FOR SWEET DISHES

In Turkey, sweet dishes also get their share of spices. Rose water, a distillation of rose petals, is one fragrance that is often used in milk-based sweets. Mastic (hardened drops of resin collected from the mastic tree) is a runner-up to rose water, but cinnamon is the spice that is sprinkled on almost every sweet. Salep is a spice derived from wild orchid bulbs that is common to all traditionally made ice creams, giving them flavor as well as their consistency. In winter, salep is boiled with milk and sugar to create a creamy hot drink that's consumed with a generous sprinkle of cinnamon and ginger.

HERBS

While tarragon is the herb of eastern Turkey, dill is the herb of western Turkey. Wild fennel, which grows in the spring and has no bulbs, is used in lamb dishes, and bay leaves are used when grilling fish and in fish stews. Purple basil is the queen of bulgur dishes, but the king of herbs is flat-leaf parsley. It is used so much that the idiom "Don't be a parsley" refers to those who think everything is their business. Thyme is used with meats where it grows wild. Most herbs are generally used dried. One that may be called a national aroma is dried mint, which is often swirled in browned butter and used as a dressing for soups. Fresh mint, however, along with fresh parsley, is a required accompaniment to kebabs in southeast Turkey.

· The Turkish Spice Rack ·

Some of these spices can be found in any grocery store. Look for the others at Middle Eastern grocers, or buy them online.

Allspice: Most likely because this New World spice was integrated into Turkish cuisine much later than other spices, its name in Turkish, *yenibahar*, literally means "new spice." It is the spice of the olive oil dolma of Istanbul, and it goes into the meat dolma and into the filling for dried vegetables, like the dried eggplant, bell pepper, or zucchini dishes of eastern Turkey.

Anise: This is used in the twice-baked hard bread known as *peksimet*. In Turkey, the beloved alcoholic drink raki is flavored with anise seeds only—no other herbs or spices are added.

Black pepper: In Turkey, black pepper is ground very finely; it is hardly visible in food, yet its taste and aroma are very strong. It is the main spice used when cooking meat, and also is prominent in egg-based dishes. Surprisingly, *laz böregi*, a sweet dessert pastry, is exceptional with black pepper added to its cream.

Cassia: This spice is often confused with cinnamon, most likely because it comes from similar-looking bark from a tree also cultivated in southern China and Indonesia. However, cassia's birthplace of Burma is a long way from cinnamon's origin in Sri Lanka. In my opinion, the deep and robust aroma of cassia is more suited to savory dishes and gives them a unique character. In more remote places such as Ula, the traditional use of cassia continues in the form of a special holiday bread, for which the hard cassia sticks are pounded at home (in contrast to cinnamon, usually bought in powder form). I have suggested cassia in some rice and meat dishes here, using the old Ottoman recipes as my guide. You may use either spice, as you prefer.

Cinnamon: Cinnamon is used ground, mostly as a spice for sweets—especially in milk desserts and sprinkled on some pastries. It is also sprinkled over salep (a hot drink made from milk and orchid root starch) and *boza* (a nourishing fermented beverage).

Clove: Clove is the main spice in all fruit compotes; it especially suits apple and quince compotes. This spice is sometimes put into tea, and people say that chewing it takes away the smell of garlic. In some areas of the Aegean region, cloves are ground and put in special breads, usually prepared for holidays.

Cumin: Cumin originated in Anatolia, and its wide use in Turkish cuisine reaffirms its origin. Cumin is an ingredient in most kinds of kofta, a condiment for the famous *çöp şiş* (tiny pieces of meat grilled on wood splinter skewers), and the dominant spice in the spice mix *çemen*, which is also used for making *pastırma*, the spicy Turkish air-dried beef.

Haspir: This spice is used only in the area surrounding the city of Gaziantep, the gastronomical center of southeastern Turkey (and one of the oldest continuously inhabited cities in the world). It has a faint aroma but gives a wonderful saffron-like color to the yogurt soups in which it is extensively used. It is thus also known as "false saffron," mostly by American cooks. But botanically speaking, false saffron (or *Carthamus tinctorius* from the *Asteraceae* family) and saffron (or *Crocus sativus* from the *Iridaceae* family) are completely different.

Mahlep: This bakery spice gives baked goods a faintly earthy, warming smell, which your nostrils will identify as unique and almost magnetic, and adds a crispiness that gives pastries a crumbly texture. A native plant of Anatolia, mahlep is produced by grinding the small seeds of a wild cherry, which look like pale, tan-colored peppercorns.

Mastic: This spice has a special place in Turkish cuisine and has probably been used since ancient times in this area (the ancient Greeks added mastic to their wine to make it tasty). Mastic has to be added with care, though, as it imparts a bitter taste if too much of it is used. Today, mastic is mostly added to milk desserts and ice cream. Its most interesting use is being mixed with oil and spread over fish. It is one of the favorite spices for the world-famous confection known as Turkish delight, called *lokum* in Turkish. I was not surprised to hear it has been added to tea. It is also used, along with clove and cassia, in the making of *bayram* (festive) bread. A pastelike dessert made with sugar, water, and mastic by Istanbul's Greeks was very famous during the Ottoman era. Mastic is grown in the microclimate of the island of Chios. In Ottoman times, almost all of it had to be sent to the palace, where the sultan's mother was given the power to distribute this spice in any way she chose.

Nigella seeds: These are literally called "pastry herb" (*çörek otu* in Turkish) because they are widely used on savory pastries. Nigella seeds are also used in a cheese made from whey, and this spice is put into amulets made to chase away bad spirits in regions where this ritual continues.

Red pepper flakes: There are two types of these ground dried red peppers: sweet and hot. The peppers are dried in open air in the shade and then ground. Sometimes the dried peppers are ground after being lightly dipped in oil, which makes them shiny. Red pepper flakes are mostly used in eastern and southeastern Anatolian cooking, especially in Maraş and Antep's regional cuisines. They are sold as Maraş or Antep pepper, and also as isot pepper

(see below), which hails from the neighboring Urfa region where it is produced in a different way. These dried red pepper flakes are sprinkled on soups and swirled with butter then added to the yogurt sauce served with *mantı* (Turkish dumplings). Quality red pepper flakes contain no seeds, for taste as well as aesthetic reasons—the heat of the seeds will burn your throat. Therefore, check to be sure there are no seeds in red pepper flakes before you buy them. Although Maraş, Antep, and isot are the most famous kinds and are offered commercially, in local markets in most areas of Turkey, village women sell homemade dried red pepper, ground almost to a powder, which would be the best choice if only one could get hold of it. These women sell sweet, medium, and hot red pepper. Commercially the heat of the ground pepper is graded too. The crushed red pepper flakes commonly found in the United States are much spicier than what we use in Turkey. Use them sparingly, or seek out milder chile flakes like Aleppo, Antep, or Mattaş pepper.

Isot red pepper flakes: Also known as Urfa pepper, isot's distinct dark color comes from being put into bags as protection from the sun during the day and taken out only during the nighttime to dry. Ideally, it should be dried uncovered in the shade, which will make it a red the color of a fez. The best time to dry isot in Urfa is between September and November when the sun is less hot. As its dark color suits the color of ground meat, isot red pepper flakes are mostly used in making the raw *köfte* (the uncooked meatballs called *çiğ köfte* that are very popular in this region). The name *isot* comes from *ıssı ot*, which means "aromatic herb."

Rose water: Rose water is added to the syrups of desserts more for its aroma than its flavor. It is also added extensively, along with powdered sugar, to the sugarless *muhallebi* (a kind of pudding) to create a dessert known as *su muhallebisi*. This *muhallebi* is literally immersed in rose water, which has a light flavor and an aroma that complements its taste, which is also very light on the palate.

It is customary to add rose water to *aşure* (page 243), a traditional dessert. The famous palace dessert *güllaç* (page 230), a light Ramadan sweet made from thin sheets of cornstarch and flour dough, a traditional artisanal product made by masters in special ateliers, is never made without rose water. When buying rose water, make sure it is for flavoring, not the kind used for cosmetics. Pharmacies sell the cosmetic rose water, whereas dessert or spice shops carry the naturally distilled rose water that's appropriate for cooking.

Saffron: This spice is derived from a cultivated plant. The three threads or stigmas in its flower are collected to be used as a spice. Since it takes eighty thousand flowers to yield a pound (half a kilo) of saffron, it has been rightly called the most expensive spice. The town of Safranbolu, on the Asian peninsula of Turkey, near Istanbul, was a center for growing saffron, hence its name. But presently most of the saffron in global markets is Iranian or Spanish. It used to be called *zaferan,* the Arabic name in the Ottoman times, but now it is called *saffron* in Turkish. We come across saffron in old rice and meat recipes. Today it is used mostly in *zerde,* a rice dessert. Saffron is sometimes put into *çemen,* the spice mixture for *pastırma.* You will also find saffron in Palace Fish Soup (page 117) and Sea Bass and Saffron Pilaf (page 151). Saffron in these recipes is used to give flavor and color. Turbo is a very light fish, and being immersed in saffron water gives it more depth. Saffron, for that matter, may be used in light soups to give them a subtle kick as long as it is used sparingly. Too much of it will make the food taste bitter.

Salep: This is the main ingredient of a winter drink known by the same name made with milk and sugar, and sprinkled with cinnamon and ginger. Salep comes from the bulb of a wild orchid found mostly in the Maraş and Muğla areas of Turkey; it gives both flavor and substance to the drink. The bulbs are boiled with milk in order to bring out the salep's taste, and then they are dried. The bulbs become unbelievably hard, so rice is added during the grinding process. Salep is one of the main ingredients in Turkish ice cream, in which no eggs are used. Turkey is a major salep producer.

Sesame seeds: Sesame seeds are a favorite in Turkish cuisine. Many pastries include their share of sesame seeds, and are all the prettier for it. One of the most popular street foods, *simit,* is a circular bread covered with sesame seeds. *Simits* are first dunked in pekmez (see page 20), and then covered with sesame seeds that have been soaked in a mixture of pekmez and water, so that both the *simit* and the seeds turn golden during baking, giving the loaves a harmonious color. (Another demonstration of how in Turkey the aesthetics of food are as important as the taste.) Turkey grows a large amount of high-quality sesame and is a major producer of tahini and tahini halva, both of which are made with sesame seeds.

· Sweeteners and Souring Agents ·

These ingredients can all be found at Middle Eastern grocers.
If you don't have one near you, you can purchase them online.

Pekmez: A ubiquitous sweetener in Turkish cuisine, pekmez is also consumed on its own as an energy tonic thanks to its iron content. Pekmez is a reduction of fresh grape juice, which is traditionally first boiled shortly with high-lime-content soil to separate particles from the grape juice. Then this mixture is left to stand for several hours to allow particles to sink to the bottom and clarify the juice. The clear juice is then boiled down to a syrupy consistency, which takes a while to reach. Mulberries and harnup are two other traditional fruits that are used for making pekmez in Anatolia. Today pekmez is made industrially as well. Note that this product is sometimes incorrectly called "molasses." Molasses is a by-product of the process of refining sugarcane or sugar beets into sugar and contains only 50 percent sugar. In Turkish, the syrupy by-product is called *melas*, and it does not taste similar to molasses at all. To maintain an authentic flavor, look for pekmez in Middle Eastern stores or online (see page 262) and do not substitute molasses in its place.

Pomegranate syrup: This typical ingredient of southern Turkey is often used instead of lemon juice in salads and other dishes that require a souring agent. Pomegranate juice is boiled until it is the consistency of olive oil and is then set out in the sun to give it a thicker consistency. The sourness of the syrup depends on the kind of pomegranate. There are sour-sweet, sweet, and sour kinds. It is best to taste before adding it to a dish. Lemon juice may always be added to lend more sourness to a syrup that is on the sweet side.

Sumac: This popular spice is made by grinding the fruits of the sumac shrub. Ground sumac has a deep purplish red color and is a popular souring agent especially in the cuisine of southeastern cities of Turkey like Urfa, Gaziantep, and Diyarbakır. It has become a condiment served at the tables of kebab restaurants all over Turkey. It is a souring agent especially used for salads or simple accompaniments like onions and parsley served with kebabs or with *lahmacun*, a very thin flatbread baked quickly with a spread of ground meat and minced onions on top. It is also used to add sourness to dolma. There is also sumac syrup, used in dolma, made from either fresh bell peppers, zucchini, eggplant and tomato, or the dried versions of the same vegetables.

Zahter (Za'atar): Za'atar is also the name of a spice mix, most commonly made from sesame seeds, thyme, marjoram, zahter, and sumac. This mix is ubiquitous on breakfast tables throughout southeastern Turkey, where it is mixed with olive oil and served as a condiment and a dip for bread.

· Other Essential Ingredients ·

HOW HOT PEPPER PASTE IS MADE

This paste is made in August, when the sun is at its hottest and peppers are abundant. The peppers, *Bursa biberi*, which actually is paprika, and *Antep biberi*, a very hot bell pepper with thinner skins, are washed, the seeds are removed, and the peppers are sliced and then crushed in a food processor. Some salt is added (2¼ pounds/1 kg crushed pepper plus 1 teaspoon salt), and then the crushed peppers are poured into shallow trays, covered with muslin, and left in the sun for three to four days until the peppers lose all their juice (depending on the temperature and the humidity, this may take up to a week). When they reach a paste consistency, olive oil in a ratio of 1 part oil to 20 parts peppers by volume is added and the mixture is transferred to jars. Before filling the jars, more salt is added if necessary. It should have enough saltiness to be used as a spread on a slice of bread or served as a dip. Today, pepper paste is also made industrially, but many households make their own out of habit and taste preference.

HOW TO MAKE YOUR OWN TOMATO PASTE

The best tomato paste is homemade. In Turkey, store-bought paste is watery and has a raw taste. That is why I suggest sautéing tomato paste in the recipes. This is not necessary with homemade paste. To start, select Italian-style tomatoes, Roma or other plum tomatoes, which are meaty, slightly oval, and not too juicy. Wash the tomatoes, cut each into four or five pieces, place them in a shallow bowl, and sprinkle them with a little salt. Then cover them with plastic wrap and leave them in the sun. (In the past, dried tomatoes were put in a container covered with a dish; today, however, plastic wrap is preferred for its better heat transference.)

When the tomatoes begin to separate from their skins, in a day or two, squeeze them thoroughly by hand to mush, and then pass them through a sieve to remove any skin or seeds. Add more salt, mix, and pour the resulting paste into enameled dishes or pots. (In the Aegean region, enameled dishes with slanted sides are used for this purpose; almost every home has one or two for making tomato paste and sun-reduced pekmez called sun's honey.) Let the paste sit in the dish for one day, under the sun, and stir occasionally. In three to four days, the paste will be reduced to the desired consistency: It's the right consistency when its top glistens. Then spoon it into jars and cover tightly. The jar will keep for more than a year if stored in a cool place, but it does not need to be stored in the refrigerator.

HOW TO COOK CHICKPEAS

These recipes call for cooked chickpeas or dried chickpeas then cooked with meat. Since cooking chickpeas takes a lot of time I make them in big batches and store them in the freezer in useful quantities. This is not only very practical, but also I have a feeling they taste better than canned ones. You are your own judge, but when a recipe calls for cooking chickpeas with meat, especially for soups, it is better to use dried ones and cook them together as it will make a great difference in the taste.

A NOTE ABOUT YOGURT

Yogurt is an essential part of Turkish cuisine, appearing on the table at every meal and as an ingredient in many dishes. Turkish yogurt is plain and unflavored with a thicker consistency than what is called Greek yogurt in the United States and a pleasant tangy flavor. If you cannot find Turkish yogurt in a Middle Eastern market, Greek yogurt is a good substitute. You may find the more commercial brands lacking in tanginess, in which case, add a squeeze of lemon juice to brighten the flavor.

• PART ONE •
SMALL PLATES (MEZE)

APPETIZERS

(ABOVE) CLOCKWISE FROM BOTTOM LEFT: OLIVE SALAD (PAGE 98), GREEN ONIONS AND RADISHES (SEE PAGE 81), MELON AND WHITE CHEESE (PAGE 24), CRISPY EGGPLANT WITH TULUM CHEESE AND PEKMEZ (PAGE 40), FRIED BALLS OF GREENS AND FIGS (PAGE 44) WITH ROASTED RED PEPPERS (SEE PAGE 81), WARM GRILLED TOMATO SALAD (*MÜNCÜR*, PAGE 84), FRIED GREEN PEPPERS WITH GARLIC YOGURT (SEE PAGE 81), BLANCHED ALMONDS (SEE PAGE 44).

The meze table brings together a tempting array of little dishes to be enjoyed communally. These small plates can include everything from stuffed grape leaves or vegetables to shish kebabs and fried calamari, typically paired with pickles, yogurt sauce, dips, and little salads. A table spread with small plates is not only appetizing, but also extends the time spent around the table with family and friends. Accompanied by drinks, usually glasses of raki, the gathering becomes festive and joyful, and what is more, meze creates an atmosphere where people can talk more freely and communicate more intimately. That is why the tables at the *meyhanes*, or taverns where meze were served, were called *çilingir sofrası*—*çilingir* meaning "the locksmith table," which implies that the table will unwind tongues, and people will talk more freely and casually. In truth, Turks value this type of conversation more than what is served, but certainly a tasty tidbit and a drink helps people relax.

The ritual of spreading the table with many different meze is more recent. In the old Ottoman days, tavern habits were more like the happy hour of the West today, where customers might enjoy a drink along with a handful of peanuts. However, after the Turkish republic was established, and men and women began socializing together as a way of life, the offerings on the meze tables became more elaborate at restaurants and homes alike.

Eventually labor-intensive dishes like *sigara börek* (cigar-shaped fried pastries) and Zucchini Pancakes *(Mücver, page 39)* would appear regularly—along with just about any type of meze the chef or hostess was capable of making. Even homey Turkish recipes, especially vegetable dishes like leeks, celery roots, and artichokes in olive oil, were added to the table around the mid-twentieth century.

One way or another, the variety keeps growing, as restaurants with an atmosphere conducive to drinking must continue to add new items to their meze platters.

It is interesting to note that meze and tapas, both of which are rooted in Arabic or Persian traditions, are becoming a popular way of eating, not only in their countries of origin but around the world. Perhaps everyone is yearning for a space in which they can truly relax and enjoy good company, with a drink and a few tasty tidbits to help set the stage.

All of the small dishes and even the fried pastry dishes in this book would be welcome additions on a meze table. You can serve just one or two meze while you enjoy a drink and conversation with a friend. Or, for a larger group, you can present a mix of hot and cold dishes, meat- and vegetable-based dishes, little salads and condiments—so many tasty tidbits that you will not even have to serve a main dish.

THIS PAIRING is a must for the raki table in Turkey. Besides the appeal of the rich variety of melons available in Turkey, the balance of sweet and salty makes this combination all that's needed for many raki drinkers. In addition, the protein-rich cheese and potassium-rich melon contain vitamins and minerals that balance the alcohol: Nature knows what she is doing. Although the expression "less is more" is true for appetizers, I offer several suggestions for cheeses to pair with the melon at the end of this recipe.

Melon and White Cheese

6 thin slices melon

3 slices (2 square inches/5 square cm) white Ezine or tulum cheese (see Note)

Serves 6 as meze

Serve the melon and cheese together on a single plate, or separately (the cheese can be cut into triangles instead of squares, if you prefer).

Note: Ezine peyniri (from the town of Ezine on the Aegean peninsula of Gallipoli) is a white cheese made from goat's, sheep's, and cow's milk; it is pickled and then ripened in tin containers. Tulum peyniri is a crumbly powerful cheese that is very special. It is made in the area surrounding Erzincan (a city in eastern Turkey) and is traditionally matured in sheepskins. Today commercial versions come in synthetic casings, and unfortunately the taste is not anything near the traditionally cured one. Look for both of these cheeses at Middle Eastern groceries or online.

Raki (Lion's Milk)

Considered the national drink of Turkey, the origins of this unsweetened anise-flavored drink go back to the Far East, where it was called *arak*, and the Middle East, where it was called *araq* in Arabic—the likely sources of the word *raki*. The famous seventeenth-century Turkish traveler Evliya Çelebi mentions that drinking raki is not a sin if you do not get drunk. Raki can be made from various fruits, including dates, but Turkish raki is made by distilling the alcohol from grapes and then redistilling the resulting liquor with anise seeds. Adding chilled water when drinking raki dilutes its high alcohol content and smoothes the taste, but the original ritual is one sip of straight raki followed by a sip of chilled water. In contrast to wine-drinking customs, sipping raki precedes tasting the appetizers. In other words, raki's distinctive taste is never mixed with another taste.

IF MELON AND CHEESE is the number one meze, this is the second. Its creamy texture and flavor justifies the name *caviar* (a term that was passed on to Western languages from its Turkish name, *hayvar*).

Turkish Caviar

3 to 4 round, Italian-style eggplants (2½ pounds/1 kg, enough to make 3 cups mashed eggplant)

1 clove garlic, pounded with a mortar and pestle

Salt

Juice of ½ lemon (about 1 tablespoon)

½ cup (120 ml) corn oil

¼ cup (60 ml) whole milk, or 2 to 3 tablespoons light cream

Serves 6 as meze

Grill the eggplants over a direct fire or a gas flame (this gives them a wonderful smoky taste) and peel while still warm (they will peel more easily this way). Wash the eggplants under running water to remove any remaining charred skin. Put in a colander for about 30 minutes to drain the bitter juices eggplants give off when grilled. Cut the eggplants into pieces and place in a food processor or chopper, or use a bowl and handmixer. Combine the garlic and a large pinch of salt, stir in the lemon juice, then whisk in the oil until emulsified. Add the dressing and then the milk and process until you have a creamy consistency. Taste and season with more salt if needed. Serve the day it is made; otherwise the garlic may become rancid.

THIS RECIPE is from eastern Turkey, where they love spicy food; in fact, its regional name, *acika*, means "heat." It can be served with toasted bread slices or toasted *yufka* slices as a part of a meze platter. Its dominant spice, coriander, was used extensively in the Ottoman times, while purple basil is the common choice for this recipe. For an older version of *acika*, made with peppers, see page 26.

Spicy Peanut Spread (*Acika* with Peanuts and Tahini)

1 cup (120 g) shelled and peeled peanuts, first toasted in their shells

2 cloves garlic, crushed or pounded

2½ teaspoons dried coriander and hot pepper spice mix (see Note)

1 teaspoon ground cumin

1½ teaspoons dried purple basil (optional)

2½ teaspoons sumac

2 tablespoons tahini

3 tablespoons vegetable oil

Serves 6 to 8 as meze; double the recipe if this is the only meze

In a food processor, combine the peanuts, garlic, spice mix, cumin, basil (if using), and sumac. Transfer the mixture to a bowl. Add the tahini with a splash of the oil and some water, up to ¾ cup (180 ml), to smooth out the texture. Add the remaining oil and the tahini, mixing in with a spoon. Serve at room temperature. It is best eaten the day it is made.

Note: To make the spice mix, grind 3 tablespoons coriander seeds with 3 or 4 dried hot peppers about 2 inches (5 cm) in length. If the peppers are not completely dry, toast them over a flame on the stovetop before grinding them. This makes enough spice mix for two batches of the spread.

MUHAMMARA IS A CLASSIC that is an indispensable meze or all-purpose spread in the eastern and southeastern regions of Turkey. It is a delicious tribute to homemade tomato and pepper pastes, which are ever present in the homes of these regions. Although its name sounds like it would be Arabic in origin, this is actually a very popular appetizer of the Circassian people, who refer to it as *acika*. (These people are known for using a lot of walnuts in their cuisine, as in the Circassian chicken on page 42.) There is a similar recipe, on page 25, also called *acika*, but it is made with tahini and peanuts instead of walnuts. However, peppers are a key ingredient, and it is certain that this dish evolved to include peppers, as in this walnut spread.

Hot Paprika and Walnut Spread (*Muhammara/Acika*)

4 slices stale white bread, moistened with cold water to soften, then squeezed dry

1½ cups (150 g) walnut halves

6 paprika peppers or mild red chiles, grilled and peeled

3 cloves garlic and a pinch of salt, pounded with a mortar and pestle

1 tablespoon hot pepper paste (page 21)

1 tablespoon tomato paste (page 21)

1½ teaspoons hot red pepper flakes

1¼ teaspoons ground cumin

⅓ cup (75 g) virgin olive oil

3 tablespoons pomegranate syrup (see page 20)

Salt to taste

Bread for serving

Serves 6 to 8 as meze; double the recipe if this is the only meze

Put the stale bread and walnuts in a food processor and process until well mixed, but not pulverized. Remove and set aside. Add all the remaining ingredients to the food processor and process until blended. Combine the walnut mixture with the pepper mixture by pounding them together in a mortar and pestle, if you are a passionate cook, or simply mixing them together with a spoon. Serve with toasted slices of good crusty bread.

THIS SPREAD, made from dried fava beans, is an all-time favorite, especially for the meze table. It keeps well and is easy to make, provided you use dried fava beans from the current year's harvest. If the beans are old, they will not cook evenly and you will have trouble making a smooth puree. As fresh fava beans have a very short season and grow in abundance, especially in the Aegean region, folks dry them and use them to make this puree. It can be eaten hot (it will be soupy) or cold (it will become firmer as it cools). Squares of cold fava puree on a serving platter make a pretty presentation when garnished with dill and red onions.

Fava Bean Puree

1 pound (500 g) dried fava (broad) beans (see Note)

1 medium onion, coarsely chopped

1 tablespoon sugar

½ tablespoon salt

⅓ cup (75 ml) sunflower oil

FOR SERVING

Fresh dill, minced

4 to 5 tablespoons virgin olive oil

1 red onion, sliced into rings

Serves 8 to 10 as meze

Pour the beans into a colander and rinse in plenty of water. Put the beans in a pot with 8¾ cups (1.8 L) cold water. Let the beans soak for 3 to 4 hours, then add the chopped onions and cook over medium heat for 50 to 60 minutes, until the beans are broken down almost into a puree. Remove from the heat, add the sugar, salt, and sunflower oil, and mix well. Press the puree through a colander into a bowl, mashing any intact beans with the back of a spoon to get rid of any chunky pieces. When cooled, garnish with dill, drizzle with the olive oil (this enriches the taste and also helps create a creamy texture), and serve with the raw onion rings.

Note: When purchasing dried beans, it is important to choose beans from the current year's harvest, if possible, so that they will puree easily. To help ensure even cooking, you may add ¼ teaspoon baking soda to the cooking water, but good-quality fava beans break down on their own.

TURKISH AND ARMENIAN cooking are very similar, so much so that it is difficult to say what recipe belongs to which culture. However, *topik* is a uniquely Armenian dish that was recently introduced to Turkish restaurants by Armenian Christians living in Istanbul, where it's become quite popular. Although this dish, made of chickpeas and tahini with an onion filling, is not classified as an appetizer (I believe, considering the ingredients, it was made during the time of fasting), I've included it in the meze section because that's how it is served today.

I first prepared this recipe with the American author Anya von Bremzen, and it was a great success. We were on a boat, so we used whatever ingredients were available. *Topik* is traditionally prepared by wrapping it in cheesecloth, but we used foil. According to the original recipe, which was given to us on the boat via a telephone call to a girlfriend who's married to an Armenian, the onions should be boiled, not caramelized, but we liked the rich flavor that caramelized onions added, and I've included them in this recipe as well.

Chickpea Balls with Tahini (*Topik*)

¾ cup (110 g) dried currants

4 cups (480 g) coarsely chopped white onions

¼ cup (60 ml) extra-virgin olive oil

½ cup (60 g) pistachios or pine nuts, toasted in the oven

1 teaspoon ground cinnamon

¾ teaspoon ground allspice

2 cups (400 g) chickpeas, soaked in water overnight, cooked until tender the next day and preferably skinned, cooking liquid reserved

2 medium potatoes, peeled, chopped, boiled (in just enough water to cover them, so that they will have substance), and mashed

3 tablespoons tahini

Salt

Sesame seeds, for serving (optional)

Pekmez, for serving (optional)

Serves 6 to 8 as meze

Put the currants in a bowl, add water to cover the currants by ½ inch (12 mm), soak for 30 minutes, then drain and dry them on a paper towel. Meanwhile, in a large sauté pan over medium heat, sauté the onions in the oil until translucent, about 7 minutes. Reduce the heat to low and cook the onions until caramelized, about 10 minutes more. Add the toasted nuts, cinnamon, allspice, and currants to the onions, toss to combine, and remove from the heat.

In a blender, puree the chickpeas with some of their cooking liquid in two batches, adding small amounts of cooking liquid as necessary. (The mixture should be very thick; add just enough liquid to keep the processor going.) Transfer the chickpeas to a large bowl, stir in the potatoes and tahini, and season with salt. (You should have a malleable but not too soft mixture; it will harden more in the refrigerator.)

Line an 8-inch (20-cm) square baking pan with plastic wrap and pat half of the chickpea and potato mixture in the bottom. Arrange the onion mixture in a uniform layer over the chickpea and potato mixture. Place the remaining chickpea and potato mixture on top, and smooth with a spatula. (A small-cupped muffin tin would work here as well). Cover with plastic wrap and refrigerate for 3 to 4 hours.

Preheat the over to 350°F (175 °C). Heat the topik until just warm. Cut into squares or rounds, sprinkle with sesame seeds, drizzle with pekmez, and serve.

THIS SPREAD was a ubiquitous meze about thirty years ago. I cannot tell you why, but all of a sudden it disappeared from menus everywhere. During the last few years, it has made a comeback in almost all fine fish restaurants. I shared this recipe in my newspaper column a few years ago and I like to think that aided its comeback. There is, however, no consensus about which fish's roe should be used. Some say carp roe, some say trout is the best—but I will stick to sea bass roe, which is used by my favorite *meyhane* (restaurant), Refik. The owner of the restaurant passed away recently, but his chef of thirty years has followed the same recipe. At Refik, sacks of roe that weigh six to eight ounces (170 to 225 g) are used, but as long as the roe you use is an orangey yellow and not red, and the eggs are almost as small as grains of sand, this recipe will work just fine. Just be sure to remove the sack that the roe comes in with care; if the roe is heavily salted, which it usually is in Turkey, you should first soak the roe in its sack in plenty of water. Repeat, changing the water several times, or your *tarama* will be very salty. You can always add more salt to the spread later if necessary.

Roe Spread *(Tarama)*

6 ounces (170 g) roe

2 slices white bread, preferably stale, crusts removed, moistened with water to soften then squeezed dry

Juice of 1 lemon, plus 1 to 2 tablespoons more if needed

1½ cups (360 ml) sunflower oil

Serves 6 to 8 as meze

Soak the roe in its sack in cold water for about 20 minutes, until the salt is removed. (Roe is hard in the summertime, so drain it once, and then soak again to soften it.) Remove the sack and squeeze the roe in your palm until no water remains. Put the bread and roe in a deep, narrow pot, add the lemon juice, and hand mix until thoroughly combined. (Never use an electric mixer, as it will break the roe and ruin the dish!) Gradually add the oil in small amounts, letting the roe mixture absorb the oil between additions, until the mixture is a little thicker than mayonnaise. Taste and add more lemon juice, if necessary. (The mixture becomes whiter every time you add lemon, but also tangier, so add in moderation.) Place the spread on a serving platter and smooth with a wet spoon. Cover with plastic wrap and refrigerate for up to 1 day. Serve chilled.

THIS APPETIZER is another favorite, sold at snack bars. Some people go to the fish market on İstiklal Caddesi, the famous promenade in Istanbul that starts at Taksim Square and goes all the way to the Old Galata District, exclusively to eat fried mussels from among all the other delicacies. This recipe lets you create a comparable taste at home.

Fried Mussels

1 recipe batter from the Crispy Zucchini Slices recipe (page 37)

20 fresh mussels, shucked, rinsed, and patted dry

Olive or sunflower oil, or a mix of the two, for frying

Serves 6 to 8 as meze

Put the batter in a shallow bowl, add the mussels, and turn them to coat. Heat the oil in a deep, heavy saucepan or pot over medium-high heat. When the oil is really hot, fry a few mussels at a time, carefully placing them in the oil one by one and leaving plenty of room between them so they fry quickly and their flesh does not dry out. Fry until completely golden, about 2 minutes. Transfer the fried mussels to paper towels to drain, then repeat with the remaining mussels in batches. Serve hot.

SARDINE BALLS are my own creation, and I think they feature an appetizing and attractive combination of ingredients. I was inspired by the zucchini pancakes known as *mücver* (page 39) and also thought that eating the sardines with some herbs would be tasty. The idea for cumin came from Tunisian cuisine, which serves fish sprinkled with this spice. Cornmeal adds a crunchy texture to the coating.

Sardine Balls

2 pounds (910 g) fresh sardines, deboned

2 large egg whites

½ packed cup (10 g) minced fresh parsley

⅓ cup (7 g) minced fresh mint

1 medium onion, minced

1 tablespoon cumin seeds, toasted for 30 seconds in a small pan

Salt and black pepper

2 tablespoons all-purpose flour

¾ cup (105 g) toasted cornmeal

Olive oil for frying

Serves 6 as meze

Chop half the sardines with a knife and chop the other half in a food processor; transfer both to a dish. Add the egg whites, parsley, mint, and cumin and mix well. Season with salt and pepper and stir well with a wooden spoon. Combine the flour and toasted cornmeal in a bowl. Use two spoons to make walnut-size balls of the sardine mixture, then coat with the flour mixture. Heat ½ inch (12 mm) of oil in a frying pan over medium heat, carefully add the balls to the oil, and fry thoroughly until the outsides are browned and the balls are slightly springy to the touch of the tongs. Drain on paper towels and serve.

THESE LENTIL balls originated in the Gaziantep region, but eventually they became an indispensable offering at ladies' teatime all around Turkey. (This way, ladies could enjoy these appetizers without visiting a tavern, which is not a common practice for women outside of cosmopolitan cities.) These are a treat for every budget and every palate. Traditionally they are rolled between the palms of your hands, but I make the balls with a *ayran* (yogurt drink; page 250) spoon, a special utensil made in Gaziantep to go with a metal *ayran* bowl. You can use an ice cream scoop instead. In Gaziantep, these lentil balls are eaten with a side of any kind of pickle, and I like to follow this tradition because it is so fitting.

Red Lentil Balls with Cornichons

1 cup (190 g) red lentils, washed

1 tablespoon tomato paste (page 21)

1 tablespoon hot red pepper paste (page 21)

1 cup (140 g) fine bulgur

2 medium onions, diced

3 cloves garlic, minced

½ cup (120 ml) olive oil

3 tablespoons minced medium-hot green chiles, such as jalapeños

1 cup (20 g) minced fresh parsley leaves

½ tablespoon fresh tarragon, or 1 tablespoon dried

Salt

3 green onions, chopped

2 stalks fresh young garlic, minced (optional, if in season; see Note)

Cornichons, cut into slices, for serving

Serves 8 as meze

Put the lentils and 5 cups (1.2 L) water in a large pot, bring to a boil, and cook until the lentils are soft and shapeless, 25 to 30 minutes, skimming off any surface foam with a slotted spoon. Add the tomato and red pepper pastes and cook for 3 minutes more. Remove from the heat, stir in the bulgur, and let cool.

Sauté the diced onions and minced garlic in the oil until the onions are translucent, then add the chiles. Set aside.

Add the parsley, tarragon, salt to taste, and the green onions to the lentil mixture and knead in with your hands. When the mixture begins to hold together, add the sautéed onion mixture and the young garlic, if using, and knead to combine. Form into walnut-size balls with your hands or an ice cream scoop. Serve with the cornichon slices.

Note: Fresh young garlic comes out in spring and is on the market for only a short time. It has a special place in Turkish cuisine and is even eaten raw as a side dish. The white parts of spring garlic eventually grow into the more familiar garlic bulbs, with a cluster of garlic cloves.

THERE IS no appetizer like rings of fried calamari, crispy on the outside and tender inside. It is served with a special mayonnaise, yogurt, and garlic dressing nowadays, but here is my version of the traditional Turkish sauce. I use pistachios instead of the walnuts typically used in the traditional version, giving it a rounder taste, provided the pomegranate syrup is not the most sour kind. (This sauce can also be served with other fish dishes.)

Fried Calamari Rings with Pistachio Sauce

FOR THE SAUCE

½ loaf stale white bread, sliced and moistened with water to soften

⅓ cup (40 g) coarsely ground pistachio nuts

2 cloves garlic

1 tablespoon pomegranate syrup (see page 20)

1 tablespoon fresh lemon juice

2 tablespoons olive oil

Chives, for serving

FOR THE CALAMARI

4 whole squid, cleaned and sliced into ½-inch (12-mm) rings

1 teaspoon sugar

½ teaspoon salt

½ teaspoon baking soda

¾ cup (180 ml) beer

3 tablespoons all-purpose flour

Olive oil or sunflower oil for frying (see Note)

Lemon wedges, for serving

Serves 6 as meze

Make the sauce: Completely squeeze the water out of the bread. Put the bread in a pot or large mortar with the pistachios and garlic and pound with a pestle. The more pasty the texture, the better it will taste. Add the pomegranate syrup, lemon juice, and oil and combine with a spoon until uniform.

Make the calamari: Put the calamari rings in a bowl with the sugar, salt, and baking soda and knead like dough. Add the beer and let sit for 10 to 15 minutes. Spread the flour on a platter, squeeze the calamari in your palm, and add it to the platter. Heat the oil in a heavy saucepan over medium heat. Roll the calamari rings back and forth in the flour, and then fry them in the hot oil for 2 to 3 minutes, until evenly browned. Place on a paper towel to drain, and then serve immediately with lemon wedges and the sauce with chives on the side.

Note: Don't fry these in extra-virgin olive oil; it imparts too heavy a taste.

THESE "BIRDS," as they are called in the Black Sea region, are traditionally made from the unique-tasting anchovies known as *hamsi*. When two of these fish are put face-to-face, they resemble a bird with the tail sticking out. I kept the preparation method but substituted sardines and made a special filling to give this dish extra flavor.

Sardine Birds

1 large egg white, lightly beaten with 1 tablespoon water

⅓ cup (55 g) all-purpose flour

2 tablespoons cornmeal

½ packed cup (10 g) very finely minced fresh parsley

1 small onion, minced

1 teaspoon black pepper

1 teaspoon ground allspice (optional)

Salt

24 sardines, deboned

Olive oil for frying

Serves 6 as meze

Put the lightly beaten egg white and water in a shallow bowl (this way you can work more easily when you are dipping the birds). Combine the flour and cornmeal on a plate, and in a second bowl, combine the filling of parsley, onion, pepper, allspice, and salt to taste. Spread each sardine out so both sides lie flat. Put 1 tablespoon of the parsley mixture on a fish and cover it with another fish to enclose the filling.

Carefully dip the filled sardines first in the egg white, then the flour (if desired, you can use a slim spatula to turn the fish around so your fingers don't get too messy). Repeat with the remaining sardines and filling (you should have 12 sardine birds in all).

Heat ½ inch (12 mm) oil over medium heat. Working in batches, lower the sardine birds slowly into the oil with a spatula, fry them on one side for 2 minutes, then turn (if using tongs, do not put pressure on the fish) and cook for 2 minutes more, or until golden. Drain on paper towels. Serve hot.

THIS MEZE DISH is one of my most popular recipes. Everyone loves it and, as easy as it is to make, it will always be a success. Just make sure your zucchini slices are drained of as much of their water as possible. You may serve these with Yogurt and Garlic Sauce (page 65), if you like. It's my favorite sauce, but I usually prefer these without it, so that the sweetness of the zucchini is not overwhelmed.

Crispy Zucchini Slices

3 to 4 medium zucchini (6 to 7 if they are petite), cut lengthwise into ½-inch (12-mm) slices

FOR THE BATTER

5 heaping tablespoons (45 g) all-purpose flour, or more if needed

¼ cup (60 ml) beer

Salt

Olive oil for frying

Serves 6 to 8 as meze

Arrange the zucchini pieces in a single layer on a baking sheet and let sit in the sun for 25 to 30 minutes, or tightly reassemble the slices and leave them in the refrigerator for a few hours. You can also lay the slices in a colander, salt them, and then dry them after they've sweat out their liquid. (Any of these methods helps the zucchini lose its extra moisture, and this is the key to crispiness.)

Make the batter: Put the flour in a large bowl. Mix the beer with ¾ cup (180 ml) water. Very slowly add the liquid to the flour, constantly stirring, to form a paste the consistency of very soft pudding; add more flour or water, if necessary. (The batter should stick to the slices, but should not be too heavy.) Season the batter with salt.

Heat just less than ½ inch (12 mm) oil in a frying pan over medium heat. Completely coat the zucchini slices with the batter and fry in batches until nicely browned on both sides, 2 to 3 minutes per side. Drain on paper towels. Serve hot.

ZUCCHINI FLOWERS are one of the many interesting ingredients used in the Aegean region. They are usually stuffed, but I think they are just as delicious fried. I tried an Italian version with cheese filling, but found that they are much lighter and crispier without cheese. The nicely browned blossoms are a real treat for both the eyes and the palate.

Fried Zucchini Blossoms

1 recipe batter from the Crispy Zucchini Slices recipe (above)

20 zucchini blossoms, picked early in the morning while still open (see Note)

Olive oil for frying

Serves 8 to 10 as meze

Fry the zucchini blossoms in the same manner as the zucchini slices in the recipe above. Drain on paper towels and serve hot.

Note: If you do not have a garden, you can buy the blossoms at a farmers' market.

WITH ITS ABUNDANCE of herbs, this was once a much-loved spring dish; people would eagerly anticipate the tableau of green pancakes with crispy edges. While zucchini is now available year-round, for some reason I still consider this a spring dish and try to serve it in season. In the Ottoman era, the spiced meatballs now referred to as kofta (*köfte*) were also called *mücver*. Both the pancakes and meatballs were cooked in special pans with indentations called *mücver tavası*. These pans are found only in antique shops today, but a spoon and a flat pan works just as well.

Zucchini Pancakes (*Mücver*)

Serves 6 to 8 as meze

5 zucchini (4 inches/10 cm long), peeled and shredded (using the grater's largest holes)

1 scant tablespoon salt

2 cups (40 g) fresh parsley leaves, chopped

½ cup (10 g) fresh dill leaves, chopped

½ cup (10 g) fresh mint leaves, chopped

3 to 4 green onions, minced (1 cup/95 g)

1 small onion, diced

4 ounces (115 g) feta cheese, grated

1 teaspoon black pepper

1 large egg, beaten

1 large egg yolk, beaten

3 heaping tablespoons all-purpose flour, plus more if necessary

Olive oil for frying

Plain yogurt, for serving

Fresh dill, for serving

Lay the shredded zucchini on a clean dish towel or cheesecloth. Sprinkle with the salt, let sit for 15 minutes, squeeze out the moisture with both hands, and place the zucchini in a bowl. Add the parsley, dill, mint, green onions, diced onion, cheese, pepper, egg, and egg yolk. Mix well, then gradually stir in the flour to make a smooth batter (if the batter seems thin, add another ½ tablespoon flour). Heat ½ inch (12 mm) of oil in a heavy frying pan over medium heat. When the oil is hot, place large spoonfuls of batter in the pan and fry the pancakes on both sides until nicely golden. Drain on paper towels and repeat with the remaining batter. Arrange on a serving dish and serve hot with yogurt and dill.

I FOUND this recipe in a cookbook about regional cooking, and the interesting combination caught my attention immediately. I would never have thought of serving all these ingredients in one dish, but here they come together in a phenomenal meze. You may also serve this meze wrapped in a very thin flatbread.

Crispy Eggplant with Tulum Cheese and Pekmez

Salt

3 large Italian eggplants, not peeled, very thinly sliced (you may use a mandoline)

Olive oil for frying

3½ ounces (100 g) Erzincan or any other tulum cheese (see Note) or any rich, ripe crumbly cheese, such as Parmesan, crumbled

2 to 3 tablespoons pekmez (see page 20)

Serves 6 to 8 as meze

Salt the eggplant slices and let sit in a colander to remove their juices. (This will yield a crisper result.) Fry the eggplant slices in batches (do not crowd them) in at least 1 inch (2.5 cm) of oil over medium heat. (Medium heat is ideal, as the longer the frying time, the crisper the eggplant will be.) Alternatively, you may deep-fry the eggplant according to the instructions for your fryer. When the eggplant slices are as crispy as a potato chip, take them out with a slotted spoon and drain on paper towels. Transfer to a serving platter, top with the cheese and pekmez, and serve.

Note: The phrase tulum peyniri *refers to all cheeses that are matured in a casing, traditionally made from goatskin; however, the most famous and sought after is the Tulum from Erzincan, a city in the eastern region of Turkey. This pleasantly sharp and crumbly cheese is made from unpasteurized sheep's milk produced by the sheep that graze on the aromatic greens of the area's numerous plateaus. The salt that is used is also very special: It's retrieved from naturally salted water collected in the ponds and lakes of nearby Kemah. The rennet is also homemade, produced by mixing a coagulated enzyme from a sheep's stomach with sugar, salt, and water. Erzincan tulumu goes well with walnuts and is always served in kebab restaurants before your kebab arrives. Tulum cheese is not eaten with a fork, but gathered up in a piece of bread, which to my mind is the most natural and human way of eating.*

NOT MANY people like liver, probably because they've never tasted it properly cooked. I did not like liver much until I tried it at one of the popular but humble restaurants in Setüstü near Kireçburnu on the Bosphoros, some twenty years ago. The secret of preparing liver is that it has to be fried in an instant, never longer than 1 minute.

Albanian-Style Fried Liver

FOR THE ONION SALAD

1 medium onion, cut into rings

1 cup (20 g) fresh parsley leaves

½ tablespoon mild red pepper flakes

FOR THE LIVER

1 lamb liver (purchase from a halal butcher), membrane removed with the tip of a knife, cut into 1-inch (2.5-cm) cubes

2 tablespoons all-purpose flour

Salt

Olive oil or sunflower oil, or an equal mix of the two, for frying

Serves 6 as meze

Make the onion salad: Toss together the onion, parsley, and red pepper flakes and spread on a serving platter.

Make the liver: Rinse the liver and let it drain in a colander. Combine the flour and salt to taste in a shallow bowl, coat the liver cubes with the flour mixture, and transfer them to a colander or sifter to shed excess flour. Heat 1½ inches (4 cm) of oil in a heavy pot over high heat. Add a handful of the liver cubes to the hot oil (only enough cubes to cover the bottom of the pot to prevent the first batch from overcooking). Fry until golden, but no more than 1 minute or the liver will stiffen and lose its flavor. (There is no need to drain the liver on paper towels.) Repeat with the remaining liver cubes until all the liver is fried. Arrange the liver on top of the salad, or serve it in a separate dish.

AN APPETIZER specialty of Istanbul and İzmir, chicory is an astringent green that's abundant in the markets of these cities. This type of chicory is more familiarly known as escarole in the States.

Blanched Chicory with Oil and Lemon

Salt

1 pound (455 g) chicory (escarole), well washed and drained

2 cloves garlic and a pinch salt, crushed together with a mortar and pestle (optional)

2 to 3 tablespoons extra-virgin olive oil

Juice of 1 lemon (about 2 tablespoons)

Serves 6 as meze

Bring 2 quarts (2 L) salted water to a boil. Add the chicory and cook for 7 to 8 minutes, until al dente. Using a slotted spoon, transfer to a colander to drain. Put the chicory on a platter. If using the garlic and salt mixture, add it to the oil, then mix in the lemon juice. Beat briefly with a fork until emulsified and then pour the dressing over the still-warm chicory. You can prepare the dressing up to 30 minutes beforehand, but the chicory tastes best if prepared at the last minute. If you need to boil the chicory earlier, you can dip the greens in very hot water for 30 seconds just before dressing and serving.

ALTHOUGH MY grandmother's mother was a Circassian beauty, Circassian chicken was not a dish made in our family kitchen. My mother always complained about its muddled look, so I was not introduced to this rich, flavorful mix of shredded chicken, walnuts, and spices until late in life. In the book *The Private World of Ottoman Women*, which is a reconstruction of women's lives in the Ottoman period, Godfrey Goodwin passes on a memory of a woman who witnessed the making of what was probably the original recipe for *çerkez tavuğu* (Circassian chicken), which had an intimidating reputation for being a labor-intensive task that took a whole day to make. As the woman who shared the recipe said:

> First, we have to start the job with eight grandmothers! [It's a job that lasts one whole day.] And don't forget the clay vases. While several women tried to break the shells of walnuts fresh enough to blacken their hands, the others shredded the chicken breasts and laid them at the bottom of the vases black from walnut oil. [They probably layered freshly cut walnuts between the pieces of chicken.] This process continued until the vases were filled to the brim. This "ambrosia" would stand all night long with a brick on top and be ready to be served only at lunchtime the next day.

Today this recipe is completed in a much shorter time, and dried walnuts are used instead of fresh ones. To prepare the tastiest Circassian Chicken, however, be sure to shell the nuts at the last minute. For results more similar to the original recipe, I also recommend pounding the nuts and bread together in a mortar and pestle with batches of chicken stock added along the way (see Note). All good things need a little bit of time and attention.

Circassian Chicken, the Easy Way

FOR THE CHICKEN

1 medium chicken (2 to 3 pounds/ 910 g to 1.4 kg), preferably free-range

1 onion

1 carrot

6 to 7 sprigs fresh parsley

2 fresh bay leaves, or ½ dried bay leaf

2 whole cloves

1 teaspoon salt

Serves 8 or more as meze

Put the chicken in a pot with the onion, carrot, parsley, bay leaves, cloves, and salt. Add cold water to cover and heat over medium heat. When the water is about to boil, skim off any scum with a spoon so that you have clear water without any residue. Cook the chicken until you can easily insert a fork into it, up to 1 hour. Let cool, remove to a cutting board, then shred the chicken meat or cut into walnut-size pieces (the skin can be included; it adds flavor to the dish).

Make the sauce: In a food processor, put the bread, two-thirds of the walnuts, ¾ cup (180 ml) of the broth, the red pepper, white pepper, and garlic-salt mixture. Mix until incorporated, then gradually add the remaining ¾ cup (180 ml) broth and process until the sauce is thick enough to coat the chicken pieces. When the desired thickness is reached, add the remaining walnuts (this crunchy batch will give a nice texture to the sauce) and coriander. In a pan, toss the chicken with the sauce until well coated. Place the chicken on a serving platter, drizzle with the walnut oil, and sprinkle with hot pepper flakes, if you like. Serve hot.

FOR THE SAUCE

4 thin slices stale white bread, crusts removed

11 ounces (310 g/about 3 cups) walnut halves, one-third of it ground with a mortar and pestle if you like (see Note)

1½ cups (360 g) chicken broth

1 teaspoon ground hot red pepper

½ teaspoon white pepper

1 clove garlic and a pinch of salt, crushed with a mortar and pestle

1½ teaspoons freshly ground coriander

FOR SERVING

3 to 4 teaspoons walnut oil

Hot pepper flakes (optional)

Note: Women used to make the topping for Circassian chicken by pounding the walnuts with pestles, then extracting their oil by squeezing the walnuts in a piece of cloth and mixing it all with hot paprika. I've simplified this method, but still recommend pounding the walnuts. Better yet, I strongly recommend pounding the bread and walnuts together in a mortar and pestle, gradually incorporating the broth as you go; it makes for a more flavorful dish because the walnuts release their tasty oil during the process.

THANKS TO the microclimates of the Aegean region, Turkey is a prodigious grower of figs. Those grown around Aydın are world famous—this area provides the entire world with dried *bardacık* figs. These figs are light green when fresh, and, since they are so abundant, farmers start drying them even when fresh ones are still on the trees. Despite their abundance, we do not use them in recipes apart from a few fig desserts, but instead prefer to eat them on their own. But I thought pairing them with fresh herbs like parsley, green onions, fresh young garlic, and pine nuts would be an interesting yet tasty combination—and it is. The sweetness of the figs creates a nice contrast to the greens and spices.

Fried Balls of Greens and Figs

2 cups (40 g) fresh minced parsley leaves

1 pound (455 g) green onions, finely minced

8 ounces (225 g) fresh young garlic, finely minced, if available (see Note, page 32); or 1 clove garlic, minced

Salt

½ teaspoon black pepper

1 teaspoon freshly ground coriander

6 to 7 dried figs, cut into chickpea-size dice

2 tablespoons pine nuts

1 cup (130 g) all-purpose flour

½ teaspoon baking powder

3 large egg whites, lightly beaten

Olive and sunflower oil (mixed half and half) for frying

Serves 6 as meze

Put the parsley, green onions, and young garlic in a bowl and add salt to taste, along with the pepper and coriander. With your hands, mix and knead. Add the figs and pine nuts and stir to incorporate. Add the flour, baking powder, and egg whites and mix with a wooden spoon until a yogurtlike consistency is achieved. Heat 1½ inches (4 cm) of oil in a heavy frying pan (see Note). When the oil is hot, place large spoonfuls of the batter in the oil (do not crowd the pan). Fry the balls until golden brown, 4 to 5 minutes, then drain on paper towels. Repeat with the remaining batter and serve hot.

Note: Since you will be frying in small batches, to economize on oil use a small, deep pot, as these fry very quickly.

White Almonds

In the spring, a plate of fresh almonds is a must in the city of İzmir on the Aegean coast. Vendors sell this delicacy from atop piles of ice to people dining in restaurants along Kordon, İzmir's seaside promenade. Fresh almonds are delicious in spring, but dried almonds properly prepared are almost as good in winter.

Buy the best-quality unsalted almonds. Place them in a bowl and add boiling water to cover the almonds by 2 inches (5 cm). Let the water cool. Peel off the skins and refrigerate the almonds, immersed in the water, for at least 12 hours. Serve between two layers of crushed ice.

I ENCOUNTERED new tastes when I first joined a raki table and shared in the meze. The selection differed according to the places we dined, but smoked mackerel was always included. I loved it. It is a meze that goes very well with raki. What I liked most was that it had a sharp, intense flavor like wind-dried meat—even though it was fish. I never guessed that one day I would meet the master of smoked mackerel, Hstro Dulidus, son of the founder of the Agora Tavern and the last of the family to operate this esteemed establishment, and learn all his secrets, which I share with you in the recipe below. Although I never had the chance to visit the Agora Tavern, I coincidentally met Hstro in Salonika. (What great luck to have come across a person who holds such an important place in Turkish *meyhane* history!) According to this master, they usually made smoked mackerel from lean mackerel, which were dried on the Agora's terrace by Jewish tenants. This tradition of drying fish continues today, but with mackerel becoming a rarity, other fish are used as well.

Smoked Mackerel

8 ounces (225 g) dried mackerel (or other dried fish)

3 to 4 tablespoons white wine vinegar (see page 102), plus more for soaking the fish

2 tablespoons olive oil

3 to 4 sprigs fresh dill

Serves 6 as meze

Scorch the fish over an open flame. (A gas stovetop burner can be used.) Wrap the fish in a vinegar-soaked cloth and refrigerate for 1 hour. Unwrap the fish and remove the softened skin. Break the flesh into shredlike pieces (a brass pestle is the traditional tool, but you could use whatever type of pestle you have). Place the shreds of fish on a serving platter, then pour the remaining vinegar and the oil over the fish. Garnish with the dill and serve.

Note: Although it is not traditional, serving the fish with a splash of olive oil will mellow the acidity.

AS THE TURKISH Greek community dwindled, many items from Turkish cuisine were added to tavern meze menus. The classic tavern recipes, however, are from the Greeks—the creators of tavern food—and to some extent from the Jewish community as well. These recipes remain, but I do not recall reading one for roasted baby bonito. To make this dish, you'll need a casserole or oven-safe earthenware pot.

Roasted Baby Bonito

1 tablespoon fresh lemon juice

1 tablespoon virgin olive oil

2 baby bonito, cleaned but left whole

2 mild green chiles, like Anaheim

1 tomato, quartered

Salt

Serves 6 as meze

Preheat the oven to 350°F (175°C). Whisk together the lemon juice and oil and brush it on both sides of the fish. Lay the fish in a casserole or earthenware pot, put the whole green chiles beside them, and place the tomato quarters wherever there is room; brush the vegetables with the remaining oil mixture and sprinkle with salt. Roast, covered, for 20 minutes, until barely brown on top. Serve hot or warm.

THE ONLY recipe shared in Evliya Çelebi's *Book of Travels*, written in the seventeenth century, is very similar to the pancake recipe below. He calls his pancakes *pilaki*, which is a vegetable dish of leeks and celery root. In the Black Sea region, this quickbread and other anchovy dishes are made with a special pan called a *döndürme tavası* (meaning "turn over"), which makes flipping the food easier.

Cornmeal Pancakes with Anchovies

10 leeks, outside layer removed and discarded, washed thoroughly, and chopped into chickpea-size pieces

2 packed cups (80 g) chopped Swiss chard

2 cups (100 g) salted anchovies, chopped

2½ cups (250 g) cornmeal

½ packed cup (10 g) minced fresh mint

½ packed cup (10 g) minced fresh parsley

1 teaspoon black pepper

⅓ cup (75 ml) corn oil for frying

Pickled plums (or pickle of your choice), for serving (optional)

Salt, only if necessary (it's not required if the fish is well salted)

Serves 6 as meze

In a bowl, rub together the leeks, Swiss chard, anchovies, and half the cornmeal so that the surfaces of the vegetables are scored. (The moisture they release will help make a better dough.) Add ½ cup (120 ml) water, the remaining cornmeal, and the mint, parsley, and pepper.

Heat the oil in an 11-inch (28-cm) pan, then press the dough carefully into the pan. Make holes in the dough with a wooden spoon in several places to help it cook evenly. Cook for 15 minutes over medium heat, then flip the pancake and cook the other side for 15 minutes; it should take on a golden color on both sides. (You can turn and flip the dough by covering the top of the pan tightly with a plate, turning the pancake upside down onto the plate, and then sliding the pancake back into the pan, cooked side up.) Serve warm with pickles, if desired, adding salt to taste as needed.

THIS IS a dish from the young chef Dilara Erbay, well known for being experimental in the kitchen. Her version of Turkish cuisine's famous *çiğ köfte* (tartar kofta) with salmon is delicious. Although the concept of the original remains, all of the ingredients have changed. I found it extremely creative and very fitting to a cuisine that is open to new tastes.

Salmon Tartar Made in the Style of Uncooked Kofta (*Çiğ Somon Köftesi*)

⅓ cup (45 g) fine dark bulgur

½ cup (10 g) minced fresh coriander

⅔ cups (15 g) minced flat-leaf parsley

Juice of 1 lime

1 tablespoon soy sauce

1 tablespoon sesame oil

Pinch of sea salt

1 teaspoon freshly ground pepper

1 tablespoon tomato paste

2 inches (5 cm) fresh ginger, grated finely

2 cloves garlic, pounded to a paste

1 tablespoon rice wine vinegar

½ pound (224 g) very fresh uncooked salmon, without the skin and bones, minced

1 teaspoon sesame seeds

Lettuce leaves

FOR THE SAUCE

⅓ cup (80 ml) soy sauce

1 teaspoon sesame oil

1 teaspoon sugar (optional)

1 teaspoon sesame seeds

Serves 6 as meze

Cook the bulgur in 1 cup (240 ml) hot water over low heat until almost soft but not mushy, 4 to 5 minutes. Set aside to cool, keeping covered until ready to use.

Combine the bulgur, coriander, parsley, lime juice, soy sauce, sesame oil, salt, pepper, tomato paste, ginger, garlic, and rice wine vinegar in a bowl and mix well. When completely combined, add the salmon. Fold the salmon into the mixture gently, taking care not to mash the fish too much.

Form the mixture into elongated balls, either by rolling between the palms or shaping with a tablespoon. Sprinkle with sesame seeds, turning the kofta gently to coat all the sides. You should have 20 to 25 kofta.

To make the sauce, combine the soy sauce, sesame oil, sugar (if desired), and sesame seeds in a bowl and stir well.

Serve on a platter lined with lettuce leaves. Pass the sauce on the side.

LATELY, PEOPLE are taking notice of the tasty green called samphire (or sea beans), which grows in dry areas of Turkey beside the sea. Interestingly, samphire and black-eyed peas have similar names in Turkish. (Black-eyed peas are called *börülce*, and samphire is called *deniz börülcesi*; *deniz* means "the sea.") This must be because the samphire resembles the slim, green black-eyed peas when they are picked fresh. (They become black-eyed once they are dried, but we also like to eat them fresh; for a recipe, see page 131.)

Black-Eyed Peas with Samphire

1 cup (200 g) dried black-eyed peas, soaked for 2 hours in cold water

8 ounces (225 g) samphire (sea beans), washed

Salt

⅓ cup (75 ml) olive oil

1 to 2 cloves garlic and a pinch of salt, crushed together with a mortar and pestle

1 tablespoon fresh lemon juice

1 teaspoon ground sumac

Serves 6 to 8 as meze

Boil the peas in plenty of water until tender, 15 to 20 minutes, depending on the age of the peas. Let stand in the cooking water. Bring a large pot of water to a boil, add the samphire, and cook until the woody inner stems loosen up, about 15 minutes. Drain and remove and discard the stems.

Drain the peas and place them in a bowl. Sprinkle with salt to taste and arrange the samphire on top. Whisk together the oil and garlic-salt mixture, and then pour this mixture and the lemon juice over the peas and greens. Sprinkle with the sumac and serve.

WILD RADISH leaves make a tasty salad or appetizer when nature offers them to us, which is in early spring.

Wild Radishes

Salt

1 pound (455 g) wild radishes

5 to 6 tablespoons extra-virgin olive oil

Juice of ½ lemon

1 clove garlic and pinch salt, crushed together with a mortar and pestle (optional)

Serves 6 as meze

Bring 2 quarts (2 L) salted water to a boil. Add the wild radishes and cook for 7 to 8 minutes, until al dente. Using a slotted spoon, transfer to a colander to drain. Put the wild radishes in a bowl. Whisk together the oil, lemon juice, and garlic-salt mixture, if using, until emulsified. Toss the dressing with the still-warm wild radishes and serve.

 GRAY MULLET caviar, most popularly called botargo (*balık yumurtası* in Turkish), is a rare delicacy made by drying the roe. An expensive food that is not served in Turkish restaurants, it is greatly prized by home cooks. Here the roe is served atop squares of baked *yufka*, a large, round sheet of paper-thin dough that is essential to Turkish pastries. Look for it online or in stores where they sell Middle Eastern delicacies. If you can't find *yufka,* tortillas will make a good replacement, providing you cut the round into 1-inch (2.5-cm) squares. Even triangles will do!

Yufka Squares with Botargo

1 sheet *yufka* (see above), cut into 1-inch (2.5-cm) squares

1 tablespoon unsalted butter

15 to 20 slices gray mullet caviar (botargo), 1/16 inch (2 mm) thick

Serves 6 to 8 as meze

Preheat the oven to 350°F (175°C).

Arrange the *yufka* squares on a baking sheet (you'll have about 50 squares in all), and bake them for about 5 minutes, until crisp. (You can store them in an airtight container after roasting for up to 15 days.) Put a lentil-size piece of butter on each *yufka* square (it will help keep the botargo in place), top with a botargo slice, and serve immediately.

THE FIRST TIME I prepared this appetizer at home, it was for my dear friends Samuel and Samantha Clark, owners and chefs of the successful Moro Restaurant in London, known for its award-winning Moorish cuisine and also some specialties from the Middle East. They added it to their menu, and I was both surprised and happy when it became their best-selling appetizer dish.

Avocado with Botargo

2 tablespoons fresh lemon juice

2 tablespoons olive oil

Sea salt

Black pepper

3 avocados

½ red onion, cut into thin rings

12 to 15 slices gray mullet caviar (botargo), very thinly sliced

3 to 5 sprigs fresh dill

Arugula leaves for serving (optional)

Serves 6 as meze

Whisk together the lemon juice and oil with salt and pepper to taste until light in color and well mixed. (In order to prevent the avocados from browning, have all the other ingredients ready.) Peel the avocados and remove the pits. Slice and open the avocado halves like a fan, without breaking the slices apart, and immediately dress with the oil and lemon juice. (If this presentation is too difficult, slice the avocados instead.) Top with the onion and then the botargo, garnish with the dill, and serve with arugula, if you like.

I GOT the idea for these from some scallop and hot mustard canapés served to me in the States. These delectable hors d'oeuvres can be made to meet any budget: You may omit the botargo, but I'd suggest a fresh onion, cut into rings, as a substitute.

Egg and Botargo Rolls

2 tablespoons olive oil

1 tablespoon hot mustard

6 thin flatbreads or lavash, if available

5 large eggs, hard-boiled, peeled, and diced

Salt

1 teaspoon black pepper

3 to 4 tablespoons grated gray mullet caviar (botargo)

10 to 12 arugula leaves

Serves 6 as meze

Whisk the oil with the mustard and brush onto the flatbreads. Add 2 tablespoons diced egg to each piece of bread. Season with salt and sprinkle with the pepper and grated botargo. Add a couple arugula leaves to each, roll up, and serve.

VARIATION

Omit the oil and mustard and substitute canned sardines (drained and deboned) for the botargo and lettuce leaves for the arugula.

Eggs with Regional Greens

Here are two regional versions of eggs with greens, both delightful on a meze platter:

Chop hard-boiled eggs and mince some lettuce. Mix together and sprinkle with olive oil (no lemon juice or vinegar is added). This recipe comes from the town of Ödemiş, which is southeast of the city of İzmir.

Mince goosefoot (chenopodiaceae), a green popular throughout the Near East (or lettuce, purslane, or any other edible leafy green), and arrange slices of hard-boiled eggs on top. Sprinkle with a mix of olive oil and lemon juice.

DOLMA AND SARMA

Many vegetables from peppers to leeks, from okra to cucumbers, have stuffed versions in Turkish cuisine. The reason these dishes are designated with the internationally recognized Turkish word *dolma* is the method of their preparation. However, not all stuffed or wrapped vegetables are dolma in Turkey. Dishes made by wrapping a filling in chard, grape leaves, cabbage, or mallow are called *sarma* because they are wrapped, not stuffed.

Dolma are divided into two groups: those with meat and those with olive oil. The meatless ones cooked with olive oil are also known as *yalancı* ("imitation"). The filling of dolma cooked with meat and butter always includes rice or bulgur. Bulgur sometimes replaces rice, and there are regional variations in which meat is replaced with other ingredients—cornmeal in the Bolu in the Marmara region or curd cheese in the Erzurum in the eastern part of Turkey. But the glory of dolma, and sarmas too, comes from the rice.

Rice, the major ingredient in dolma, was first brought to Anatolia in the fourteenth century and held a special place in Turkish culture and cuisine. While Asian rice was the staple food of the Ottoman army, it was still used only as medicine in the Western world. And, as Ibn Battuta, an intrepid fourteenth-century Moroccan traveler, revealed, butter, flour, and rice were the traditional Turkish traveling provisions. The variety of rice dishes served in the palace of Sultan Mehmet, the fifteenth-century conqueror of Istanbul, included rice with chickpeas, cooked rice, rice soup, a rice dish eaten in the mornings, and a saffron and rice dessert that eventually made rice popular in the West. During this era, Westerners referred to pilaf, the most ubiquitous Turkish rice dish, as "Turkish rice." Summarizing the Turks' affinity for rice, explorer Pietro della Valle wrote, "If it does not contain rice, it is not called a Turkish dish."

WHILE TURKS consider stuffed mussels to be a great appetizer, it is also a wonderful fast food sold by street vendors and eaten on the run. Turks tend to frequent their own regular vendors, and purchasing and eating the mussels is a sort of street ritual in Istanbul. The vendor serves with flair, giving the mussels a squeeze of lemon juice as he hands them over. No fork is necessary! The diner uses the top half of the shell for a spoon. The stuffing in this recipe includes currants and pine nuts, if you want to make it Istanbul style, but you may also use plain rice cooked in olive oil (Aegean style).

Stuffed Mussels

FOR THE ISTANBUL-STYLE STUFFING

1 cup (240 ml) virgin olive oil

4 medium onions, chopped

3 tablespoons pine nuts (optional)

2½ cups (500 g) medium-grain rice

1 teaspoon ground cassia, if available (optional; see page 17)

1 teaspoon ground allspice

1¼ teaspoons black pepper

4 tablespoons dried currants (optional)

FOR THE MUSSELS

30 large fresh mussels, still in the shell (if using small mussels, you'll need more; see Note)

10 to 15 lemon wedges for serving

Serves 6 to 8 as meze

Make the stuffing: Heat the oil in a large pan over medium heat. Add the onions and sauté until transparent. Add the pine nuts, if using, and sauté for 1 minute. Add the rice and sauté until the rice sizzles. Add the cassia (if using), allspice, pepper, and currants (if using); stir well and add 2¼ cups (540 ml) water. Cover and cook for 5 minutes over medium heat until the rice grains are al dente. Remove from the heat, cover, and let cool.

Prepare the mussels: Scrub the mussel shells until clean. With a small sharp knife, open the shells halfway, but leave them attached. Wash the insides of the shells without damaging the meat, then stuff with the rice mixture.

Put a strainer or colander in a pot and arrange the mussels in the strainer, open ends facing upward. Add 1 cup (240 ml) water to the pot, and instead of using a lid, carefully and completely cover the mussels with a thoroughly moistened piece of parchment paper. Cook over very low heat for 25 to 30 minutes, until the rice is thoroughly cooked (check by lifting up a corner of the parchment). If the rice is still not tender, re-cover and cook until done. (The water added should be thoroughly evaporated; if necessary, sprinkle with ¼ cup/60 ml tepid water and cover tightly again to lengthen the cooking time.) Let the mussels cool, then arrange on a serving dish. Serve with the lemon wedges.

Note: To have a few extra mussels is always a good idea; it is very easy to divide the stuffing among them and you can easily end up using it all.

STUFFED MACKEREL used to be a classic dish in Istanbul. There are still a few chefs who prepare it, but most are put off by the idea of deboning the fish. I got the idea of stuffing sardines instead from Sicilian cooking, and I had fun adapting the recipe to Turkish cuisine. I substituted rice for bread, and I thought using grape leaves was a good idea—especially since they appear in the markets at the same time that the sardines begin to run.

Stuffed Sardines on Grape Leaves

½ recipe stuffing for Istanbul-Style Stuffing (page 54), cooled

1 cup (20 g) fresh parsley leaves, minced

½ cup (10 g) fresh fennel fronds, if available, minced (optional)

18 sardines, cleaned and deboned

18 fresh grape leaves (see Notes)

Juice of 1 bitter orange (see Notes)

½ tablespoon olive oil

1 orange, halved and sliced

Serves 6 or 7 as meze

Preheat the oven to 425°F (220°C). Generously grease a baking pan.

Combine the stuffing, parsley, and fennel, if using.

Place a sardine, stomach side up, on a grape leaf. Spoon as much cooled stuffing mixture as you can into the fish's cavity. Wrap up the sardine and stuffing in the leaf and place on the prepared pan. (The head of the fish should peek out of the leaf.) Repeat with all the sardines and grape leaves, arranging rolls on the prepared baking pan so that they touch one another. Whisk together the bitter orange juice and oil and brush on the rolls. Arrange the orange slices over the rolls. Bake for 10 to 12 minutes, then turn off the oven and let the sardines sit in the oven for 5 minutes. Remove from the oven and serve immediately.

Notes: If fresh grape leaves are not available, you can substitute brined grape leaves.

Bitter oranges are also called Seville oranges; their juice is very acidic and aromatic. In Turkey, only their peels are used for making jam. If you can't find bitter oranges, you can use the juice of 1 regular orange plus 2 tablespoons fresh lemon juice.

MY MOTHER was very conservative about food. She rarely liked food that others had prepared, and even more rarely did she ask for a recipe. İzmir-style stuffed artichokes was on the list of great dishes my mother learned to cook later in her life. Her artichoke dolma was very successful because of her expertise with other olive oil dolma. I replicated her recipe by taste; the only change I made was the addition of green onions.

Stuffed Artichokes, Olive Oil Style

1 medium onion, minced

½ cup (120 ml) virgin olive oil

6 to 7 green onions, chopped

1½ cups (300 g) medium-grain rice, washed

Salt and black pepper

1 cup (20 g) fresh dill, chopped

1 tablespoon dried mint

Juice of 2 lemons

8 artichokes

1 large egg

Serves 8

In a pot, sauté the minced onion in the oil, add the green onions, and cook until the minced onion is translucent. Add the rice and sauté over medium heat. Add ½ cup (120 ml) water, cover, and cook over low heat for 2 to 3 minutes, until the water is absorbed and the rice begins to swell (it will not be tender yet). Add salt and pepper to taste, along with the dill and mint, remove from the heat, and let cool.

Fill a bowl with cold water and add half of the lemon juice. Trim the artichokes by removing all the outer leaves, cutting down to the heart, and retaining the soft inner leaves. Cut off any remaining thick, hard pieces; trim off the stem for a flat bottom. Remove the hard inner leaves, spoon out the choke, and discard it. Wash the artichokes and place in the lemon water.

Stuff the artichokes with spoonfuls of the rice mixture, tapping the artichoke on the work surface so the rice grains settle but aren't compressed. Keep the other artichokes in the lemon water so they don't brown.

Pack the stuffed artichokes beside each other in a pot. Pour 2 cups (480 ml) cold water in the pot and place the pot over medium heat. Whisk together the egg and the remaining lemon juice and, when the water begins to steam (in 4 to 5 minutes), brush the egg mixture on top of the artichokes. Cover the pot and cook over low heat, 30 to 35 minutes, until all the liquid is absorbed. If the artichokes are tender and there is still too much liquid in the pot, uncover and let the liquid evaporate. Serve warm or at room temperature.

IN TURKISH *yalancı* means "imitation"—or, literally "liar"! This meatless stuffed vegetable dish may rightly be called "imitation," since it appeared after the original version with meat in the filling. The Spanish prisoner of war Pedro raves about the meat version in his sixteenth-century manuscript, but no document mentions meatless stuffed peppers and eggplants until the nineteenth century. Coincidentally, dishes made with olive oil began to appear at the same time.

Turkish bell peppers are light green and have very thin skins. They also have a delicate fragrance that can be destroyed if too many spices are added to the filling. Outside of Istanbul, the filling is seasoned only with black pepper. In Istanbul, however, cooks use currants, pine nuts, sugar, and spices. Restaurants generally do not add tomatoes (for fear that the filling they stuff will go bad too quickly); they make do with spices.

Stuffed Peppers and Eggplant (*Yalancı* Dolma)

3 Japanese eggplants

Salt

10 medium green bell peppers (1½ pounds/680 g total)

2 large or 3 medium onions, coarsely chopped (plus 1 more onion if you add the Istanbul-Style Stuffing Seasoning to the dish)

1½ cups (360 ml) virgin olive oil

1¾ cups (350 g) medium-grain rice, rinsed well and drained

2 tomatoes, cut in half and grated, peel reserved (see Notes, page 60)

1 cup (20 g) minced fresh parsley

1½ tablespoons dried mint

1 cup (20 g) fresh dill leaves (optional)

1 recipe Istanbul-Style Stuffing Seasoning (see Notes, page 64, optional)

1½ teaspoons black pepper

Serves 8

Cut the eggplants in half and hollow them out with a knife. (In Turkey we have a special utensil to hollow out eggplants, but a sharp paring knife will do.) Chop the eggplant flesh you removed, sparsely salt it, and set aside. Cut the tops off the peppers. (You also can remove the tops by pressing gently all around the stem part with your thumb, as we do in Turkey. This will break off the stem from the pepper.) Cut off the seedy part and reserve the tops. Remove the seeds and pith from the hollowed-out peppers. Wash the peppers and the eggplants. Drain the peppers upside down for about 10 minutes, or until all the water has drained out. Sparsely salt the peppers all over, using your fingertip to distribute the salt. Salt the eggplants, leaving them open side up, to extract the water. Turn them upside down after about 5 minutes to drain this juice. The vegetables are now ready to be filled.

In a heavy skillet, sauté the onions and pine nuts, if using Istanbul-Style Stuffing Seasoning, in the oil until the onions are translucent. Add the rice, sauté for 2 to 3 minutes, then add the tomatoes. Stir thoroughly and cook over low heat, stirring occasionally, for about 3 minutes. When the tomato liquid is almost entirely absorbed, add ½ cup (120 ml) tepid water and cook for about 3 minutes, or until the water is absorbed and the rice grains are nearly al dente, then squeeze the excess juice from the chopped eggplant and add it to the skillet, along with the parsley, mint, and dill, if using, and black pepper. Add the Istanbul-Style Stuffing Seasoning, if using. Remove from the heat, cover the pan, and let sit for 15 minutes to allow the rice to cook further and absorb any juices that may not be visible.

(continued)

Using a spoon, pack the filling into the peppers and hollowed-out eggplants, leaving no empty spaces. (Tap the bottom of the peppers to ensure that the rice has settled.) Cover the eggplants with thin slices of the reserved tomato peel and cover the peppers with their cut-off tops.

Arrange the stuffed vegetables in a single layer in a pot. Add 1½ cups (360 ml) water, cover the pot, and cook for 6 to 7 minutes over high heat (see Notes). Continue cooking for 20 minutes over medium heat and then 15 minutes over low heat. (If the water has boiled away before the 20 minutes of cooking, add ½ cup/120 ml water. If there is still too much liquid after the vegetables are cooked, uncover and increase the heat to high so the water boils away.) Serve hot.

Notes: To grate a tomato, cut it crosswise in half so that the stem is on one half and the bottom part with no stem composes the other half. This way, when you grate the flesh, the peel is left in your palm, without tearing.

The peppers and eggplants will give away water once cooking starts that becomes part of the cooking liquid—that is why not much cooking water is added. Also, do not be surprised by the large amount of oil. The rice requires a lot of oil, and it is the oil that blends with all the other ingredients in the filling to make this a memorable dish.

(ABOVE) UÇHISAR, CAPADOCIA.

KALE IS ONE of the healthiest greens we know and very trendy to eat these days; the leaves are also very easy to work with. The people of the Black Sea region have been using it for ages in many of their dishes. That cornmeal is used instead of rice also makes it very typically *Karadenizli* (from Black Sea).

Kale Dolma (Sarma Style)

20 kale leaves, all the size of your palm (if smaller, increase the number; you may use two leaves together or make smaller dolma)

1 pound (448 g) medium-fat ground beef

1½ cups (210 g) cornmeal

1 tablespoon corn oil or butter

1 medium onion, finely chopped

1 teaspoon ground allspice (optional)

½ teaspoon black pepper (use 1 teaspoon black pepper if optional allspice is omitted)

2 cloves garlic, minced (optional)

Salt

Serves 8 as meze

Double the recipe to serve as a main dish

Blanch the kale leaves in hot water for 30 seconds, then run them under cold water. Let them sit in a colander to drain until ready to use. Mix together the ground beef, cornmeal, oil or butter, onion, allspice (if using), pepper, and garlic (if using) and season with salt. Add up to ⅓ cup (75 ml) water to loosen up the mixture.

Lay a leaf with the stem end facing you and place about 1 heaping tablespoon of filling on the leaf. Pull the stem end up and over the filling and roll to the end of the leaf. Continue with the remaining leaves and filling.

Place the filled kale leaves close to one another in a pot. After placing a small plate on top of the dolma, add 1⅓ cups (315 ml) warm water and cook over medium heat for 25 to 30 minutes. The water will have been absorbed. (Add about ⅓ cup/75 ml or more water if the liquid is absorbed before the cooking is finished.)

YAPRAK SARMA, rolled or stuffed grape leaves, have always been and still are indispensable, as both an appetizer and a side dish. My mother used to boast about being able to roll them almost as thin and long as a pencil. You could pick one up, always by hand, and finish it in three or four bites. Alas, nowadays, they make them much smaller, just enough for a bite, so that you are tempted to grab a plateful of them to ensure that you'll be satisfied. Here, I share two different recipes for stuffing. The Aegean-style stuffing has a clean flavor; the taste of the grape leaves comes across best if you use fresh ones. On the other hand, the Istanbul-style stuffing, a variation on the Aegean, is more sophisticated and complex.

Stuffed Grape Leaves with Olive Oil (*Yaprak Sarma*)

3 large onions, chopped

1¼ cups (300 ml) extra-virgin olive oil

2½ cups (500 g) medium-grain rice

1 large tomato (or 2 medium), halved and grated (optional; see Notes, page 60)

1 tablespoon dried mint

⅓ cup (7 g) minced fresh dill (optional)

½ cup (10 g) fresh parsley leaves, chopped

Salt and black pepper or Istanbul-Style Stuffing Seasoning (optional; see Notes, page 64)

11 ounces (310 g) fresh grape leaves, soaked; or 22 ounces preserved grape leaves, dipped in salted water (see Notes, page 64, for further instructions)

Serves 10 as meze

In a large frying pan, sauté the onions in the oil over medium heat until translucent, 6 to 8 minutes. Add the rice, sauté briefly over low heat, then add the tomato (if using), dried mint, dill, and parsley and cook, stirring constantly. Add ½ cup (120 ml) water and continue stirring. Season with salt and pepper or Istanbul-Style Stuffing Seasoning. Cover the pan, remove from the heat, and let stand for about 10 minutes to let the stuffing cool and the rice fluff.

Remove the stems from the grape leaves. Arrange the leaves on a plate, stem side facing you (shiny side down). Place about 1 heaping tablespoon of filling on a leaf (the amount will differ according to the size of the leaf, but be generous with the filling, especially if you are using preserved leaves), and then roll the leaf up tightly. Repeat with the remaining leaves, using the large, tough leaves to line the bottom of a large pot (or line the pot with parsley stems or lemon slices).

Arrange the rolls on the lining in the pot, packing them tightly together, and then weigh the rolls down with a heavy plate. Add 1½ cups (360 ml) water and cover the pot tightly. Cook for 5 minutes over medium heat, then reduce the heat to low and cook for 40 to 45 minutes, until almost all the liquid is absorbed. (If the rolls are cooked but there is still too much liquid in the pot, remove the lid and allow the liquid to boil away until the bottom is almost scorched. This adds an extra deliciousness.) Remove from the heat and let sit for 2 hours. Invert the pot onto a serving dish or, better yet, arrange the rolls one by one on a platter.

(continued)

(OPPOSITE) VEGETABLE VENDORS AT THE *PAZAR* (A WEEKLY MARKET).

Notes: If you prefer spicy stuffing you can leave out the tomato; instead add ⅓ cup (75 ml) more water to precook the rice partially.

To make Istanbul-Style Stuffing Seasoning, combine 3 tablespoons pine nuts, ¼ cup (35 g) dried currants, ½ teaspoon ground cinnamon, 1 teaspoon ground allspice, and 1 teaspoon sugar.

If using fresh grape leaves, dip them briefly in plenty of hot salted water for not more than 30 seconds. When using preserved leaves, soak them in plenty of cold water for 30 minutes to take out the extra salt, and rinse under running water before rolling.

VARIATION

Stuffed Lettuce

When making stuffed or rolled vegetables, you often have leftover stuffing and no more veggies to stuff. This dilemma led me to explore alternative wraps. When I happened upon the idea of stuffing lettuce leaves, it turned out to be delicious. You may be similarly inspired to experiment—after all, cherry leaves were once used to make *sarma* with meat stuffing. For this preparation, you will need 1 head romaine lettuce.

Remove and discard the outside leaves from the romaine. Break off the rest of the leaves, leaving them whole; wash and pat dry. Dip the leaves in hot water (this is to soften them and make them easier to roll), then stuff and roll the leaves. (A large leaf is perfect for one roll. If the leaves are small, overlap two.) Tightly pack the stuffed leaves into the pot so they hold each other together.

THIS DISH is so tasty, its fame is well earned. No wedding banquet in Turkey is prepared without it, and it is still the star of traditional banquet tables. Many countries that were once part of the Ottoman Empire still cook this meaty concoction. On a visit to Romania, I learned that it is the national dish, served with yogurt and garlic sauce, just as we do. Greeks serve it with lemon and egg sauce instead.

Grape Leaves Stuffed with Meat and Rice (*Etli Yaprak Sarma*)

FOR THE YOGURT AND GARLIC SAUCE

1 cup (240 ml) plain Greek yogurt

1 clove garlic and 1 teaspoon salt, crushed with a mortar and pestle

FOR THE GRAPE LEAVES

10½ ounces (300 g) fresh grape leaves, or 1 pound brined grape leaves, stems removed and reserved

1 pound (455 g) ground lamb or veal or a combination (lamb delivers a fuller taste)

⅓ cup (65 g) medium-grain rice, washed in a sieve

1 cup (10 g) minced fresh parsley leaves (optional)

½ cup (10 g) minced dill (optional)

1 tablespoon dried mint

1 large onion, minced or grated

1 medium tomato, halved and grated (see Note, page 60)

2 tablespoons butter, melted (olive oil may substituted, but butter supplies a more fulfilling taste)

Salt and black pepper

2½ cups (600 ml) hot water

FOR SERVING

2 tablespoons browned butter (optional; see Note)

Serves 8

Make the yogurt and garlic sauce: Beat together the yogurt and garlic, then let sit at room temperature.

Make the grape leaves: Blanch fresh grape leaves in boiling water for a few seconds to soften them. (If using brined leaves, soak them for at least 30 minutes in lots of warm water, then wash each leaf to remove the salt.) In a large bowl, combine the lamb, rice, parsley (if using), dill (if using), mint, onion, tomato, and butter, and season with salt and pepper. If the filling is too thick, add a few spoonfuls of water. (A looser filling gives a softer texture.)

Arrange a grape leaf on the work surface, shiny side down, stem end facing you. Place 1 heaping tablespoon filling on the side of the leaf nearest to you (the amount will differ depending on size of leaf, but be generous, especially if you are using preserved leaves); make sure to leave ½ inch (12 mm) on both sides too, which will be used to cover the filling. Roll the grape leaves: Secure the sides by folding them over the filling, then tightly wrap the stem side of the leaf over the filling and start rolling away from you, as tightly as you can, enclosing the filling as you go to create a tight bundle. (Aesthetically, the bundle should be rather slim, not plump.) Repeat with the remaining grape leaves and filling. Line the bottom of a pot with the reserved grape leaf stems.

Pack the rolls tightly in the pot, add 3 to 4 tablespoons cold water, weigh the rolls down with a heavy plate, and cover the pot tightly. Cook for 5 minutes, until the water is absorbed (this step ensures that the leaves will not open up!). Pour the 2½ cups (600 ml) hot water over the plate and cook for 30 minutes, until almost all the liquid is absorbed. Arrange on a platter, drizzle with the browned butter, if desired, and serve with the yogurt sauce.

Note: To brown the butter, heat it over medium heat until it gives off a nice aroma and is almost brown. Pour into a heatproof cup; if it is kept on the heat or in the hot pan too long, the particles in the butter will burn and make it bitter.

THIS DELICIOUS dish is from Tokat, a city that's situated on the border of the Middle Anatolia and Black Sea regions. This recipe is sure to become a favorite of vegetable lovers, as it pairs fresh fennel fronds with fresh or dried fava beans, but any other aromatic greens you favor may be used instead. Be sure to use only the freshest spices. Tokat is also famous for its grape leaves, as they are thin and the veins are hardly visible. In fact, they are the most sought-after grape leaves in Turkey because they turn a nice golden color once cooked.

Tokat-Style Meatless Grape-Leaf Rolls

FOR THE STUFFED GRAPE LEAVES

1 cup (125 g) shelled fresh fava (broad) beans, coarsely chopped (see Notes)

1½ cups (210 g) fine bulgur

Large pinch of minced wild fennel (see Notes)

1 teaspoon mild red pepper flakes

1 teaspoon ground cumin

Salt and black pepper

1 tablespoon tomato or red-pepper paste, dissolved in 1 cup warm water

1 pound (455 g) very fresh grape leaves, briefly blanched

FOR THE COOKING LIQUID

1 large onion, thinly sliced

3 to 4 tablespoons olive or sunflower oil

1 tablespoon tomato or red-pepper paste

About 1 cup (240 ml) warm water

Serves 6 to 8 as meze

Mix together the beans, bulgur, fennel, red pepper flakes, cumin, and salt and black pepper to taste in a bowl; add the diluted tomato or red-pepper paste. The filling should be runny.

Make the stuffed grape leaves: Arrange a grape leaf on the work surface, shiny side down, stem end facing you. Place 1 heaping tablespoon filling on the side of the leaf nearest to you (the amount will differ depending on size of leaf, but be generous, especially if you are using preserved leaves); make sure to leave ½ inch (12 mm) on both sides too, which will be used to cover the filling. Roll the grape leaves: Secure the sides by folding them over the filling, then tightly wrap the stem side of the leaf over the filling and start rolling away from you, as tightly as you can, enclosing the filling as you go to create a tight bundle. (Aesthetically, the bundle should be slim, not plump.) Repeat with the remaining grape leaves and filling. Pack the rolls tightly in the pot.

Make the cooking liquid: Fry the onion in the oil until translucent, then stir in the tomato or red-pepper paste. Pour in the warm water and bring to a boil. Pour enough of the liquid into the pot to just cover the rolls, weighing them down with a heavy plate so they don't open during cooking. Cook over medium heat for 40 to 45 minutes, until the water is absorbed and the rolls are cooked through. (Stuffed vegetables should never be cooked in too much water or at too high a temperature. If the water has boiled away and the rolls are still not cooked, add more water.) Serve warm.

Notes: Dried green lentils or dried fava beans may be substituted. Soak for 2 to 3 hours in warm water before chopping.

When you find fresh wild fennel, buy a bunch, blanch it, and store in batches in the freezer to use as needed. You may use mint, purple basil, or dill as a substitute.

EXCITING AND exotic for vegetarians, this dish features truly nomadic ingredients. It's from Erzurum, a city right in the heart of eastern Anatolia. *Lor* is a curd cheese; the preferred kind contains some fat and has a sweetish taste. If you can't locate *lor*, you can substitute ricotta cheese.

Grape Leaves Stuffed with *Lor* Cheese

7 ounces (200 g) fresh grape leaves, or 10½ ounces (300 g) brined grape leaves, or 9 ounces (255 g) Swiss chard

1 large onion, minced

2 tablespoons virgin olive oil

1 cup (140 g) coarse bulgur

1 pound (455 g/1 cup) *lor* cheese

1 pound (455 g/1 cup) skim-milk cottage cheese, strained if too watery

1 cup (240 ml) warm milk or stock

1 tablespoon unsalted butter

2 cloves garlic, crushed with a mortar and pestle

1 cup (240 ml) plain Greek yogurt

2 tablespoons browned butter (see Note, page 65)

Black pepper

Serves 8

Preheat the oven to 350°F (180°C).

Blanch fresh grape leaves in boiling water for a few seconds to soften them. (If using brined leaves, soak them for at least 30 minutes in lots of warm water, then wash each leaf to remove the salt. If using chard, blanch the leaves for a few seconds.)

Sauté the onion in the oil until translucent, about 5 minutes. Transfer to a bowl and stir in the bulgur, *lor* cheese, and cottage cheese to make the filling.

Place a grape leaf on a flat surface, shiny side down. Arrange 1 heaping tablespoon stuffing on the edge of the leaf closest to you, about ½ inch (12 mm) away from the edge; make sure it is also about ½ inch (12 mm) away from both sides. To roll the grape leaf, first secure the two sides by folding the extra part of the leaf in over the stuffing, then start rolling the leaf away from you to enclose the stuffing, as tightly as you can. Arrange the stuffed leaves in an ungreased casserole dish. Pour the warm milk or stock over the rolls, dot with the butter, cover, and bake for 20 to 25 minutes. Let sit for about 10 minutes for the flavors to meld (also the yogurt sauce will curdle if the grape leaf rolls are too hot). Whisk together the garlic and yogurt, then pour the yogurt mixture over the grape leaves. Top with the browned butter, sprinkle with pepper, and serve.

STUFFING CABBAGE leaves with a meat and rice filling was probably adopted after the Turks conquered the Balkans in the fourteenth century, and then passed along to the Swedes, who make a similar dish they call *kaldolmar*. After losing a war with the Russians, the Swedish king Charles XII took refuge in Turkey en route to his home, and his cooks stayed on for a while as guests of the sultan. Either the cooks really liked the dish or it was served to them far too often, because they brought the method back to their own country. I find cabbage rolls easier to prepare than grape-leaf rolls: Even if not uniform in shape, cabbage leaves cook up nicely and assume a convenient shape for rolling. In Turkey, cabbage rolls are served with lemon, unlike grape-leaf rolls, which are always served with garlic-yogurt sauce.

Cabbage Rolls Stuffed with Meat
(*Etli Lahana Sarma*)

1 cup (20 g) fresh parsley leaves, chopped, with stems reserved

1 medium green cabbage (with loose, not tightly packed, leaves)

1 large onion, diced

1 tablespoon butter or sunflower oil

1 tablespoon tomato paste

1 pound (455 g) ground lamb or veal (or a mixture of the two)

¾ cup (150 g) rice, washed in a sieve

¼ teaspoon ground allspice

½ teaspoon white or black pepper

Salt

Fresh lemon juice for serving

Serves 6 to 8

Line the bottom of a pot with the reserved parsley stems; set aside. Remove the cabbage leaves from the core (without tearing them) until you get to the small leaves surrounding the core. In a large pot, parboil the leaves only until soft enough to roll. Sauté the onion in the butter or oil in a frying pan until soft. Add the tomato paste and sauté until aromatic. Remove from the heat and let cool. Add the meat, rice, allspice, pepper, salt to taste, and parsley leaves and knead with you hands until uniform. If the stuffing mixture is too stiff, add a few tablespoons water. (A looser filling gives a softer texture.)

Cut the cabbage leaves into uniform-size rectangles. Place a generous spoonful of filling on the bottom edge of a rectangle and roll it up tightly. Pack the rolls firmly into the parsley-lined pot and weigh them down with a heavy plate. Add enough hot water just to cover the rolls and cook over medium heat for 40 minutes. Let the rolls cool, then sprinkle them with lemon juice just before serving.

THIS GIFT from Anya von Bremzen to the appetizer world is a result of our endless discussions about the culinary arts. Since she has written many books about several cuisines, she comes up with the most fascinating combinations using indigenous ingredients, as in this simple meze with a complex taste, which she created using common Turkish ingredients. Here *pastırma* and halloumi, a hard and salty but meltable cheese from Cyprus, are wrapped and grilled in grape leaves and dressed with two native ingredients: pomegranate syrup and pekmez. For another delicious *pastırma* recipe, see Amulet-Shaped *Pastırma* Pies on page 210.

Grilled Halloumi and *Pastırma* Grape-Leaf Wrap

12 brined grape leaves

2 quarts (2 L) hot water

12 finger-length pieces *pastırma* (spicy air-dried beef)

12 finger-length pieces halloumi cheese, or any meltable hard cheese, such as pecorino

1½ tablespoons extra-virgin olive oil, plus more for drizzling

2 tablespoons pomegranate syrup (see page 20)

¼ teaspoon pekmez (see page 20)

Serves 6 as meze

Soak the leaves in the hot water for 5 minutes to rinse off the salt. (If the leaves are still salty, let soak a while longer). Remove the leaves from the hot water, rinse with cold water, and drain on paper towels. On each leaf, shiny side down, place 1 piece of *pastırma* and 1 piece of halloumi on top of each other. (If the cheese extends beyond the edges of the grape leaves, cut it off.) Wrap as described in Stuffed Grape Leaves with Olive Oil (page 63), and drizzle a little oil over them.

Preheat the broiler to medium. Place the wraps under the broiler and broil on each side for 1½ minutes, or until the cheese is melted (see Note). Whisk together the oil with the pomegranate syrup, pekmez, and 1 tablespoon water. Arrange the wraps on a serving platter, pour the dressing over them, and serve.

Note: The wraps also can be pan-fried or cooked in a sandwich grill, taking care not to crush them.

SHISH KEBABS AND KOFTA

The shish kebab is a world-renowned dish that owes its fame to the Turks. In fact, Turks came from Asia with the knowledge of making shish kebabs—cubes of meat threaded on a skewer and grilled in no time. Not only are shish kebabs easy to make, they also make a great impression: They're aesthetically appealing and with a taste that pleases all palates. Turks use lamb exclusively in their shish kebabs, and, considering the top quality of lamb in Turkey, it's an excellent choice. Although sometimes beef is used in other places, it is tougher and does not deliver the traditional flavor of lamb. Turks also place pieces of fresh tomatoes and peppers in between the meat cubes, which makes the dish more festive and special.

Kofta (or *köfte*) is another tantalizing meze that has long been popular, most likely because it is both economical to prepare and perfect for sharing. It is no wonder that these walnut-size fried meatballs are a preferred offering at communal gatherings of all sorts, including cocktail parties. You cannot go wrong with kofta, especially if you serve them with a nice side or sauce. Yogurt and Garlic Sauce (page 65) is an old standby, but I've provided several other recipes for dips that you can serve with kofta, including Tahini and Onions (page 91) and Hot Paprika and Walnut Spread (page 26).

WALNUT-SIZE fried meatballs, what we call *köfte*, are a ubiquitous offering, especially with drinks at cocktail hour. Even though they can be found everywhere, we are always happy to be served *köfte*—and, since they are easily picked up with a toothpick, they are often our first choice from the meze platter. This recipe is similar to the typical recipe, but my addition of walnuts, plus a drizzle of tahini and a sprinkle of cumin for serving, will make it more exciting.

Meatballs with Parsley and Walnuts (*Köfte*)

2 pounds (910 g) minced or ground lean veal

3 cups (60 g) loosely packed fresh parsley leaves, chopped

1 large onion, chopped

¾ teaspoon black pepper

¾ teaspoon salt

1 cup (120 g) ground walnuts

½ cup (55 g) all-purpose flour

2 tablespoons unsalted butter, plus more as needed

1 cup (240 ml) sunflower oil, plus more as needed

Tahini for serving

Ground cumin for serving

Seves 6 as meze

In a stand mixer with the dough hook attached, mix the meat with the parsley, onion, pepper, and salt until well combined. (If the bowl of the mixer is small, mix in two batches.) Knead the meat mixture with the walnuts by hand until incorporated. Form the mixture into walnut-size balls (you should have 30 to 40 meatballs) and roll the balls in the flour to coat.

Melt the butter with the oil in a skillet over medium heat. Fry the meatballs in batches until they are golden on all sides, 8 to 10 minutes, adding more butter and oil as needed. Transfer to paper towels to drain. Drizzle lightly with tahini and sprinkle with cumin to serve.

THIS KIND of shish kebab is prepared in the style of the Gaziantep kebab masters (see Note). *Tike* means "cube" in Turkish. In certain areas of India today, where Turkish-Mughal culture was once dominant, cubes of meat or chicken marinated and then grilled on skewers is called *tikka*. Although the *tike kebab* is now popular worldwide, it seems likely that it first spread to South Asia via the establishment of a Turkish-Mughal dynasty in the Indian subcontinent from the sixteenth to the mid-eighteenth centuries.

Tike Shish Kebab (*Tike Kebab*)

FOR THE *KEBAB TERBIYE* (MARINADE)

2 tablespoons olive oil

1 tablespoon tomato paste

1 tablespoon red pepper paste

¼ teaspoon black pepper

½ teaspoon ground allspice

2 cloves garlic, crushed with a mortar and pestle

FOR THE LAMB

2 pounds (910 g) lamb, cut into walnut-size cubes

3½ ounces (100 g) lamb tail fat (purchase from a halal butcher; optional)

FOR THE KEBAB CONDIMENTS

2 pounds (910 g) tomatoes, diced

3 to 4 small mild, green chile peppers, such as Anaheim

½ teaspoon mild red pepper flakes

1 tablespoon minced fresh thyme

Salt to taste

Serves 6

Make the *kebab terbiye:* Mix together all the ingredients with 3 to 4 tablespoons water. Add the meat cubes to the *terbiye*, generously coat each piece, and marinate in the refrigerator for at least 12 hours or up to 24 hours.

Prepare the lamb: Preheat an outdoor grill to medium-high heat. Put the meat cubes on skewers, with a piece of lamb tail fat in between, if using. Assemble the condiments in a bowl. Grill the kebabs for about 10 minutes, turning occasionally. (Cooking longer than this will dry out the meat.) Serve the kebabs on the skewers with the condiments alongside.

Note: In Gaziantep, a cube of raw eggplant and a piece of green pepper or even loquat (if in season) are placed between the meat cubes.

THIS KIND of kebab—a combination of kofta and onions—is normally eaten in a kebab restaurant. It certainly tastes better there because the meat is grilled over a wood fire and cut with a *zırh* (a special heavy butcher's knife for cutting meat into small pieces), which gives it a wonderful texture. In addition, the meat is lamb and has fat, and shallots can be used instead of onions. (I have given away the trade secrets!) My addition of walnuts gives the extra crunch that kofta can miss because of modern grinding techniques.

Onion Kebab

3 to 4 medium onions, sliced about ½ inch (12 mm) thick, or 15 shallots, peeled and cut in half

1 pound (455 g) ground lamb (preferably with some fat), or a mix of ground lamb and ground beef (ask your butcher to run either meat through the grinder only once)

½ packed cup (10 g) fresh parsley, minced

1 to 2 cloves garlic, finely minced

½ cup (50 g) walnuts, roughly chopped

Salt

½ teaspoon black pepper

¼ teaspoon ground coriander (optional)

½ tablespoon unsalted butter

¾ cup (180 ml) lamb, beef, or chicken stock

¼ cup (60 ml) pomegranate syrup (see page 20)

Hot red pepper flakes, for serving

Serves 6 to 8

Wrap the onions or shallots in foil and heat in a preheated 400°F (205°C) toaster oven for 5 minutes or in a 400°F (205°C) oven for about 15 minutes, until softened. Transfer to a sauté pan and set aside.

Knead the meat with the parsley, garlic, walnuts, salt to taste, the pepper, and the coriander, if using. Form the meat mixture into walnut-size balls. Put the butter in a preheated frying pan and add the kofta as soon as the butter melts. Shake the pan so the kofta are browned on all sides, but don't overcook them. When the kofta are browned, transfer them onto the onion slices. Add the stock and pomegranate syrup and simmer for 15 to 20 minutes to cook the kofta through and to meld the flavors. Serve straight from the pan and sprinkle with red pepper flakes, if desired.

Note: If you prefer, after browning, transfer the pan to a 350°F (180°C) oven for 15 to 30 minutes to finish cooking.

THIS KOFTA, the pride of eastern Turkey, gets its flavor from the butter in the filling. Since you won't cook this every day, don't feel guilty about being generous with the butter. Anyone stingy with the butter will end up with dry kofta—a pity after all that work. Preparing the thin shell requires expertise. I have eaten ones with a shell as thin as chicken skin. Mine are not that thin, but you can't succeed if you don't try! These kofta will taste good anyway—as long as there is plenty of butter.

Kofta with Filling (*İçli Köfte*)

FOR THE CASING

8 ounces (225 g) very lean ground beef (see Note)

2 cups (280 g) fine bulgur

1 large egg

1 tablespoon all-purpose flour

1 tablespoon semolina flour

Mild red pepper flakes

Salt and black pepper

FOR THE FILLING

3 medium onions, chopped

7 tablespoons (100 g) unsalted butter

1 tablespoon olive oil

1 pound (455 g) ground lamb (with some fat)

2 cups (200 g) walnut halves

1 tablespoon mild red pepper flakes

1 tablespoon red pepper paste

1 teaspoon ground allspice

1 packed cup (20 g) minced fresh parsley

Serves 6

Make the casing: Mix all the ingredients in a food processor three times, sprinkling with a little water each time. Let the mixture sit while you make the filling.

Make the filling: In a large pan, sauté the onion in the butter and oil until soft, then add the meat and sauté until cooked through. Add the walnuts, red pepper flakes, red pepper paste, allspice, and parsley and mix well. Let the filling mixture sit until cool.

In a large pot, bring plenty of water to a boil, then reduce the heat to a simmer (otherwise, the kofta will break). From the casing mixture, take a walnut-size piece. Spread it out on your palm until slightly bigger than your palm. Press on it in the middle, but don't make a hole. Place a spoonful of filling in the middle and cover it by folding over the rest of the casing (try to keep the thickness uniform). Pinch to close. Carefully add the kofta to the simmering water one by one. When done, they will rise to the surface. Carefully remove them with a slotted spoon and place in a warm oven until serving time. The leftovers can be fried in a little oil until heated through.

Note: Be sure to use lean ground beef for the casing. If there is too much fat in the meat, the kofta will break in the simmering water.

THIS IS the most popular street food in Turkey. It takes its name from the sound the patties make when placed on the grill. When there is a football game, the mobile *cızbız kofta* makers with their special carts fitted with grills, will take their place—with tomatoes and peppers already cut—all around the arena. The air is filled with the appetizing aroma of the grilling kofta and, if you are close enough, you can hear the "cız cız" sound. The secret of their *cızbız* is that they make thin patties that are fast and economical to grill.

Cızbız kofta is also a popular fast food in Turkey, made in unique restaurants called *köfteci*. My mother used to make a similar kofta, but it was fried and didn't really taste the same. I devised this method after questioning a lot of *cızbız* makers—if I used a fattier meat, it would taste almost the same as the street *cızbız*. But this less fatty version is still very good and is now a regular dish on our menu at home. The other secret is that the fewer breadcrumbs are used, the better the taste.

Cızbız Kofta

1½ pounds (672 g) ground beef (see Notes)

2 tablespoons breadcrumbs

Juice from 1 grated onion, pulp discarded

6 stems parsley; cut the stems and mince the leaves

1 heaping teaspoon ground black pepper

Salt

1½ tablespoons vegetable oil (optional; use only if the meat is very lean), plus more for greasing the pan

2 tomatoes, sliced and grilled (see Notes)

2 green peppers, sliced and grilled (see Notes)

Bread or flatbread for serving

Serves 8

In a stand mixer or by hand, mix together the beef, breadcrumbs, onion juice, parsley, and pepper. Season with salt and add the vegetable oil, if using. Mix for about 3 minutes.

Form the mixture into 24 round or elongated patties about ½ inch (12 mm) thick. Grease a nonstick pan or flat griddle lightly with oil and preheat the surface.

Place the kofta in the hot pan for 1 minute then turn them. Continue to turn them each minute for about 5 minutes. They should be cooked through but not overcooked. If there is room in the pan, cook the tomatoes and peppers at the same time (see Notes). Serve immediately, with the grilled tomatoes and peppers, on warm sliced bread or flatbread.

Notes: For a more authentic version, replace one-third of the ground beef with lamb ground from a fatty cut.

Since the kofta have to be served right away, it is better to grill the peppers and tomatoes beforehand if your pan or griddle is too small for you to cook them together. If you are making several batches, it is best to hold those already cooked in the pan, covered with a thin slice of bread, so that they will stay hot.

THIS IS a popular kofta of the eastern region. In Turkish cuisine, meat is paired with yogurt or yogurt mixtures. The tanginess of the yogurt makes for an appealing accompaniment to the spicy kofta.

Fried Kofta with Bulgur
(*Bulgurlu Kimyon Köfte, Tavada*)

FOR THE PARSLEY AND WALNUT
 CACIK

1 cup (240 ml) plain Greek yogurt

1½ cups (30 g) minced fresh parsley

2 cloves garlic, crushed with
 a mortar and pestle

½ cup (50 g) walnuts, coarsely
 broken

FOR THE KOFTA

1 cup (140 g) fine bulgur

1¼ pounds (570 g) lean ground lamb
 or beef

1 medium onion, diced

2 cloves garlic, finely minced

1½ teaspoons ground cumin

½ teaspoon black pepper

1 tablespoon mild red pepper flakes

Salt

Vegetable or olive oil for frying

Serves 8 to 10 as meze

Make the parsley and walnut *cacik*: Mix together the yogurt, parsley, garlic, and walnuts (don't add the garlic more than 2 hours before serving).

Make the kofta: Cook the bulgur over low heat, sprinkling with 1 cup (240 ml) water by hand while cooking. When the water has been absorbed, in 3 to 5 minutes, remove from the heat. Let cool. When cooled, mix the bulgur with the meat, onion, garlic, cumin, black pepper, and red pepper flakes, season with salt, and knead for 3 minutes with wet hands. Break off walnut-size pieces from the meat mixture and form them into elongated or round balls. (You should have about 20 elongated or 30 round kofta in all.)

Heat 1 inch (2.5 cm) oil in a pan over medium heat. Working in batches, fry the kofta slowly in the oil, until golden on all sides and cooked through, 6 to 8 minutes per batch. Drain on paper towels. Serve warm or at room temperature with the *cacik*. The *cacik* can be served under the kofta (which will make the presentation really special), or separately.

THIS IS one of the most popular vegetable dishes stemming from the legacy of Jewish cuisine in Turkey. Why it never became popular among the Turkish people is a puzzle as it is so easy to make and very tasty and economical.

Leek Kofta (*Albóndigas de Pırasa*)

2 ½ pounds (1.3 kg) leeks

½ pound (250 g) ground beef or lamb

1 large egg

Salt and freshly ground pepper

Vegetable oil for frying

Serves 8 as meze

Trim the leeks, wash them well, and chop them into small pieces. Bring a pot of water with enough water to cover the leeks to a boil. Add the leeks and when they are soft, strain them and squeeze them in a clean kitchen towel to remove any remaining moisture. Place the leeks in a bowl and add the meat and egg. Season with salt and pepper and mix well. Form the mixture into balls slightly larger than the size of a walnut. You should have 25 to 30 kofta. Heat 1 inch (2.5 cm) of oil in a pan over medium heat. Working in batches, fry the kofta slowly in the oil, until golden on all sides and cooked through, 6 to 8 minutes per batch. Drain on paper towels. Serve warm or at room temperature.

THIS DISH, a favorite of classic Turkish cuisine, can be bought at delicatessens in Turkey; however, it is never as tasty as the homemade version. Even though the name literally means "lady's thigh," the kofta is the size of a rabbit thigh. Its unique taste comes from sautéing half of the ground meat before mixing in the rest of the ingredients. Coriander is not used traditionally, but it makes a nice addition.

Lady's Thigh Kofta (*Kadınbudu Köfte*)

⅓ cup (35 g) medium-grain rice

2 onions, chopped

1 tablespoon unsalted butter

2 pounds (910 g) lean beef, or a combination of lean beef and lean lamb (the combination will taste better)

¼ cup (5 g) fresh parsley leaves, chopped

Salt and black pepper

½ teaspoon ground coriander

⅓ cup (40 g) all-purpose flour

2 large eggs, beaten

Olive oil for frying

Serves 6

Cook the rice in ½ cup (120 ml) water. Cook the onions in half of the butter over medium heat until softened. In a separate pan, sauté half of the meat in the remaining butter, until all the liquid evaporates. In a large bowl, thoroughly combine the rice, onion, sautéed and raw meats, and parsley. Season with salt and pepper and add the coriander. Remove egg-size pieces from the meat mixture and roll them one by one between your palms into elongated balls. Let sit for 30 minutes, then roll the balls in flour and then in the egg. Heat ½ inch (12 mm) of oil in a frying pan and fry the kofta over medium heat until golden on all sides and cooked through. Drain on paper towels. Serve hot or warm.

SALADS AND CONDIMENTS

When serving an assortment of meze, or appetizers, Turks typically pair them with a selection of side salads and condiments. Turkish dishes do not contain a lot of ingredients, so they may require supplemental flavors to complement them or whet the appetite. Even raw onion will do. (Our favorite condiment to serve with *tarhana* soup at home, for example, is onion.) In *The Cooks' Shelter (Melceü't Tabbahin)*, the first published book about Turkish cuisine (1844), these accompaniments were aptly called "asides." Turkish cuisine's most common side salads are shepherd's salad in the summer (a juicy combination of fresh seasonal tomatoes, cucumbers, peppers, raw onion, and parsley) and leaf lettuce in the winter. These are dressed with olive oil and either lemon juice or vinegar, or in some regions with either pomegranate syrup or sumac. But I have included recipes for other tempting accompaniment salads, from instant pickled peppers to tahini with cumin. Such small asides may very well be part of a meze table, too, providing you serve fresh bread with them.

All-Purpose Asides

Onion with parsley: Slice an onion thinly, salt liberally, and knead the salt into the slices to remove the bitterness or strong taste of the onion, then rinse. (Nowadays onions are rather sweet. If so, you may use them without salting and rinsing.) Mince fresh parsley and mix with the onion rings. This is a great accompaniment to fried or grilled food like Albanian-style liver or roasted baby bonito fish, fried kofta, and grilled meats.

Parsley with sumac: Mince fresh parsley and sprinkle with freshly ground dry sumac. This aside goes well with fried meatballs, sardine birds, cornmeal pancakes with anchovies, and fried liver. Minced onion, or especially chopped green onion, can also be added.

Cumin and hot red pepper flakes: These are great seasonings for grilled meats and also go nicely with fried meatballs. They can be used separately or combined to create a single seasoning.

Garlic yogurt: Crush 1 or 2 cloves garlic, add immediately to a small bowl of yogurt, and serve. (If the garlic sits for more than 1 hour, it becomes bitter.) Garlic yogurt is wonderful with cooked greens like spinach and chard, and with stuffed grape leaves. *Note: Yogurt, with or without garlic, is a standard side dish for vegetable-filled* börek *(savory pastry).*

Summer Asides

Sliced peppers, cucumber, and tomatoes: These vegetables can function as appetizers, eaten raw with a drink before a meal, or they can be served as accompaniments on a meze platter. They are known as *söğüş,* meaning uncooked vegetables served as salads or side dishes.

Roasted fresh peppers: Roast long green peppers, preferably hot ones, over a gas flame or charcoal, peel as well as possible, and serve with meze or with a main dish. They go well with soups and stews.

Pan-fried green peppers: Prick whole bell peppers once or twice (to ensure that the oil will not splatter) and fry in hot olive oil for a couple of minutes, until softened. Remove from the oil and peel, if desired. Mix minced garlic and the juice of a bitter orange, pour over the peppers, sprinkle with salt, and serve as an aside. *Note: Bitter orange juice possesses a unique tartness. If bitter oranges are not available, you can substitute lemon juice mixed with a little white wine vinegar.*

Winter Asides

Onions and red or white radishes: Slice onions and radishes into very thin rounds or wedges. This is a great accompaniment to *tarhana* or lentil soups, meat dishes, and bean or chickpeas dishes.

Roasted dried peppers: Fry mild or hot peppers or roast them in an oven or in a charcoal grill; serve whole or cut up. They go nicely with soups and sprinkled over salads.

Pickles: Not that long ago, a Turkish table was never set without a plate of pickles; in fact, they were a staple on the tables of the sultans. Pickling was a respected, specialized craft, but families also made their own homemade pickles. While the practice of pickling at home is gradually dying out, store-bought pickles are still quite popular. None of these, however, compares to the delicious homemade varieties (pages 94 to 102).

SHEPHERD'S SALAD is always found on summertime tables. The juice of fresh seasonal tomatoes is so delicious that simply dipping bread into the juice makes a meal! This salad is best when the vegetables are chopped but not overhandled. Make the salad just before serving, as the onions will give off a heavy odor if left to sit for even a half hour. If you must cut up the rest of the vegetables in advance, you should cut them not more than an hour before and keep them in the refrigerator, preferably covered. Add the onions, salt, lemon juice, and oil, and mix briefly, just before serving. If you want to get more taste out of the tomatoes, you may sprinkle them with salt when you are preparing the salad. Don't salt the cucumbers, though, or they will wilt and lose their crispness.

Shepherd's Salad

2 large ripe but firm tomatoes, peeled, if preferred, and chopped (firm tomatoes will peel easily with a small sharp knife)

2 medium cucumbers, peeled and thinly sliced (about 1½ cups/180 g)

1 long mild green chile, such as Anaheim, seeded and chopped

1 small onion, minced

Leaves of 2 to 3 sprigs fresh parsley, minced

Salt

2 to 3 tablespoons extra-virgin olive oil

Juice of ½ or 1 lemon (4 to 5 tablespoons/60 to 75 ml; see Note)

3 to 5 olives, for garnishing

Serves 6 as meze

Put the tomatoes, cucumbers, pepper, onion, and parsley in a shallow dish. Sprinkle with salt to taste. Drizzle with the oil and lemon juice and toss gently. Garnish with olives, if using, and serve.

Note: You may use wine vinegar instead of lemon juice. As lemons are not native to Turkey, most likely they were initially thought of as a delicacy, hence their current popularity as a souring agent.

I WAS INTRODUCED to this dish at the breakfast table of a family from Thrace (the westernmost area of Turkey). A hot and garlicky appetite-teaser, it goes well with eggs and cheese at breakfast and is a nice accompaniment to fish or meat. It is messy to prepare this dish over a gas flame, but you know the saying: "Who loves the rose must put up with its thorns."

Warm Grilled Tomato Salad (*Müncür*)

4 medium tomatoes

4 long mild green chiles, such as Anaheim

Salt

2 cloves garlic, crushed with a mortar and pestle

2 to 3 tablespoons extra-virgin olive oil

Mild red pepper flakes (optional)

Serves 8 as meze

Using tongs, cook the tomatoes and peppers directly over a gas flame until the skins of the tomatoes are charred and the peppers are softened (see Note). When cool enough to handle, peel and chop the tomatoes and mince the peppers; combine them in a bowl and add salt to taste. Mix together the garlic and oil, pour over the roasted vegetables, and mix well. If you want it even hotter, sprinkle with red pepper flakes; serve warm.

Note: Alternatively, place the tomatoes and peppers on a sheet of foil in a preheated 400°F (205°C) oven. Roast the peppers for about 10 minutes, according to their size and how soft you want them. Roast the tomatoes for about 15 minutes; when they begin to blacken in places remove from the oven and peel.

AN UNUSUALLY tasty side dish! The recipe was created by Civan Er, a very young chef who has achieved great success with his exciting, experimental use of Turkish spices.

Roasted Red Pepper Salad

3 cloves garlic

Pinch of salt, plus more to taste

10 pickled roasted red peppers, diced (see Note)

Grated zest and juice of 2 lemons

2 fresh or dried hot peppers, seeds removed and diced

1 tablespoon dried mint

1 tablespoon ground coriander

1 tablespoon cumin, whole or ground (if using whole, toast the seeds briefly first)

5 tablespoons (75 ml) extra-virgin olive oil

Serves 6 to 8 as meze

Crush together the garlic and a pinch of salt with a mortar and pestle. Mix together the pickled peppers, lemon zest and juice, garlic-salt mixture, hot peppers, mint, coriander, cumin, and oil. Season with salt to taste and serve.

Note: Pickled roasted red peppers are available in cans or jars from stores selling Turkish food. If you cannot find them, roast red peppers over a gas flame or in a preheated 400°F (205°C) oven; when cool enough to handle, peel, rinse, and drain. Add 5 to 6 tablespoons (75 to 90 ml) wine vinegar (see page 102) and let marinate in the refrigerator for 24 hours.

THIS SIMPLE salad was a winter favorite in my family and, for me, a nice reminder of my mother. The crispness and faint sweetness of the uncooked cabbage, not at all like the flavor of cooked cabbage, gets substance from the olive oil and is enhanced by the flakes of freshly roasted pepper, which is aromatic in its own special way and makes this a dish that everyone loves. In Athens, I ate the same salad, minus the pepper flakes, sprinkled with feta cheese and dressed with a lot more olive oil. With cheese on top, it was almost a meal on its own! But this salad goes well with any kind of dish—even just rice on kofta.

Cabbage Salad, Aegean-Style

1 to 2 cloves garlic

Pinch of salt

⅓ cup (75 ml) olive oil

Juice of 1 lemon

½ medium white cabbage, thinly sliced, washed, and drained (about 4 cups/280 g)

1 dried red chili pepper, roasted over a gas flame (see Note), for garnish

Serves 6 to 8 as meze

Crush together the garlic and salt with a mortar and pestle. Whisk the garlic-salt mixture, oil, and lemon juice into a dressing, drizzle it over the cabbage, and mix thoroughly. Wearing gloves, chop the pepper and sprinkle it over the salad. (Do not let the hot pepper touch your skin!) Serve at room temperature.

Note: With tongs, hold the dried pepper over a gas flame for 30 seconds or until slightly roasted. Let it cool; it will become crisp and easy to crush.

VARIATION

Cauliflower Salad, Aegean-Style

Instead of cabbage, use 1 medium head of cauliflower. Break into florets and discard the thick stems. Boil the cauliflower in plenty of water until tender yet still firm, about 5 minutes. Pour the dressing over the cauliflower and garnish with the roasted dried pepper. This is best served warm.

A SIMPLE recipe I created in memory of a Jewish family now living in Tel Aviv. They served this for breakfast over toast and I found it unusual but tasty; the lemon and dill are my addition. You can omit the cucumbers and pour the dressing over thinly sliced red or black radishes, if you prefer. When using black radishes, peel them before slicing.

Cucumber with Tahini

FOR THE DRESSING

1 clove garlic

Pinch of salt, plus more as needed

3 tablespoons tahini

Juice of ½ lemon, mixed with 3 tablespoons of water

3 medium cucumbers, peeled and sliced

½ cup (10 g) chopped fresh dill

Serves 6 as meze

Make the dressing: Crush together the garlic and salt with a mortar and pestle. Mix the tahini with ⅓ cup (75 ml) water, then add the lemon juice and garlic-salt mixture.

Mix in the cucumber, taste, and add more salt, if needed. Garnish with the dill and serve.

THIS INTERESTING combination of green beans and purslane is from a cookbook written in the mid-nineteenth century, a time when new recipes were being added to the classical cooking of the palace and bourgeoisie. This was mostly due to the influence of prestigious and affluent foreign visitors, including ambassadors and the adventurous rich, who had begun to travel to Istanbul at the end of the Ottoman era. The city had always been a curiosity magnet, but the arrival of the *Orient Express* and the opening of luxurious hotels like the Pera Palace Hotel made travel to this exotic destination more possible.

Green Bean Salad with Purslane

1 pound (455 g) green beans, the fresher the better, picked over and strings removed

3 cups (130 g) purslane, woody stems discarded

3 to 4 tablespoons extra-virgin olive oil

Juice of ½ lemon

2 to 3 tablespoons chopped fresh dill

½ onion, thinly sliced

Serves 6 as meze

Add the beans to a pot of boiling water and cook until tender, about 8 minutes. Immediately drain and rinse under cold running water to stop the cooking. Transfer to a bowl and add the purslane. Whisk the oil and lemon juice together until smooth, pour over the beans and purslane, and mix well. Garnish with the dill and onion and serve.

WE MAKE this salad at home, but it is a classic salad in kebab restaurants. Known in Turkey as mashed eggplant, it is always one of the appetizers on offer because the sour taste of the yogurt goes well with both raki and kebabs. This salad can be prepared thick, but I prefer it on the thinner side. It's a must-have summer dish around the Muğla region, especially in Ula, my mother's hometown.

Eggplant Salad with Yogurt

2 to 3 Italian eggplants or 4 Japanese eggplants (each about 8 inches/20 cm long), roasted directly over gas or charcoal flame

2 long green peppers, roasted directly over gas or charcoal flame (optional)

1 to 2 cloves garlic and a pinch of salt, crushed with a mortar and pestle

1½ cups (360 ml) plain Greek yogurt

½ teaspoon salt

2 tablespoons olive oil

Serves 6 as meze

Peel the roasted eggplants while still hot, if possible, because they peel faster. (The best method is to peel with a knife, holding each eggplant by its stem.) Rinse under running water. Skin the roasted peppers, if using, and rinse under running water. Let the vegetables drain and cool for 30 minutes in a colander, then dice. Mix the garlic-salt mixture into the yogurt. Add the eggplant, peppers, if using, and salt to the yogurt mixture and toss to combine. Transfer to a platter, drizzle olive oil on top, and serve.

VARIATION

If you like, you can spread some sweet pekmez (see page 20) on top to balance the taste of the yogurt—if it is on the sour side—as is done in *nazkhatun,* an Anatolian dish that's also made with eggplant and soured, strained yogurt. Sometimes this dish is also topped with roasted almonds.

THIS SALAD was served to me by Filiz Hösükoğlu, who is an expert in the cooking of Gaziantep. I took the recipe over the phone, and her instructions were so detailed, it was successful the first time I made it. My son loved it and told me that I could serve it to him anytime instead of the purslane salad he loves, so we now have a new family favorite. The crushed ice adds a lot to this salad by making the radishes crunchier. Like most salads from eastern Turkey, this salad is prepared without olive oil, as it is hard to get it where olive trees are not part of the landscape.

Anatolian Gypsy Salad

2 cups (230 g) diced red radishes

½ cup (10 g) finely chopped fresh mint or tarragon

¾ cup (15 g) finely chopped fresh parsley

2 teaspoons sumac

1 large clove garlic, crushed

1 tablespoon tomato paste, diluted with 2 tablespoons cold water

3 tablespoons pomegranate syrup (see page 20)

3 tablespoons crushed ice (optional)

Salt

Serves 6 as meze

In a bowl, toss together the radishes, mint or tarragon, parsley, sumac, and garlic. Add the diluted tomato paste, pomegranate syrup, and ice and toss. Season with salt to taste and serve immediately in a chilled bowl.

TRADITIONALLY, PURSLANE was picked and cooked only in select regions of Turkey where wild purslane grew in abundance. Wild purslane grows among cultivated vegetables and is still known in some regions as *bostan guzeli* (beauty of the vegetable garden). These greens became very popular throughout the land as a salad, however, when cultivated purslane (*semizotu*) appeared on the market; today it has become an indispensable salad ingredient that's regularly praised for its health benefits, which has made it even more popular. Cultivated purslane has larger, thicker leaves than the wild variety. Although the leaves are quite bland and not crisp, they take very well to a seasoning of lemon and garlic, and impart a juiciness to salads. Purslane wilts quickly, so use it within a day or two.

Purslane Salad

6 cups (170 g) purslane, washed well, tough stems and wilted leaves discarded

1 medium cucumber, diced

1 green onion, minced

2 tablespoons crumbly Turkish tulum cheese (see Note, page 24) or any rich, ripe crumbly cheese, or grated Parmesan

2 tablespoons olive oil

¼ cup (60 ml) fresh lemon juice

1 clove garlic, crushed with a mortar and pestle

2 dried hot chile peppers, toasted over a gas flame (see Note, page 85), for garnish

Serves 6 as meze

Layer the salad ingredients in a salad bowl, starting with the purslane, then the cucumber and green onion, and ending with the cheese. Whisk the oil, lemon juice, and crushed garlic together and pour over the salad just before serving. Toss the salad. Wearing gloves, chop the hot peppers, sprinkle them over the salad, and serve.

IN GAZIANTEP in southeastern Turkey, this is served as an accompaniment to meatballs tartar (*Çiğ Köfte*), but it can also be used as a salad dressing or an accompaniment to any kind of kofta.

Tahini and Onions

4 teaspoons ground cumin

⅓ cup (75 ml) tahini

5 to 6 tablespoons (75 to 90 ml) fresh lemon juice

½ teaspoon mild red pepper flakes

Salt

1 medium onion, sliced into thin rings

1 teaspoon black pepper

Serves 6 as meze

Make a paste with the cumin and a generous 3 to 4 tablespoons (45 to 60 ml) water. Drizzle in the tahini and lemon juice. (Add in batches to make the emulsification process easier.) Add the red pepper flakes and salt to taste and whisk together until smooth. Mix in the onions and stir until the onions are completely coated with dressing. Sprinkle with black pepper and serve it alongside the kofta of your choice.

Note: Make sure the tahini is as runny as it's supposed to be. If its oil has separated, stir it until completely reincorporated.

THIS IS a specialty of the Antalya region, located on the Mediterranean coast of southwestern Turkey. *Piyaz* is usually made with olive oil, but here they dress it with tahini.

Dried Bean Salad with Tahini
(*Tahinli Piyaz*)

2 cups (400 g) white beans, soaked overnight

1 cup (180 g) Tahini and Onions (above)

1 cup (20 g) minced fresh parsley

Serves 6 as meze

In a pot, combine the beans and 1½ quarts (1.4 L) water (add more water if the water does not cover the beans by at least 1 inch). Cook over medium heat for 45 minutes or until the beans are soft but still firm. Drain and, while the beans are still warm, add the Tahini and Onions, mixing slowly until the beans are thoroughly coated with the dressing. Spoon into a serving dish, garnish with the parsley, and serve.

THIS RECIPE was created by me at sea. We were out on our boat cruising near the Mediterranean coast of Turkey, and I put together what I had on hand. The cookbook author and writer Anya von Bremzen was one of the guests and she liked this salad so much that she submitted it to *Food and Wine*. The magazine presented this as one of the healthiest dishes in the world, which came as a wonderful surprise.

Hot Bulgur Salad

6 to 7 dried tomatoes, drained of oil, if necessary, and chopped to chickpea size

3 to 4 tablespoons olive oil

1 cup (140 g) fine bulgur

1 cup (150 g) cooked chickpeas

1¾ cups (420 ml) warm water

Salt

1 teaspoon ground hot red pepper

2 tablespoons pomegranate syrup (see page 20)

2 tablespoons fresh lemon juice

15 cherry tomatoes, quartered

10 to 15 fresh mint leaves, minced

3 tablespoons chopped fresh dill

3 to 4 tablespoons pomegranate seeds for garnish

¾ cup (75 g) walnut pieces for garnish

Serves 8 as meze

In a deep skillet over medium heat, lightly sauté the dried tomatoes in the oil. Add the bulgur and chickpeas and stir until the bulgur is translucent and the chickpeas are crisp, about 2 minutes. Do not stir as you add the warm water, and salt to taste; cook over low heat for 3 to 4 minutes, then turn the heat down to very low and cook for another 2 to 3 minutes. Remove from the heat and let sit for 5 minutes, until the bulgur is tender. Add the red pepper, pomegranate syrup, lemon juice, cherry tomatoes, mint, and dill. Stir thoroughly and spoon into a serving dish. Garnish with the pomegranate seeds and walnuts and serve.

IN TURKEY, pickle making is primarily a family tradition. The most popular pickle makers in Istanbul today hail from Bursa. They maintain that, along with the city's white wine, it is Bursa's pure water that gives their pickles a unique taste. My taste buds tell me that the ratios of vinegar, salt, and water are as important as the actual ingredients. But when I started to learn pickle making from my green-grocer, Necmi Akbulut, I immediately saw that he doesn't measure anything. When I asked him how he knew the right quantities, he answered, "By tasting." I told him that my cookbook wouldn't come with taste buds, and immediately found some measuring cups and spoons. What follows is the recipe we came up with, right there in his shop.

Mixed Pickles with Store-Bought Vinegar

FOR THE BRINE

1½ quarts (1.4 L) filtered or spring water

2 cups (480 ml) white vinegar (see page 102)

4 heaping tablespoons (60 g) kosher salt

FOR THE PICKLES

10 very fresh cucumbers, each pierced with a needle in 4 or 5 places

2 pounds (910 g) cabbage, chopped into egg-size pieces

8 to 10 hot red peppers

3 carrots, peeled and thinly sliced lengthwise

20 fresh green beans, trimmed

5 to 6 sprigs fresh parsley

3 to 4 sprigs fresh mint

5 to 6 sprigs celery leaves, minced

4 to 5 sprigs fresh fennel or dill fronds

4 to 5 cloves garlic, chopped if large

2 bay leaves

1 teaspoon citric acid

Makes 1 (3-quart/2.8-L) jar, or 3 (1-quart/960-ml) jars

Make the brine: Put the water, vinegar, and salt in a large bowl or pan.

Make the pickles: In a clean 3-quart (2.8-L) glass jar, pack the cucumbers, cabbage, hot peppers, carrots, and green beans, sprinkling with the parsley, mint, celery leaves, fennel or dill, garlic, and bay leaves at intervals. Press firmly on the vegetables, leaving as little space in the jar as possible. (If necessary, add carrot slices at a diagonal to the other vegetables.) Pour the brine mixture into the jar, add the citric acid, and close the jar tightly. Some liquid may spill out, but this will help ensure that no air enters the jar.

Wipe the outside of the jar with a damp cloth and place the jar in a cool, dark place. When the cucumbers have yellowed, the pickles are ready; about 15 days in hot weather and 20 days in cool weather.

Pickles Fit for the Sultan

In Ottoman times, the most delicate and delicious produce was collected just for pickles for the sultan's table. Pickled cabbage was the palace favorite, but Ottoman royalty also enjoyed cucumber, zucchini, eggplant, and other vegetables pickled with *şalgam* (rutabaga) juice. Most of the pickles were made in the palace's "halvah kitchen"; however, pickled capers came from Osmancık, near the Black Sea, and pickled apples came from Amasya in northern Turkey, which is famous for its apples; all were brought into Istanbul on mules. The tradition of pickles for the palace made from grapes from Gelibolu on the Dardenelles strait dates back to 1470, the time of Sultan Mehmet II, the conqueror of Istanbul.

I CAME across this simple dish served as a meze at one of the famous fish restaurants in Dalyan near Çeşme, the resort town of İzmir. As simple as it was, it boosted my appetite because the peppers were hot and, with vinegar added, even more appetizing.

Instant Pickled Green Peppers

2 cloves garlic

Pinch of salt

8 to 10 long green peppers (whatever kind you like)

¼ cup (60 ml) white vinegar, preferably homemade (page 102)

Virgin olive oil (optional)

Serves 6 to 8 as meze

Crush the garlic and salt together with a mortar and pestle. Roast the peppers directly over a gas flame (see Note, page 85). Peel and discard burnt portions. Chop the peppers or leave them whole. Mix the garlic-salt mixture with the vinegar and the oil, if using, and pour over the peppers. Serve immediately, or store in the refrigerator for up to a day or two.

WITH THEIR color and delicious flavor, pickled beets are a popular addition to any pickle selection.

Instant Pickled Beets

2 pounds (910 g) beets, washed, trimmed, and peeled

1½ cups (360 ml) white vinegar, preferably homeade (see page 102)

½ teaspoon kosher salt

¼ teaspoon sugar

3 cloves garlic, minced

2 teaspoons olive oil (optional)

Makes about 4 cups

Boil the beets whole for 20 to 30 minutes, until they can be pierced easily with a knife. Drain and let cool, then slice, chop, or cut into wedges, as you prefer. Place the beets in a deep bowl. Whisk together the vinegar, salt, sugar, garlic, and 1 cup (240 ml) water, and pour over the beets. Add the olive oil, if you like. Let marinate in the refrigerator for at least 1 day before serving. Stored in the refrigerator, these pickles will keep their flavor for at least 3 weeks, ready to eat whenever you want.

EGGPLANT PICKLES rank among the most popular kinds of pickles in Turkey; they are great with macaroni and cheese, pilafs, and egg dishes. Eggplant is best pickled with the vinegar at full strength (undiluted by water) because the meaty eggplant will keep better in a more acidic solution. Tastewise, somehow this is not that acidic to the palate.

Stuffed Eggplant Pickles

FOR THE BRINE

1½ quarts (1.4 L) white vinegar, preferably homemade (page 102)

4 to 5 tablespoons (60 g) kosher salt

FOR THE STUFFED EGGPLANTS

4½ pounds (2 kg) small Italian eggplants (no more than 4 inches/10 cm long), stems removed

2 carrots, peeled, thinly sliced lengthwise, and cut into 4-inch (10 cm) lengths

5 meaty red paprika peppers, sliced into rounds

10 to 15 cloves garlic, sliced

2 cups (40 g) minced fresh parsley

25 pearl onions, peeled (optional)

10 green tomatoes, thinly sliced

Leaves and tips from 20 celery stalks

Makes 5 to 6 quarts (5 L)

Make the brine: Combine the vinegar and salt and stir to dissolve.

Make the stuffed eggplants: Cook the whole eggplants in plenty of boiling water until soft, about 10 minutes. Drain and transfer to a strainer. Place a cutting board on top of the eggplants, weight the board with something heavy (I use a well-washed rock or a brass mortar, but a can of tomatoes would work too), then let the juice drain from the eggplants. Once most of the juice is drained, remove the eggplants from the strainer and slit them open lengthwise.

Stuff each eggplant with some carrots, red pepper, 1 or 2 garlic slices, and about 1 tablespoon parsley. Tie up each of the stuffed eggplants with kitchen twine and place them in a clean 5- to 6-quart (5 L) glass jar, interspersing the onions, if using, and slices of tomato among the eggplants as you fill the jar.

Cover the eggplants with the remaining parsley and the celery leaves and tips, firmly press the vegetables down into the jar (traditionally, a washed stone or piece of wood would be used for this), and then fill the jar to the rim with the brine.

Cover tightly with the lid and store in a cool, dark place or the refrigerator. Give the jar a shake or two every morning to ensure that the brine is getting to all the vegetables. The pickles should be ready to eat in 1 to 1½ weeks. You can store the pickles in the refrigerator for 6 to 8 weeks after opening.

Note: If the mixture foams, add more vinegar. If the eggplants are kept under the vinegar by putting a weight on them, they will keep for at least another 4 weeks in the refrigerator.

WHEN WE Turks think of olives, we think of the Aegean region, which is in the west, bounded by the Aegean Sea, but this recipe is actually from Gaziantep in Turkey's southeast. Freshly cured olives are definitely required to make it. This side salad can also be served on fresh purslane leaves or slices of bread to create a meze dish similar to bruschetta, or used as a filling for *börek* with *pastırma* (Amulet-Shaped *Pastırma* Pies, page 210).

Olive Salad

1 pound (455 g) freshly cured green olives (preferably sliced, hammered, or broken), pitted and diced

2 medium tomatoes, peeled and diced

4 green onions, chopped

2 stalks fresh young garlic (if available; see Note, page 32), chopped; or 2 to 3 cloves garlic, finely minced (about 1 tablespoon)

1 to 2 tablespoons olive oil

3 to 4 tablespoons pomegranate syrup (see page 20)

½ cup (50 g) walnut pieces

Seeds from ½ pomegranate

Serves 8 to 10 as meze

Mix together the olives, tomatoes, green onions, and garlic. Sprinkle with the oil and pomegranate syrup. Garnish with the walnuts and pomegranate seeds and serve.

Green and Black Olives

Breakfast without olives can never be considered a real breakfast in Turkey. Green or black, there must be at least one type of olive on the table; even better if they have been dressed with some premium (extra-virgin) olive oil and lemon juice or lemon slices. Those who like their food sour will squeeze on some extra lemon juice. Olives also are indispensable for the meze table. In this context, you can sprinkle the olives with any spice you choose, though hot red pepper flakes are the most common addition. Even a sprinkling of ground nuts and a little drizzle of virgin olive oil will transform olives into a new dish.

In Turkey, we generally classify olives into just two groups—by their color, black or green—but there are actually scores of varieties.

One of my favorites is the wrinkle-skinned black olive called *sele*, named for the shallow baskets the olives are salted and packed in (which allows their bitter juices to drain off). Their skins become puckered from the weight of all the olives pressing in on each other. Before selling, the olives are mixed with a little olive oil so they keep longer. *Kuru sele*, meaning dry *sele*, are usually kept for the farmer's own use as they don't store well and are only on the market for a short time.

Sele curing can be done at home. All you need is a basket and some kosher salt. The freshly picked olives are placed in the basket and sprinkled with a layer of salt. Hang the basket so that the liquid can drain (if you're hanging the basket inside, put a plate underneath to catch the drippings). In about two weeks they will have lost their bitter juice. When they are cured to your taste, wash the olives and coat them with olive oil. They are ready to eat!

Olives blackened on the tree, and then picked and dried for one day before being packed into jars with oil are called *yaglık* or oiled olives. These are ready to eat immediately.

Green olives are called by a variety of names in Turkey, which are typically based on the curing method or the region where they are grown. Green olives slit with a knife to drain the bitter juices are called çizik ("scratched") or *dilme* ("sliced"). Olives struck with a mallet are called çekiçte ("with the mallet"), while olives broken with a stone are called *kırma* (broken). The last two varieties can be eaten four to five days after processing. The broken-skinned olives are sprinkled with salt, put in a muslin bag, and hung for four to five days, until they lose their bitter juice, then washed before consuming.

In all of these methods, the goal of curing is to remove the bitter juices from the olives. In the United States, asking for traditionally cured olives may help you to get one of these types. If you ever have the opportunity to buy freshly picked olives, it is great to cure them at home; their flavor will be more vibrant than already cured store-bought olives.

THIS IS a good mixture to make from end-of-the-season vegetables. Use whatever kind and mixture of vegetables you wish. An important note: You can judge whether your pickles are pickled correctly and will taste as they should by looking at the peppers. Whether long or bell peppers, they will turn yellow as they mature. Greenish peppers that do not turn yellow in a week or so indicate that the pickling process did not go right.

Mixed Pickles with Homemade Vinegar

FOR THE BRINE

3 cups (720 ml) filtered or spring water

4 heaping tablespoons (45 g) kosher salt

4½ cups (1 L) white wine vinegar, preferably homemade (page 102)

10 to 12 long green peppers, preferably with thick flesh (see Note)

8 to 10 small green or red bell peppers

5 to 7 small cauliflower florets (Ping Pong ball size); or 3 small beets (tennis ball size), peeled and quartered; or 6 to 7 pieces of cabbage, cut to the size of a medium tomato; or 3 to 4 carrots, cut into 2-inch (5-cm) pieces

5 to 7 jalepeños or similar hot chiles

3 cups (300 g) roughly chopped celery stalks and leaves

1½ cups (200 g) garlic cloves, peeled

Makes 1½ gallons (5.7 L)

Make the brine: Combine the vinegar and salt and stir to dissolve.

Wash all the vegetables and let them dry. Pierce the peppers once or twice so they will absorb the vinegar (it makes tastier pickles). Place all the vegetables nicely in a 1½-gallon (5.7-L) plastic or glass lidded jar. After placing a few peppers or vegetables, add the celery leaves and garlic cloves so that they are distributed evenly in the jar. Continue layering in the vegetables with the celery and garlic, packing everything tightly until there is almost no space left. When the jar is packed full, add the brine to the very top.

Immerse the vegetables by pressing on a few large green peppers, making sure the vinegar comes to the top. Secure the cap loosely the first day to allow room for any extra foam that might form and then screw the cap to form a tight seal the following day.

Keep the pickle jar in a dark, cool place for 2 days before moving to a cellar or even the refrigerator. It may take a week to 10 days for the pickles to be ready, but remember they will have a more delicate taste if you wait.

Note: End-of-season peppers are normally used. They have stayed on the plant past their prime and have tougher skins, which makes them better for pickling.

THESE SMALL, tangy pickles with just a bit of spice, are served everywhere in Turkey and throughout the Middle East.

Pickled Cucumbers

FOR THE BRINE

4 ½ cups (1 L) white or red wine vinegar, preferably homemade (page 102)

3 cups (720 ml) spring or filtered water (see Note)

3 heaping tablespoons kosher salt

4 pounds (1.8 kg) gherkin cucumbers, about 2 inches (5 cm) long

2 cups (200 g) roughly chopped celery stalks and leaves

1 ½ cups (200 g) cloves garlic peeled

3 to 4 hot green or red chile peppers, dry or fresh (optional, although heat adds a good taste)

Makes about 3 pounds (1.5 kg)

Make the brine: Combine the vinegar and salt and stir to dissolve.

Pack the gherkins in a ½-gallon (2-L) plastic or glass lidded jar, layering the gherkins with the celery, garlic, and chiles so that they are distributed evenly in the jar.

When the jar is packed full, add the brine to the very top. Secure the cap loosely to allow room for any extra foam that may form and then screw the cap to form a tight seal the following day.

Keep the pickle jar in a dark, cool place for 2 days before moving to a cellar or even the refrigerator. It may take a week to 10 days for the pickles to be ready, but remember the pickles made with white grape vinegar will have a more delicate taste if you wait.

Note: If using red wine vinegar, use 4½ cups (1 L) spring or filtered water.

I WAS so proud of myself the first time I made my own vinegar and used it to make pickles. I had made a nomadic product right in my own home and both the vinegar and the pickles were perfect! The red grape vinegar was outstanding but the yellow vinegar was to die for. Now I understand why the pickles for the sultans had to be made with yellow vinegar: The taste is much more delicate, with a very slight sweetness.

Homemade Vinegar

8 pounds (3.6 kg) red or white grapes

Makes 6 ½ cups (1.5 L)

Process the grapes in a juicer (don't mind the small stems). Transfer the must (the remaining pulp, skins, and stems) to a ½-gallon (2-L) plastic or glass jar with a lid. Pour the grape juice over the must and fill the jar completely—there should be no air at the top. Tightly close the jar and move it to a sunny spot. If the sun is strong, the grape juice will ferment (see Note).

After the second or third day, foam will begin to form on the grape must. This foam increases every day. After 4 days, taste the vinegar. If it is not strong enough for your taste, give it another 2 to 3 days in the sun. (You will know that the grapes have given their all and the fermentation has stopped when all of the grape must looks foamy.)

Strain the vinegar through a very fine-mesh sieve into a bottle or jar. Pour a glass of water on the residue to take all of the vinegar left behind and use this water to dilute the vinegar, filling the bottle or jar to the top. Discard the must left behind. Store your vinegar in a cool place to prevent it from becoming more sour.

Note: Since grapes do not ripen before mid-August, depending on where you live and the weather conditions, there may not be enough of the strong sunshine required for fermentation. If so, you can put the jar in a very low (175°F/80°C) oven for the whole day or even overnight. Take care not to let the jar cool from one day to the next by placing it on a wooden surface and covering with a cloth.

WE CAN say that this dish either flavors cucumbers or spices up yogurt. However we describe it, there is nothing like this cold soup on hot summer days. Traditionally served with ice cubes, it is a must for Turkish tables when the weather heats up. Each person is served a bowl of it. In Turkey, dried mint is more popular for sprinkling over the top than fresh.

Cold Yogurt and Cucumber Soup (*Cacik*)

2 cloves garlic

1½ teaspoons salt

2 medium cucumbers (7 inches / 17 cm long), peeled and minced

1¼ cups (300 ml) plain Greek yogurt

1 tablespoon wine vinegar (see page 102) (optional; add only if the yogurt is not tangy enough)

2 tablespoons extra-virgin olive oil

3 tablespoons chopped fresh dill or mint or 3 teaspoons dried, for garnish

Serves 6 as meze

Crush together the garlic and 1 teaspoon of the salt with a mortar and pestle. Sprinkle the cucumbers with the remaining ½ teaspoon salt, mix, and let sit in the refrigerator for 1 hour. This helps the cucumbers release some of their juice. This makes a more tasty *cacik*, for the soupy yogurt is enhanced by the juice of the cucumbers.

Meanwhile, mix together the yogurt and garlic-salt mixture until well combined. The consistency should be slightly thicker than cream soup; if necessary, add up to 1 cup (240 ml) water to thin the soup. Add the cucumbers and mix well; taste and add the vinegar, if needed. Drizzle with the oil and garnish with the dill or mint. Serve cold. (One or two cubes of ice is usually added on very hot days to keep the *cacik* as cold as possible. Since it is not too soupy, the addition of ice is welcomed.

THIS EASTERN Anatolian version of *cacik* is garnished with an abundance of fresh herbs. It can be diluted to make it soupier, according to preference. It pairs well with stews or grilled meats.

Cold Yogurt and Cucumber Soup (*Cacik*) with Green Onion

1 cup (240 ml) plain Greek yogurt

1 or 2 long green peppers, sliced into rings

2 green onions, minced

1 clove garlic, crushed with a mortar and pestle

Chopped fresh dill for garnish

Chopped fresh mint for garnish

1 tablespoon pekmez (see page 20; use only if the yogurt is too sour)

Serves 6 as meze

Thoroughly mix together the yogurt, peppers, green onions, and garlic. Spoon into a serving bowl and garnish generously with the dill and mint. Drizzle with pekmez, if using. Serve cold.

SOUPS

Soup had symbolic meaning during the Ottoman era. The phrase "drinking from the soup" referred to the janissaries' consumption of the soup offered by the palace on payday, indicating their satisfaction with their quarterly wages. The term "soup man" (*çorbacı*) referred not only to a soup cooker or seller, but also to a rank in the army, and officers could be titled novice soup man or janissary soup man. In those days, soups were not only eaten at lunch or dinner, but in fact mostly at breakfast. Some records indicate that the hospices of Sultan Mehmet the Conqueror and Sultan Bayezid II prepared a nourishing rice soup with parsley for breakfast.

Nowadays, the healthful soups of Turkey encompass a wide variety of ingredients, including fresh vegetables, lamb or beef, fish, grains and legumes, such as chickpeas and favas, plus fresh herbs, lemon juice for tartness, and spices. Red lentil soup and curd and flour soup are the most popular soups nationwide, and consommés, chicken broth soups, and eastern Turkey's delicious yogurt soups are also favorites. Chicken vermicelli soup is made especially flavorful with the addition of lemon and eggs; this is a favorite dish and also the first one that comes to mind when you catch a cold. The soup that tops them all is *tarhana*, the basic ingredient of which is made at home in villages throughout Turkey.

There are also soups that are often served as main-dish meals, including lentil (either red or green), *tarhana*, and yogurt soups; all are always served with plenty of bread. During Ramadan, at the special dinner for breaking the fast known as *iftar*, a main-course soup is a must. When we say soup, we typically think of it as piping hot, but in eastern regions of Turkey, yogurt soups are made with wheat grains and are eaten at room temperature and as a main dish too. *Cacik*, the yogurt and cucumber dish with a soupy consistency (page 103), is served cold too, but we think of it as a sidedish rather than a soup.

(OPPOSITE) RED LENTIL SOUP (PAGE 106)

THIS IS an inexpensive, easy-to-make dish loved by one and all. Prepared in every home in Turkey, every cook has a favorite way of making this traditional soup. The soup is always topped with a drizzle of browned butter, or *kızdırılmış yağ*, which means "heated a lot" in Turkish. To prepare it, butter is cooked in a pan until it is the color of hazelnuts (*beurre noisette* in French). Note that butter is always browned when it is added as a finishing touch to cooked food in Turkey. Melted but not browned butter is used during the cooking process.

Red Lentil Soup
(Kırmızı Mercimek Çorbası)

1½ cups (285 g) red lentils, picked over and rinsed

1 large onion, coarsely chopped

1 fresh seasonal tomato, grated (see Note, page 60), or ½ tablespoon tomato paste if tomatoes are not in season

1 small potato, peeled and grated

1½ cups (150 g) chopped celery

Salt

1 tablespoon dried mint

2 tablespoons unsalted browned butter (see Note, page 65)

Red onion slices, chopped, for serving (optional)

Hot pepper flakes, for serving (optional)

Serves 6

Put the lentils, onion, tomato, potato, and celery in a pot with 1½ quarts (1.4 L) water and cook over medium heat until creamy, about 25 minutes. (Puree with an immersion blender if you want a smoother soup.) Add salt to taste. Garnish with the mint and browned butter and serve immediately. Serve with red onion and hot pepper flakes, if desired.

THIS IS another version of Red Lentil Soup, a very tasty dish that one finds in all kebab houses, humble restaurants, and especially roadside taverns. As simple as it is, it tastes amazingly sophisticated. I would serve it at an elegant dinner.

Traditional Red Lentil Soup

1½ cups (300 g) red lentils

1 medium onion, coarsely chopped

4½ cups (1 L) cold water

2 cups (480 ml) chicken or meat stock, to bring the soup to preferred consistency

Salt

FOR THE ROUX

1½ tablespoons butter

1 tablespoon flour

Serves 8

Wash the lentils and place in a pot with the chopped onion. Add the water and cook over medium heat until the lentils have broken down and the onion is soft. Set aside.

Make the roux: Melt the butter in a small saucepan over medium heat. Add the flour and stir to combine; let the roux cook for a few minutes, but do not let it brown. Add a few tablespoons of the soupy lentils to the roux. (Don't worry if the mixture starts to firm up.) Return this mixture to the cooked lentils, stirring all the while. Using an immersion blender, blend in enough stock to bring the soup to a creamy consistency. Add salt to taste. You may garnish the soup before serving with mint and browned butter, as with Spicy Red Lentil Soup (opposite), and with croutons, desired.

THIS RECIPE combines both Turkish and Egyptian cooking traditions. For more than three hundred years, between the sixteenth century and the end of the nineteenth, the borders of the Ottoman Empire included Egypt, which was ruled by Turkish governors appointed by the sultan. Thus there are many similarities in their cuisines, like this meatball soup. The versions are similar, but in Turkey, it is made with egg and lemon; I like the delicacy of this Egyptian-inspired broth, which reminds me of consommé. In the Turkish version, the rice is incorporated into the meatballs, whereas in this recipe, it is cooked separately. Both the Turks and the Egyptians share the tradition of spicing soup with either cinnamon or cassia, although the two spices are not much alike (see page 15). The Ottomans chose these spices because they aren't as hard on the throat as black pepper—especially in broths. Try this recipe and see for yourself!

Meatball and Parsley Soup

FOR THE VEGETABLE BROTH

1 celery stalk

1 carrot

1 onion

1 leek

1 tomato

FOR THE MEATBALLS

11 ounces (310 g) ground beef

1 medium onion, grated

1 clove garlic, finely minced (see Note)

All-purpose flour

Butter or good-quality olive oil for frying

⅓ cup (35 g) medium-grain rice, washed and then broken in a food processor

Leaves from 6 or 7 sprigs fresh parsley

Serves 6

Make the vegetable broth: Wash the celery, carrot, onion, leek, and tomato well and add to cold water in a narrow but deep pot (this way, the water does not evaporate as much). Bring to a boil, and simmer until the vegetables are very soft, about 40 minutes. Strain out and discard the vegetables and return the broth to the pot. Bring to a boil.

Make the meatballs: Knead the beef with the onion and garlic. When the meat mixture is smooth, roll it into hazelnut-size balls. Coat the balls with the flour and fry in butter or oil until browned on all sides. Add the meatballs and rice to the boiling broth and cook until the rice is tender, 12 to 15 minutes. Garnish with parsley leaves and serve.

Note: Garlic should be crushed or minced right before using it, or it will get bitter. This is true for every recipe that uses crushed garlic.

I LIKE this soup because it has a lot of healthy ingredients and is filling. It is one of those soups that may be served as a main dish, especially for lunch, providing you have a few sides on hand to serve with it. For a redder, richer soup, use both the tomatoes and tomato paste.

Green Lentil and Noodle Soup
(Yeşil Mercimek Çorbası)

2 medium onions, diced (about 3 cups/360 g)

½ cup (120 ml) olive oil

1 or 2 fresh seasonal tomatoes, grated (see Note, page 60), or 1 tablespoon tomato paste if tomatoes are not in season

2 quarts (2 L) beef or vegetable broth

1½ cups (285 g) green lentils, picked over, rinsed, and soaked in cold water for 1 hour

1 cup (114 g) flat noodles, preferably broken by hand, or any small pasta

1 tablespoon tarragon (optional)

1 to 2 dried hot chiles

Serves 6

Sauté the onion in the oil until golden, then add the grated tomatoes. (If using the tomato paste, sauté it in the oil for 1 minute, then add the onions and cook until all the liquid is absorbed.) Add the broth and lentils and cook over medium heat. When the lentils are soft, after about 15 to 20 minutes, add the noodles, tarragon (if using), and chiles and cook for 3 to 4 minutes more, until the noodles are soft. Serve hot.

Note: This soup thickens as it sets or if kept in the refrigerator. You can dilute it by adding a little more stock when reheating.

THIS RECIPE is from a nineteenth-century Ottoman manuscript. I did not make the recipe until I ate a very similar, absolutely delicious soup one winter night at La Bottega del 30, a restaurant in a hamlet outside of Siena, Italy. It occurred to me that the soups were the same except for the butter and cassia in the Ottoman recipe and the olive oil and rosemary in the Italian version. Here is the Ottoman version. Ideally, you should use chickpeas from this year's harvest.

This soup thickens as it sits, so you may have to add more broth when you are ready to serve it. Keep some hot broth on hand just in case!

Palace Chickpea Soup

1 pound (455 g) chickpeas, washed and soaked overnight in 12 to 14 cups water

1½ quarts (1.4 L) chicken, beef, or vegetable broth (or any combination)

1 teaspoon cinnamon or ground cassia (see page 17), for serving

2 tablespoons extra-virgin olive oil or browned butter (see Note, page 65), for serving

¼ cup (10 g) snipped chives, for serving

Serves 6

Cook the chickpeas in their soaking water over medium heat. (Add more water during cooking, if necessary, but make sure the water you add is hot.) Once the water comes to a boil, reduce the heat to low and let the chickpeas simmer (this way the water does not evaporate as quickly). If the chickpeas are from the current year's harvest, they should take about 45 minutes to cook. Drain the chickpeas, setting aside ¼ cup (40 g) of the chickpeas and reserving all of the cooking water. Peel off and discard the skins of the remaining chickpeas, and puree the chickpeas in a blender, or with an immersion blender, with some of the broth or reserved cooking water. Stir this concentrate into a pot containing the broth. Bring the soup to a boil and ladle into bowls. Garnish with the cinnamon or cassia and the oil or browned butter. Top with the reserved whole chickpeas and the chives and serve piping hot.

ALMOST LIKE a restorative with its abundant legumes and vegetables, this unusually thick soup from Gaziantep in southeastern Turkey is a meal on its own. *Pirpirim* is another name for the wild purslane common in and around Gaziantep.

Purslane Soup

1 cup (200 g) chickpeas, soaked overnight

1 pound (455 g) lean lamb or beef, cut into ½-inch (12-mm) cubes

1 medium onion, minced

3 to 4 tablespoons extra-virgin olive oil

1 tablespoon tomato paste

2 medium tomatoes, grated (see Note, page 60)

1 cup (190 g) green lentils, picked over, rinsed, and soaked overnight

1 cup (200 g) black-eyed peas, soaked overnight, then cooked until soft in water that covers them by 1 inch (2.5 cm)

4 to 6 cups (175 to 260 g) purslane, including stems, minced

½ cup (70 g) coarse bulgur

2 dried hot red peppers

Salt

3 cloves garlic, crushed with a mortar and pestle

2 tablespoons pomegranate syrup (see page 20)

2 tablespoons fresh lemon juice (optional, if a tangier taste is desired)

2 tablespoons dried mint

Serves 6

Put the chickpeas and meat in a large pot with 10 cups (2.4 L) water and cook until the chickpeas are soft, 40 to 50 minutes. (Skim off the foam that will appear in the first 5 minutes, then cover and continue cooking.) After the water boils, turn the heat to low so the stock will not reduce too much. If necessary, you may add water so that there is plenty of stock for the soup.

Sauté the onion in a little of the oil in a large frying pan until golden, add the tomato paste, sauté for 30 seconds, add the tomatoes, and cook for a couple minutes, until the tomatoes release their juice and become pulpy, but not so much that they stick to the bottom of the pot.

Add the meat, the chickpeas with their cooking liquid, the lentils, black-eyed peas, purslane, bulgur, dried peppers, and some salt to taste; cook until all are soft.

Remove from the heat, mix the garlic with the pomegranate syrup and lemon juice, if using, and add to the soup.

Heat the remaining oil, add the mint, mix well with a spoon, and drizzle into the soup. Let the soup sit for 2 minutes before serving to allow the flavors to settle.

I CHANCED upon this traditional soup recipe. I knew that Anatolians used to sweeten yogurt with pekmez, but the idea of using almonds in this soup comes from Moorish Andalusian cooking that I happened to encounter in Córdoba, where Arab-Islam influences are still very evident. Interestingly, "almond soup" was one of the dishes offered at the tables of Suleiman the Lawmaker and his family at the circumcision banquets of his sons Şehzades Beyazıd and Cihangir in 1539. There is no clue as to how the soup was prepared then, but in *almond sübye*, the milk of the almond is extracted to serve as a drink. I crushed the almonds instead, as it's more fitting for the soup.

Romaine lettuce, with a squeeze of lemon juice, is usually eaten cold and uncooked as a side dish, or even instead of fruit after a meal. In dishes like lamb stew or braised lettuce, however, the romaine is cooked. This refreshing soup, with such a fascinating history, turns out to be perfect for hot summer days.

Summer Soup with Romaine Lettuce

2 cups (480 ml) plain Greek yogurt

1 head romaine lettuce, tough leaves discarded, washed well, and diced

½ cup (75 g) blanched almonds, ground in a food processor and combined with 3 tablespoons water in a mortar and pestle

3 tablespoons dried currants, soaked in 1 cup (240 ml) water until soft, then drained

1 green bell pepper, cored, seeded, and finely diced

2 tablespoons pekmez (optional; see page 20)

FOR SERVING

2 tablespoons extra-virgin olive oil (optional)

3 tablespoons minced fresh dill

1 tablespoon chives, minced

3 tablespoons blanched almonds, sliced lengthwise

1 tablespoon hot red pepper flakes (preferably isot; see page 18)

Serves 8

Slowly add about 1 quart (960 ml) water to the yogurt (use less or more depending on the yogurt's consistency), stirring constantly until smooth. Put the lettuce and ½ cup (120 ml) water in a large pot and cook until al dente, 7 to 8 minutes. Add the yogurt mixture to the pot, along with the ground almonds, currants, and bell pepper; stir to combine. (Add the pekmez if the soup is too tart.) Let cool in the refrigerator. Serve cold, drizzled with the oil, if using, and sprinkled with the dill, chives, sliced almonds, and red pepper flakes.

THIS IS a festive spring soup from Gaziantep. Usually served as a side dish during the short period it's in the markets, fresh young garlic is used here as an ingredient in the soup.

Fresh Young Garlic and Yogurt Soup (Şiveydiz)

1 lamb roast (preferably from the shoulder), with bones (deboned meat can be used, but has less flavor)

1½ cups (300 g) chickpeas, soaked overnight

1 large egg

2½ cups (600 ml) plain Greek yogurt

4 to 5 stalks fresh young garlic (see Note, page 32), chopped

4 to 5 green onions, chopped

3 tablespoons extra-virgin olive oil

1 tablespoon dried mint

Serves 8

Put the meat and chickpeas in a pot with 1½ quarts (1.4 L) water and bring to a boil. Cook, covered, skimming off the foam that will appear in the first 5 minutes, until the meat and chickpeas are very soft, 45 minutes to 1 hour; strain and set the broth aside. Debone the meat and cut into cubes, discarding the bones. Return the broth to the pot, adding some hot water if necessary, along with the cooked meat and chickpeas.

While the broth comes to a boil, beat the egg and yogurt together. Spoon 5 to 6 tablespoons (75 to 90 ml) of the broth into the yogurt mixture, then slowly add this to soup. Add the young garlic and green onions. Cook and stir over low heat for 1 minute; do not allow the broth to boil. Ladle into serving bowls. Warm the oil in a small pot, add the mint, and stir well. Drizzle the seasoned oil into the soup and serve.

A POPULAR story about Nasreddin Hodja, a thirteenth-century Turk known for his satirical stories, has him at the shore of a lake, carefully spooning a bowl of yogurt into the water. "Hodja, what are you doing?" the passersby asked. Hodja replied that he was making yogurt. They laughed at him and told him that he couldn't make yogurt from water. He replied, "But what if?"

This wonderful yogurt soup is both delicious and easy to make. Yogurt and false saffron are put on a pedestal in this concoction, which without them would be an ordinary dish.

Yogurt Soup with Safflower (*Haspir*)

1 cup (200 g) chickpeas, soaked overnight

10 ½ ounces (300 g) lean veal or beef, cut into small cubes

2 large potatoes, cut into small cubes

Salt

1 large egg

2 cups (480 ml) plain Greek yogurt

2 tablespoons unsalted butter

1 tablespoon vegetable oil

¼ cup false saffron (also known as *haspir,* see page 17)

1½ teaspoons coarsely ground black pepper

Serves 8

Put the chickpeas and meat in a pot with 1½ quarts (1.4 L) water and bring to a boil. (You may add more water during cooking, but make sure the water you add is hot.) Cook, covered, until the meat and chickpeas are soft, 45 minutes to 1 hour, skimming off the foam that will appear in the first 5 minutes. Add the potatoes, season with salt, and continue cooking. (There should be at least about 1 quart/960 ml water left in the pot; if necessary, add more.) Beat the egg with the yogurt until well mixed. When the potatoes are tender, spoon some of the broth into the yogurt mixture and stir thoroughly. Once the yogurt mixture is warm, add it to the soup, stirring all the while, and cook over very low heat for 2 to 3 minutes more, stirring constantly and making sure the soup does not come to a boil. (If it boils, the egg and yogurt will separate.) Salt to taste.

Melt the butter in a small pan over medium heat and cook until almost browned. Add the oil, false saffron, and black pepper and remove from the heat so the butter does not burn. Stir the soup once or twice, then drizzle with the seasoned butter and serve (see Note).

Note: The presentation is especially nice if you add the oil-and-pepper butter individually to each bowl of soup as you serve it. The soup is especially delicious if it sits a day or two, but take care not to bring it to a boil when reheating. Stirring while reheating will help prevent this.

THIS RECIPE is from a nineteenth-century manuscript of Ali Eşref Dede, who reached *Dede* ("wise man") status in the Sufi order in the western Turkish city of Edirne. He states in his recipe that using wheat berries instead of eggs to thicken the soup gives it a more delicate flavor, and that the lightness of the pulp of the wheat offsets the softness of the fish. I do not strain out all of the wheat, because I like a little texture in the soup. I guess we have lost the very refined taste of palace cooking, but doubtless this is much more sophisticated than the flour- and egg-thickened fish soups that Turkish restaurants serve today.

Palace Fish Soup

FOR THE FISH BROTH

3 or 4 sprigs fresh mint

5 or 6 sprigs fresh parsley

6 tablespoons (90 ml) extra-virgin olive oil

10 ½ ounces (300 g) whole scorpion fish (or any fish that is good for boiling), scales removed

7 or 8 sprigs celery leaves

1 carrot

1 leek, washed well

1 green bell pepper

10 whole black peppercorns

1 ½ cups (250 g) pounded wheat (see Notes)

6 sea bass fillets (about 2 pounds/910 g total)

Pinch of saffron threads

Juice of 1 lemon

Finely minced fresh parsley

1 teaspoon ground cinnamon or cassia (see page 17)

Serves 6

Make the fish broth: Sauté the mint and parsley sprigs in the oil in a large pot. Add 2½ quarts (2.4 L) water along with the whole fish, celery, carrot, leek, bell pepper, and peppercorns (see Notes). Cook over medium heat for 45 minutes. Strain out the solids and set the broth aside.

Meanwhile, cook the wheat in 2 quarts (2 L) water over very low heat until the wheat opens and releases its starch, 45 minutes to 1 hour. Strain half the wheat through a colander and keep the other half to use whole.

Cook the fish fillets on a charcoal grill or a grill pan for about 3 minutes per side, until the flesh is white throughout. Put 5 cups (1.2 L) of the fish broth in a large saucepan, crumble in the saffron, bring to a boil, and reduce the heat to low. Add half the pounded wheat and heat thoroughly. Remove the pan from the heat, add the remaining unstrained wheat, and add the lemon juice (more broth can be added for a thinner soup; more wheat mixture can be added for a thicker soup). Arrange the grilled fillets in soup bowls and pour the soup over them. Garnish with parsley and sprinkle with either cinnamon or cassia and serve warm (not piping hot).

Notes: Those who prefer a stronger taste may fry the scorpion fish and the vegetables before adding the water to produce the broth.

This is a special wheat that we call dövme, *in which the hard outside casing is removed by sprinkling water on the wheat berries to soften them, then beating the berries to loosen the casing and get rid of this hard peel. This enables the wheat to cook faster. You may find pounded wheat in specialty stores where they sell ethnic ingredients. If not, you can replace it with rice.*

TARHANA SOUP MIX (the soup itself is called *tarhana*) is probably one of the most ancient "instant" foods in history. Made from a fermented mixture of flour and yogurt, there are two kinds of *tarhana* mix found in Turkish cuisine. One is an older version of nomadic origin, made with only roughly ground wheat and yogurt. A soup made from the dried patties of this mix is cooked with stock and dried black-eyed peas, especially in the Aegean region. It is a substantial winter soup that is still made in areas like Muğla, Gaziantep, and Maraş, areas where Turcoman-nomadic culture still prevails, especially in the ways of food.

The second recipe contains New World ingredients and seems to be a pre-prepared version of the fresh *tarhana* mix made in the palace. According to the short description given for the palace *tarhana*, it is made from bread of the finest quality, which is pounded with yogurt (most probably strained and rather sour) and then cooked with stock.

This recipe makes a lot of soup mix, an appropriate amount to last through the winter months. The amounts are easily reduced, keeping the proportions the same. If the recipe intrigues you, but the method does not, you may also find ready-made *tarhana* mix in Middle Eastern markets.

Tarhana

5 ½ pounds (2.5 kg) large long red frying red peppers with a tough skin

5 ½ pounds (2.5 kg) red tomatoes

3 ¼ pounds (1.5 kg) onions

5 ½ pounds (2.5 kg) plain Greek yogurt (for the best result, strain until it is very thick)

5 ½ pounds (2.5 kg) hard-wheat bread flour

½ pound (250 g) semolina

Salt

Makes 20 servings

Cook the peppers with 2 cups (480 ml) water in a tightly covered pot over medium heat until soft. Let them cool and then peel the peppers, reserving the cooking water. Cook the tomatoes with 1 cup (240 ml) water in a tightly covered pot over medium heat until soft but still solid. Let them cool, and then peel the tomatoes, reserving the cooking water. Cook the onions with 2 cups (480 ml) water in a tightly covered pot over medium heat until thoroughly softened. Let them cool, reserving the cooking water.

Pulse the peppers, tomatoes, and onions—along with their cooking waters—in a food processor in batches. The result should be very watery.

Transfer the pureed vegetables to a large pot. Add the yogurt in batches, mixing well to incorporate each addition. Add the flour and semolina in batches, then season with salt and stir well. The mixture should be very liquid, similar to the consistency of tempura batter. Cover the pot tightly and let the batter sit for 4 to 5 days, mixing occasionally each day.

Once the dough has fermented, cover a large surface (like a table) with plastic and spread an old, clean bedsheet on top. You should be working outdoors in the shade or in a well-ventilated area. Spread a thin layer of the *tarhana* batter across the sheet. Cover the surface with muslin or another light material, and let it dry for 2 days.

(continued)

After 2 days, the *tarhana* will have lost almost all of its water. Lift the sheet from underneath and press the mixture with the palm of your hands and then press it through a colander. Spread the crumbled *tarhana* on the table, covered with plastic and clean sheets. Cover again with muslin and let it sit for about 10 days to dry completely.

Crumble the dried *tarhana* (at this point, it should be like sand) and store it in tightly sealed jars until ready to use for soup.

 THIS USE of *tarhana* soup mix is a family favorite. Contrary to many versions I have encountered, our family always adds one or two cloves of crushed garlic to the finished soup. Rather than describe something as "to die for," the Turks say "don't eat it, sleep with it." It's an appropriate phrase for this soup, especially on cold winter days. My mother always served it with grilled fresh chiles in summer and dried chiles in winter, but it is a very basic soup that can be garnished however you like.

Tarhana Soup (*Tarhana Çorbasi*)

½ cup (70 g) *tarhana*, homemade (opposite) or store-bought

1 or 2 medium tomatoes, grated (⅓ to ½ cup; see Note, page 60)

1½ to 2 tablespoons butter

4½ cups (1 L) chicken stock

2 cloves garlic, crushed and set in 2 tablespoons cold water

Salt, if needed

1½ cups (255 g) cooked black-eyed peas (optional)

3 hot chiles or sweet peppers, depending on your preference, grilled, peeled, and minced, for serving

Serves 8

Soak the *tarhana* mix in 1 cup (240 ml) of water for 10 minutes.

Meanwhile, in a large pot over medium heat, cook the grated tomatoes in butter until all the juice is gone. Add the chicken stock and, when it comes to a simmer, add the soaked *tarhana* and stir. Keep stirring until the mixture comes to a boil, and then for another 3 to 4 minutes, until all of the *tarhana* particles are blended into the stock and the soup reaches a smooth consistency.

Let the soup simmer for another 5 minutes over low heat, stirring occasionally. Just before taking it off the heat, ladle some of the hot soup into a small bowl and add the garlic and water mixture. Salt to taste, if needed, but the *tarhana* mix has salt, so add carefully. Add this back into the soup pot and stir to combine completely. Stir in the black-eyed peas just before serving, if using. Remove the soup from the heat and serve immediately. Pass the minced pepper at the table.

Note: This soup may be reheated. It may get thicker as it cools down. If so, add some hot stock to bring it to the preferred consistency, but it should not be diluted too much.

VEGETABLE DISHES

Vegetables and wild greens are widely used in Turkish cooking, cooked either alone (usually with plenty of olive oil) or with meat to extend the precious protein, resulting in dishes that are both tasty and economical. Vegetables grown in Turkey are uniquely flavorful, especially in the western and southern parts of the country, where the sunny and hot weather is an advantage for vegetable farming. Because of the terroir—the climate and characteristics of the soil—the variety and delectability of Turkish vegetable dishes is hard to surpass.

Many vegetables, fruits, and wine are mentioned in Mahmut from Kaşgar's Turkish to Arabic dictionary (*Divanü Lügati't-Türk*), which he wrote in Baghdad for the Arabs, beginning in 1072. We can understand from the listed Turkish words that Turks ate vegetables like eggplants, carrots (including white carrots), as well as gourds. They also used herbs like wild mint and basil and spices like pepper and cumin; even mastic was known. As the Turkish tribes established nations in other lands with different produce and started to live a more urbanized life, certainly this list became longer. This is confirmed by the list of foods that were served to Mehmet the Conquerer in the fifteenth century, including leeks, cabbages, spinach, pumpkins, and Swiss chard. The palace also was partial to rare vegetables, as shown by the cultivation of asparagus from the sixteenth century on. With the introduction of tomatoes, paprika and other kinds of peppers, and beans, the diversity of Turkish vegetable dishes was further enriched.

Cooking methods for vegetables can be grouped this way: meatless vegetable dishes (including vegetables with olive oil), vegetables cooked with meat, fried vegetables, boiled vegetables, and roasted vegetables.

Down to the oil: This method, the general style of cooking vegetables with olive oil, is to cook the vegetable with onion and (usually) tomato over very low heat until all the liquid evaporates. The long cooking time over low heat dries up the moisture in the vegetable, and both the oil and the vegetable end up with a peerless taste.

Stewed marrow (*kalya*): Although this term has been used for cooking meat or liver, most likely cut in cubes, today it is used in reference to cooking cubed zucchini and eggplant in olive oil.

Şakşuka: This method of cooking vegetables with olive oil differs from region to region. In Balikesir in northwestern Turkey, green tomatoes are used. In southern towns on the Mediterranean coast, *şakşuka* is a dish of fried eggplant, pepper, and potato. A tomato and garlic sauce, prepared with the same oil and poured over the fried vegetables, gives the dish a new taste.

Pan-frying (*tava*): With this method, vegetables such as potato, eggplant, zucchini, carrot, and peppers are fried in a pan and served with yogurt and garlic or with a tomato sauce made with the oil. Vinegar can also be added to this sauce to make it lighter.

Sautéed (*kavurma*): In this method, with regional variations, vegetables are boiled until al dente and then sautéed in butter or olive oil. (The same term is used for meat dishes.) In the Aegean region, fresh black-eyed peas are often cooked in this manner. In the Black Sea region, a dish made with pickled or dried beans is a sort of sautéed vegetable.

Borani and yoğurtlama: A dish known throughout history, the roots of *borani* are either an eggplant dish mentioned in Persian cuisine or a beautiful Persian queen. In modern times, however, *borani* refers to parboiled spinach leaves sautéed with rice or bulgur. Fresh black-eyed peas or green beans are cooked in a similar way, but are called *yoğurtlama*. Though the names are different, they are both served with garlic and yogurt sauce; however, *borani* is understood to be made only with spinach. There may be other dishes named *borani*, like the *urfa borani* in this book (page 164), but it is probable that the creator fancied the name and called it *borani* regardless of the vegetable featured in the dish.

Nut and garlic sauce (*tarator*): Boiled vegetables are always served with this sauce, made with olive oil, lemon, and bread (plus ground walnuts or almonds, if desired). In the Aegean region, fresh black-eyed peas or spring greens are often served this way.

RECIPES FOR this rich, creamy dish date back to the nineteenth century, when it was first prepared for a sultan who liked it. *Beğendi* means "it is liked"—hence the name. Even though I give the recipe for just the eggplant dish here, it is never eaten alone; it is always served with some kind of stewed or grilled meat, chicken, or even fish. Many foreigners like this dish best when it has the consistency of mashed potatoes, but I add more milk because I prefer it more saucelike.

Eggplant Puree (*Beğendi*)

1½ tablespoons unsalted butter

1 heaping tablespoon all-purpose flour

1 cup (240 ml) warm milk, plus more if reheating

4 to 5 Italian eggplants (2 pounds/ 910 g total), roasted (but better grilled over a flame), peeled, and chopped

3 tablespoons *kaşar* or other mildly aged cheese, grated (optional; see Note)

Salt

Serves 6

Melt the butter, add the flour, and make a roux by stirring constantly over low heat with a wooden spoon until the butter and flour are thoroughly mixed, taking care that the flour does not brown. Remove from the heat and let cool a little. Add the warm milk and stir until smooth. Return to the heat, add the chopped eggplant, and stir constantly with a wooden spoon, making it almost a puree, until the mixture comes to a boil. If desired, add the cheese, stirring until it melts into the eggplant. Season with salt to taste. Serve hot. You can make this ahead of time, but add some milk and stir often so that it doesn't burn when you reheat it. Adding milk returns the cold puree to the desired consistency by loosening it up.

Note: I prefer this dish without cheese; others insist that it needs cheese. The taste becomes stronger with cheese, and it may overpower the meat you are serving it with.

Eggplant: The Turkish Caviar

Eggplants are the veritable sultan of Turkish cuisine and are featured in everything from the most sophisticated dishes to the humblest of pickles. Although originally from India, the eggplant is now a representative ingredient of Turkish cooking. Once they have tasted our eggplant dishes, many foreigners refer to it as caviar. No matter what they are called, fresh eggplants are cooked until they are soft and creamy; hence the caviar metaphor. Dried eggplant has a rather leathery consistency that makes it a perfect casing and imparts a delicious flavor when stuffed. All of Turkey's many eggplant recipes are delicious, including the world-famous *imam bayıldı* ("the priest fainted," page 127), featuring creamy eggplants immersed in olive oil, and the empress of summer, *karnıyarık* (eggplant boats, page 128).

The most treasured eggplants come from the lovely town called Brick in the country's southeast, but as far as I am concerned the long thin seedless variety (similar to Japanese eggplants in the States) grown around Muğla in the southwest is the best. They fry so well because their firm flesh does not absorb much oil. (Turks love to fry eggplants, so much so that during the last century of the Ottoman era, Istanbul suffered from "eggplant fires"—fires caused by housewives frying eggplants that engulfed whole neighborhoods! Typical Turkish homes of the period were made of wood, which had a special architectural—albeit dangerous—charm.

AS SIMPLE as it is, this is a ubiquitous dish, especially in the coastal Mediterranean area and the Aegean region. This is logical, considering the fact that everyone there grows vegetables in their own gardens (or at least used to) and eggplants grow particularly well. Because it's delicious and quick to put together, everyone in the region makes fried eggplant and green peppers often. In the Aegean, it is called *yoğurtlama*, which means it has been sauced with yogurt. All you need to serve with this is Shepherd's Salad (page 82) and lots of fresh bread. It is good for summer lunches, but also is served as part of a meze spread.

Fried Eggplant and Green Peppers

2 tablespoons salt

3 long thin Japanese eggplants

Olive oil for frying

4 or 5 long green frying peppers or green bell peppers, washed, dried, and pierced in several places with the tip of a knife

¼ cup (60 ml) plain Greek yogurt

2 to 3 cloves garlic, crushed with a pinch of salt with a mortar and pestle

Serves 6

Add the salt to a generous amount of water in a bowl. Peel the eggplants in a zebra pattern (removing only alternating strips of peel), cut in half horizontally, slice the halves lengthwise, and add the slices to the salty water. Let soak for 15 to 20 minutes, then remove from the water and dry thoroughly with a clean cloth or absorbent paper towel. (Omit this step and the eggplant will splatter oil.)

Heat ½ inch (12 mm) of oil in a frying pan over medium heat until hot, but not to the smoking point. Add the eggplant slices one by one (the oil should sizzle when it contacts each slice), fry until both sides are nicely browned, and remove to a serving platter. Add the peppers and cover the pan so the oil doesn't splatter. Shake the pan every 30 seconds or so. When the splattering dies down, remove the cover and turn the peppers over to fry the other side; this will go faster, as the peppers will already be heated through. (Do not let peppers with thin skins fry for too long; 2 minutes should be enough. Fry fleshy peppers for about 4 minutes.) When the peppers are done, remove them to a platter. Mix together the yogurt and garlic-salt mixture and generously spoon the sauce on top of the vegetables, allowing some vegetables to peek through (see Note). Serve immediately.

Note: You can drizzle a couple tablespoons of the frying oil over the fried vegetables after they are dressed with the yogurt sauce; this is both attractive and flavorful.

I HAVE slightly modified this traditional recipe, from the town of Ula in southwestern Turkey, by putting the yogurt at the bottom of the dish, adding some dried tomatoes, and enriching it with ground meat. (*Ala Nazik* is a similar popular dish served in the Gaziantep area.) The rest of the world thinks that dried tomatoes are Italian in origin, but Turks have long used dried tomatoes in many of their dishes. The combination of yogurt and butter in this dish makes it loved by all.

Grilled Eggplant Topped with Yogurt

2 cups (480 ml) plain Greek yogurt

1 to 2 cloves garlic, crushed with a mortar and pestle

Salt

2 pounds (910 g) Italian eggplants, roasted over a gas flame or grilled (see Note)

1 tablespoon olive oil

2 tomatoes, peeled and diced

1 long thin green pepper (preferably hot), sliced into thin rings

1 cup (200 g) diced dried tomatoes

3 tablespoons unsalted butter

½ pound (225 g) ground beef or lamb

1 tablespoon minced fresh parsley

½ tablespoon mild red pepper flakes (optional)

Fresh or toasted sliced bread for serving

Serves 6

Beat the yogurt, garlic, and salt to taste until smooth, then spoon the mixture into the bottom of a serving dish and let it come to room temperature.

Peel the eggplants while hot (they're easier to peel that way), then transfer to a strainer and let drain. Heat the oil in a frying pan and sauté the fresh tomatoes, peppers, and dried tomatoes for 3 to 4 minutes, until the juice from the fresh tomatoes is absorbed. Dice the eggplants and add them to the pan. When the eggplants are heated through, spoon the eggplant mixture over the yogurt mixture.

In a pan, melt the butter. Add the ground meat and cook until the butter is aromatic and almost browned. Pour the meat over the eggplant. Sprinkle with the parsley and red pepper flakes, if using, and serve immediately with plenty of slices of fresh or toasted bread.

Note: You may roast the eggplants in an oven, but they will not have the same flavor.

LIKE TURKISH delight, I think this dish is representative of Turkish cuisine mostly to non-Turkish people. It seems its popularity is due to foreigners visiting Turkey who liked its taste and were intrigued by its name. There are various stories about this. One is that there was an imam (a man who leads prayers in a mosque) who was rather tight-fisted. When he saw how much olive oil his wife had used in this dish, he fainted on the spot. (Sometimes "imam" is replaced by "priest," and I'd guess rightly because, due to their heritage, the Greek community uses a lot more olive oil than the Turkish people.) Whether the story is true or not, this dish does use a lot of olive oil. Another popular story is that the imam liked the dish so much that he fainted with delight. This may also be true, as this is indisputably a delicious dish. My addition of pine nuts and currants, which are not traditional, infuses an interesting taste into this dish.

The Priest Fainted (*Imam Bayıldı*)

6 medium Italian eggplants (no more than 6 inches/15 cm long)

Salt

3 large onions, sliced into thin rings

2 tablespoons pine nuts (optional)

1 cup (240 ml) olive oil

2 tablespoons dried currants (optional)

10 to 12 cloves garlic

1 tablespoon tomato paste

2 medium tomatoes, peeled, seeded, and diced

⅓ teaspoon sugar

½ cup minced fresh parsley

Black pepper

Serves 6

Peel the eggplants lengthwise in a zebra pattern (removing only alternating strips of peel) and place in 3 to 4 cups (720 to 960 ml) salted cold water. In a large frying pan, cook the onions and pine nuts, if using, in the oil over low heat until caramelized, about 10 minutes; add the currants, if using, and set aside. Remove the eggplants from the water, squeeze out the excess water, and pat dry. Fry in the same oil over medium heat until both sides are nicely browned. (Do not burn the eggplants.) Remove the eggplants from the pan, add the garlic to the pan, and sauté until aromatic. Remove the garlic from the pan and set aside. Add the tomato paste and tomatoes to the pan and sauté. When the liquid has evaporated, remove the pan from the heat. Sprinkle the tomato mixture with the sugar, parsley, and pepper to taste.

Preheat the oven to 350°F (175°C). Arrange the eggplants in a single layer in an oven-safe baking dish with a lid or aluminum foil to use as a lid. Slice an opening in the eggplants, lengthwise, and fill with half of the fried onion mixture, then divide the tomato mixture among the eggplants. Cover with the rest of the caramelized onions and stick several garlic cloves in each eggplant. Add enough water to just cover the eggplants. Cover and cook for 15 minutes over medium heat. Uncover and bake for 25 to 30 minutes, until most of the liquid is absorbed. Turn off the oven and let the dish cool for 1 to 2 hours. Serve warm or at room temperature.

THIS IS a dish not to be missed at any of the *esnaf lokantası* (restaurants for working people that serve only lunch). They make the best ones, with a lot of tasty juice to mop up. I am sure some people go there just to eat this. Eggplant boats are easy to prepare but a little time consuming. When you taste what you get in the end, you will know it was well worth all the time it took to make it.

Eggplant Boats with Meat Filling (*Karnıyarık*)

6 long thin Japanese eggplants (8 to 10 inches/20 to 25 cm long), peeled in alternating 1-inch stripes

Corn oil for frying

1 medium onion, diced

3 to 4 tablespoons unsalted butter

½ pound (225 g) ground lamb, beef, or a combination

1 tablespoon tomato paste

2 medium tomatoes, peeled, cored, and diced, plus 6 slices of tomato

⅓ cup (7 g) minced fresh parsley

Salt and black pepper

2 long green peppers, cored and cut into 6 pieces

3 cups (720 ml) hot water, plus 1 cup (240 ml) more if needed

Serves 6

Fry the eggplants in the oil until all sides are golden. Remove them to paper towels to drain.

Fry the onion in the butter until translucent; add the meat and sauté until cooked through. Add the tomato paste and stir to mix. Add the diced tomatoes and cook until all juices are evaporated, then add the parsley and salt and pepper to taste and mix well. Place the fried eggplants on a shallow, ovenproof pan. Slit them diagonally along the middle to create openings for the meat filling. Evenly divide the meat filling among the eggplants and place a piece of green pepper on top of each, accompanied by a slice of fresh tomato. Gently pour the hot water into the pan so that it almost reaches the filling but does not disturb it. (Most of the water will be absorbed during cooking.) Cover and cook over medium heat for about 30 minutes. Do not let it dry out; add more water while cooking, if needed.

Meanwhile, preheat the oven to 350°F (175°C) and arrange a rack in the center of the oven.

Uncover the eggplant boats and transfer the pan to the oven. (If the water has diminished, add another cup of hot water before placing the pan in the oven.) Bake for 20 minutes, until the meat filling is a little browned. Serve hot. (This dish may be reheated on the stovetop, so it is fine to cook it ahead of time, then reheat and serve.)

TURKS ROAST eggplants over a flame for many different uses, and each region has its own recipes. Here is one from Denizli, the area in southwest Turkey where my father comes from, in which roasted eggplant is stuffed into pita bread. A *dürüm* (wrap) is also a very popular way of eating shish kebabs—consider it a nomadic version of the sandwich. When eating at home, everyone makes their own wraps. The meat or filling is put on a special bread that is made like *yufka* (the thin, round sheet of pastry used for making *böreks*). These breads are scorched on a hot, concave sheet of iron, called a *sac*. The breads become hard, which enables them to be kept for a long time, and they are moistened before eating.

Roasted Eggplant Wrap

2 pounds (910 g) whole Italian eggplant, roasted over a gas flame or on a grill, peeled, and chopped

2 medium onions, diced, or sliced into rings (see Notes)

2 long thin green peppers, roasted, peeled, and diced

2 medium tomatoes, peeled, cored, and diced

3 pita or *yufka* breads, halved (see Note)

Tulum cheese (see Note, page 24), or any other strong-flavored, crumbly cheese (optional)

Pomegranate syrup (see page 20)

Serves 4

Mix together the roasted eggplant, onions, roasted peppers, and tomatoes in a bowl. Keep warm, or warm before using. Scoop the vegetable mixture into pitas, add the cheese, if using, and drizzle with pomegranate syrup.

Notes: Cook the onion rings on a panini press, or wrap them in foil and roast them in the oven. This will give them a sweeter taste.

You can substitute toasted regular bread for pita and make a bruschetta instead; it is the same idea.

Borani is a classic spinach and yogurt dish with a small amount of rice that was cooked even in the time of Sultan Mehmet the Conquerer, according to kitchen archives from the fifteenth century—although, according to this listing, it was made with just spinach and rice. There was always some rice in this olive oil dish when my mother cooked it too. We also made it with garlic yogurt and burnt butter; it was a winter favorite of our family. *Borani*, the name of a Persian queen, is also said to be the inspiration for an eggplant dish. This is not unusual: The names and contents of dishes may change over time and among different cultures.

Make sure that the yogurt is at room temperature, but mix in the crushed garlic while the spinach is cooking. Cold yogurt will cool the spinach and the butter sauce too quickly. This dish does not reheat well, so consume it all just after cooking.

Spinach with Rice and Garlic-Yogurt Sauce (*Borani*)

1 medium onion, diced

3 to 4 tablespoons extra-virgin olive oil

1½ pounds (680 g) spinach, roots removed, washed thoroughly, drained, dried, and chopped

4 to 5 dried hot peppers

1½ tablespoons rice

4 to 5 tablespoons (75 to 90 ml) plain Greek yogurt, at room temperature

2 cloves garlic and ½ teaspoon salt, crushed with a mortar and pestle

2 tablespoons unsalted butter

1 tablespoon vegetable or corn oil

½ tablespoon good-quality tomato paste

1 teaspoon hot red pepper flakes (optional)

Serves 6

In a large pot, sauté the onion in the olive oil until translucent. Add the spinach, dried hot peppers, and rice and mix well. Cover and simmer uncovered for a couple of minutes. If necessary, add ⅓ cup (75 ml) water (the spinach usually releases enough water, but the rice may need extra water) and cook until the rice is soft and the liquid is completely absorbed. Spoon into a serving dish.

While the spinach is cooking, stir together the yogurt and garlic-salt mixture. Spoon the sauce onto the spinach. Heat the butter and oil and, when the butter becomes aromatic and nicely browned, stir in the tomato paste and red pepper flakes, if using. Drizzle the tomato glaze over the yogurt and serve warm.

THIS IS a dish to inaugurate summer dining. Even though beans are now available year round, I only cook them in season. Served cooled, this meze is a summer favorite thanks to its light texture. What's more, it tastes even better after sitting for a few days. Some cooks use sugar in this dish, but to my taste, the beans are much lighter without it.

Green Beans in Olive Oil
(*Beans à la Turka*)

10 to 12 pearl onions (or 1 large or 2 medium onions, minced), peeled but left whole, stems attached

1 tomato, sliced into rounds, plus 3 medium tomatoes, halved and grated (see Note, page 60)

2 pounds (910 g) fresh green beans, strings removed (either whole or snapped)

Salt

½ or 1 teaspoon sugar (optional)

1¼ cups (300 ml) virgin olive oil

Serves 6, or 8 to 10 as meze

Lay the onions and then the tomato slices in the bottom of a large pot. Add one or two layers of beans over the tomatoes. Add the grated tomato on top of the beans. Add the remaining beans, salt to taste, the sugar, if using, and oil. Cover tightly and cook over high heat until steam appears (or until the lid is very hot to the touch). Reduce the heat to low and cook for 30 minutes. Check the beans; if needed, add 1 to 1½ cups (240 to 360 ml) water. Cook for another 10 minutes over medium heat (only a very little liquid should remain in the pot and, toward the end of the cooking time, if you let the bottom scorch a little, it will be even more delicious). Let the beans sit for 2 hours, to cool and absorb the cooking liquid. Pour off and set aside any remaining liquid. Invert the beans onto a serving platter and pour the liquid over the beans. Serve, with or without the onions.

PEOPLE AROUND Muğla, a city in the sealess part of the Aegean region, use a lot of fresh black-eyed peas in their cooking. Other traditions cook with dried black-eyed peas, but only here have I seen whole fresh beans used, the peas still in their pods. The secret of this distinct dish is the olive oil: the more the better.

Fresh Black-Eyed Peas Braised in Olive Oil

1 medium onion, diced

½ cup (120 ml) olive oil

2 large tomatoes, seeded and grated (see Note, page 60; about 3 cups)

2 long green peppers, preferably hot, or 2 to 3 hot red peppers

1 pound (455 g) very fresh black-eyed peas still in their pods, strings removed, snapped in half

Salt

Serves 6

Sauté the onion in the oil in a pot until translucent. Add the tomatoes and peppers, then the black-eyed peas, and season with salt to taste. Cook over very low heat, without adding any water. (If all the liquid is absorbed but the peas are not sufficiently soft, add 1 cup/240 ml hot water and cook over medium heat until the liquid is almost entirely absorbed.) When the bottom of the pot starts to sizzle, remove from the heat. Serve warm or at room temperature.

THE JERUSALEM artichoke is called "apple of the earth" in Turkish, and rightly so, as it is a tuber that is taken out of the soil. This *zeytinyağlı* (olive oil) dish is full of flavor. You just have to be careful not to overcook the Jerusalem artichokes so they don't break apart (which is a not very pleasant sight).

I was served a raw Jerusalem artichoke salad with the same ingredients as below except for the raisins. It's another delicious way to serve this vegetable: Simply slice the Jerusalem artichoke very thin (use a mandoline), dress with olive oil and lemon juice, and sprinkle with fennel and hazelnuts.

Jerusalem Artichokes with Raisins in Olive Oil (*Zeytinyağlı Yerelması*)

1 medium onion, minced

⅓ cup (75 ml) virgin olive oil

1 tablespoon fresh lemon juice

Salt (optional)

1 teaspoon sugar

1½ pounds (680 g) Jerusalem artichokes, peeled, surfaces smoothed, and cut crosswise into 1-inch rounds

¼ cup (60 ml) warm water

2 tablespoons seedless (Smyrna) raisins, sautéed in 1 tablespoon olive oil (see Note)

2 tablespoons minced wild fennel (see page 156; or the green fronds of cultured fennel)

2 tablespoons sliced hazelnuts, preferably roasted

Serves 6 to 8 as meze

Sauté the onions in the oil in a pot. Add the lemon juice, salt to taste, sugar, if using, the Jerusalem artichokes, and warm water (the water should not cover the vegetables); cook, partially covered, over medium heat until the Jerusalem artichokes are soft and all the liquid is evaporated. (If the Jerusalem artichokes are done before the water has been evaporated, uncover, raise the heat to high, and cook until the water is gone.) Remove from the heat, add the sautéed raisins, cover, and let cool. Garnish with the fennel and hazelnuts and serve warm or at room temperature.

Note: Sautéing the raisins in olive oil gives them shine and extra chewiness.

BECAUSE VEGETABLES cooked in olive oil are traditionally eaten cold, they are generally considered summer dishes. Unlike the summer specialties green beans or cranberry beans, however, leeks and celery root are winter favorites. While celery root is for banquets, leeks are an essential home staple. Leeks look more attractive when cut on the diagonal and taste wonderful served barely warm. Leeks should be thoroughly cooked but still maintain their shape.

Leeks in Olive Oil

2 pounds (910 g) leeks, cut diagonally into 1-inch (2.5-cm) pieces, washed thoroughly and drained

8 ounces (225 g) carrot (1 large carrot), cut diagonally into ½-inch (12-mm) slices

¼ teaspoon sugar

2 tablespoons fresh lemon juice

½ teaspoon salt

¾ cup (180 ml) virgin olive oil

1½ tablespoons medium-grain rice

1 cup (240 ml) warm water

Lemon wedges, for serving

Serves 6

Put the leeks and carrot in a large pot. Add the sugar, lemon juice, salt, and oil. Cover and cook over high heat until steam appears from under the lid. Immediately reduce the heat to low and cook until the leeks are yellow but not quite done. Make a hollow with a spoon in the center of the leeks and pour in the rice and warm water. Cover and cook for 10 minutes, until the rice is cooked but still holds its shape. (Add 3 to 4 tablespoons hot water and cook for 1 or 2 minutes more, if desired.) Serve warm, with a squeeze of lemon juice.

ALTHOUGH A humble vegetable, celery root braised in olive oil has always been an important dish at modern banquets in the winter, much like braised artichokes typically making an appearance at spring banquets. Here, I share a more humble home-cooked dish that is enjoyed by celery lovers. This dish can be served right out of the pot or rewarmed; either add the *terbiye* (lemon and egg sauce) just before serving, or reheat the dish over low heat, taking care not to boil it. It is soupy, and when you dip bread in its tangy sauce, it becomes a full meal. It also can be served as part of a meze spread; just make sure it is served warm.

Celery Roots in Lemon and Egg Sauce (*Terbiyeli Kereviz*)

10 shallots, peeled and cut in half

4 celery roots, each with a 2-inch (5-cm) circumference, peeled, cut in half, with a well scooped out in the center of each half (see Note)

1 carrot, peeled, halved lengthwise, and chopped into ⅓-inch- (8-mm-) thick half moons

1 small potato, peeled and cut into ½-inch (12-mm) cubes

½ cup (120 ml) virgin olive oil

2 cups (480 ml) warm water

Juice of 1 lemon

1 large egg, beaten

Salt and black pepper

1 tablespoon finely minced fresh parsley

Serves 8 as meze

Sauté the shallot halves, celery roots, carrot, and potato in the oil for about 3 minutes over medium heat. Add the warm water and cook, covered, over medium heat until the vegetables are al dente, about 10 minutes. Remove from the heat and keep the vegetables covered (there should be about ¾ to 1 cup/180 to 240 ml cooking water left in the pot). Whisk the lemon juice into the egg until well mixed and add 1 tablespoon of tepid water to dilute. Quickly add the lemon-egg mixture (*terbiye*) to the vegetables, stirring well to keep it from separating. Season with salt and pepper to taste and give the pot a quick shake to completely mix in the *terbiye*. Serve warm with a sprinkle of pepper and the parsley.

Note: If you can only find small celery roots, the size of a small apple, buy eight and just chop off the top quarter of each, then make small wells for the filling.

NOW A veritable staple of Turkish cooking, dried beans have become popular only in the last two centuries or so. The arrival of beans and tomatoes from the New World was surely a turning point for Turkish cooks. Those who prefer to stay away from meat may of course cook beans without adding meat, but you really do need either chicken or beef stock to get more flavor. I find beans cooked with chicken broth to be tastier.

If you want this dish to be a thick soup, do not allow all the liquid to boil away. If you want this to be a dinner-plate dish, boil it down more and serve next to rice. The aim is a slightly soupy dish that can be eaten with either a fork or a spoon. When you turn the heat off, the top should glisten like a red sea with just the tops of the beans showing.

Beans: The Classic Recipe

2 cups (400 g) dried beans (see Note), soaked overnight in plenty of water, then drained

2 medium onions, minced

2 tablespoons sunflower or olive oil

3 tablespoons unsalted butter

1 heaping tablespoon tomato paste

2 large tomatoes, seeded and grated (see Note, page 60)

2 or 3 dried hot red peppers, pierced in one or two places

Salt

3 to 4 cups (720 to 960 ml) hot chicken broth, preferably homemade

Serves 6

Put the beans in a pot, cover with water by 2 inches (5 cm), and bring to a rolling boil. Reduce the heat to medium and simmer until the beans are soft but still hold their shape. (If the water is boiling too much, the beans will pop open.) Check the beans quite frequently as there is no way to know beforehand how quickly or slowly they will cook (see Note).

Put the onions, 2 to 3 tablespoons water, the oil, and butter in a pot and sauté over medium heat. When the onions are about to turn golden, add the tomato paste and sauté, stirring constantly, until nicely aromatic but not burned. Add the tomatoes, dried peppers, and salt to taste, cover, and let simmer until all the liquid is evaporated. Add the broth and beans. Cook for 15 minutes over medium heat to blend all the flavors. Remove from the heat and let sit for 30 minutes. If necessary, reheat before serving.

Note: When buying beans, make sure they are of the current year's harvest. Old beans each cook in a different length of time, giving the chef difficulties. Some stay uncooked, while some become mush as they cook!

FROM THE highland town of Bolu, this lentil dish will surprise everyone with its unusual mixture of ingredients. Quince alone does not have much taste, though it does have a faint but distinct aroma. In this dish, its contribution is strictly aromatic. Pumpkin chopped into ½-inch (12-mm) dice would be a nice alternative to the quince, adding color and a delicate fragrance. The vanilla and cassia are my additions to this regional dish.

Lentils with Quince and Mint
(*Meksenye*)

2 medium onions, diced

4 tablespoons (60 ml) unsalted butter

1 tablespoon virgin olive oil

1 large quince (see sidebar), diced, soaked in water and lemon juice to prevent browning, or 2 cups (500 g) diced peeled pumpkin

½ cup (95 g) green lentils, soaked in warm water for at least 30 minutes

1 cup (200 g) medium-grain rice, soaked in hot water with ½ tablespoon salt for 30 minutes

⅓ vanilla bean, split, seeds scraped out, and cut into pieces

1 (2-inch/5-cm) cassia stick (optional; see page 17)

Fresh mint leaves

Serves 6

Sauté the onions in the butter and oil until soft and about to turn golden; add the quince or pumpkin and sauté a few minutes more. Drain and add the lentils, rice, and 2½ cups (600 ml) water. Bring to a boil over high heat, then reduce to medium heat, add the vanilla pod pieces and cassia stick, if using, and cook for 10 minutes. Reduce the heat to low and cook until the lentils and rice are soft, about 5 minutes more. If one of the ingredients seem a little uncooked after the specified cooking time is complete, you can always add 1 or 2 tablespoons hot water and continue cooking for another 2 to 3 minutes. (The dish should be somewhat moist.) Remove and discard the cassia stick and vanilla bean, and serve garnished with mint leaves.

Selecting Quince

The Turkish expression "to eat quince" has unpleasant connotations, meaning one who eats quince will have trouble. It is used mockingly for those who get married, especially for men, implying that being married is a disadvantage for a man, and one who takes a bite of a quince may find out this implication is not at all misleading. A quince may have a beautiful smell, but it will not be pleasant to eat if it is not the juicy kind known as *ekmek ayvasi* (literally "bread quince"). *Ekmek ayvasi* are big (as heavy as 9 to 12 ounces/255 to 240 g), juicy, and good to eat raw. In season, they're served as a meze with raki. While the hard *limon ayvasi* (literally "lemon quince") has a dense, feathery peel, *ekmek ayvasi* barely has any such peel at all. Unfortunately, in Turkey, fruit sellers remove this hairy part by rubbing it off with a cloth, so it is difficult to correctly identify the type of quince. Hard *limon ayvasi* is good for making quince jam. At least there is a use for it.

PINTO BEANS are a never-fail dish on the tables of İzmir, the ancient and busy port on the Aegean, a cosmopolitan city where the inhabitants love to enjoy life together with food. The pleasant weather allows a long spring and autumn, and people take advantage of the temperate seasons to eat and drink outdoors along the coastline. Light mezes like wild greens, quick-pickled green peppers, eggplant caviar, and pinto beans are part of the spread, and fish from the Aegean Sea—like gilt-head bream, red sea bream, and red mullet, to name the most popular ones—are served as the main dish after the mezes. There are luxury restaurants along Kordon, the city's famous coast, but eating at small restaurants in the area used to be a memorable experience, as they were rustic and as fresh and spontaneous as could be.

The pinto beans may turn white if you add lemon while cooking, or take on a darker color if no lemon is added. I prefer them dark and add a squeeze of lemon juice before eating. This dish is good to have on hand when you feel too lazy to cook, because the beans taste just as good—if not better—when they are cold.

Fresh Pinto Beans with Cinnamon and Vegetables

2 pounds (910 g) fresh pinto beans

3 medium onions, diced

⅓ cup (75 ml) virgin olive oil

3 cloves garlic, minced

3 medium tomatoes, peeled, seeded, and diced

1 carrot, diced (optional)

1½ teaspoons sugar

1 tablespoon fresh lemon juice, (optional)

1 teaspoon crushed dried hot red peppers, or 2 to 3 fresh long green chiles

1 cinnamon stick, preferably from Ceylon

Salt

1 tablespoon minced fresh parsley

Serves 8 as meze

Boil the beans in plenty of water for about 30 minutes, until soft, and drain.

Sauté the onions in the oil until golden, then add the garlic and sauté for 30 seconds; add the tomatoes and cook until all the liquid is evaporated. Add the carrot, if using, the sugar, lemon juice (if using), hot peppers, and cinnamon stick, and sauté until aromatic. Add the beans and 2 cups (480 ml) water and cook for 20 minutes over medium heat until most of the water boils away. Season with salt to taste, remove from the heat, and let cool. Remove and discard the cinnamon stick, garnish with the parsley, and serve.

(OPPOSITE) JARRED PICKLES FOR SALE IN FRONT OF A *TURŞU* (PICKLE) SHOP.

138 • ESSENTIAL TURKISH CUISINE

RICE AND BULGUR PILAFS

The pilaf, made from rice, butter, and stock, is a simple dish that's seductively light and velvety. For Turks, it is a dish that can be appreciated on its own, without embellishment, provided it is accompanied by a glass of *ayran* (a cold yogurt beverage), *cacik* (a cold yogurt and cucumber "soup"), *hoşaf* (a fruit compote), or any kind of salad on the side. In Ottoman times, a huge dish of rice would be served at the end of a banquet, most likely to make sure everyone left the banquet with a full stomach. Mrs. Ramsey, an English lady who traveled to Anatolia with her archeologist husband, wrote that when the pilaf came at the end of the banquet, she had already counted some twenty dishes that had been served, one after the other. But the most celebrated dish was the white pilaf, or pilaf with chickpeas (page 145) and meat cooked *tandir* style. Nowadays, pilafs are also served with a meat and vegetable dish (or *yahnis*; see page 175) or alongside grilled meat like chops or shish kebabs (see page 70).

Traditionally, pilafs are made with baldo, a polished, starchy, medium-grain rice, but Arborio rice may be substituted. Likewise bulgur has been used to make tasty and nutritious pilafs since ancient times (see sidebar, pages 156–157). Cooking in chicken or beef broth makes pilafs more flavorful, and authentic Turkish pilafs are always topped with hot butter. To make perfect pilaf, choose from one of two methods:

The soaking method: Let the uncooked rice (medium-grain baldo or Arborio) soak in hot salty water until the water is cool. (Do not cover during soaking.) Soaking removes the starch so that the grains won't stick together. Drain and rinse the rice until the water runs clear. Add the rice to premeasured stock boiling in a pan (this action is known as *salma*). Generally speaking, the ratio is 1 measure of rice to about 1¼ measures of water, but Turkish mothers tell their daughters that the water should cover the rice by a finger-width, and this always proves right. If using Arborio rice, you may need to add a little extra water because the grains are fatter than baldo grains. If you do not use meat or chicken broth, rice generally takes a little longer to cook; add another ⅓ cup (75 ml) water.

Cover the pot and cook over medium heat for 5 minutes, then reduce the heat to low and cook for another 5 minutes, until you see "eyes" on the surface of the rice and all of the liquid is absorbed. Then, lower the heat to the lowest possible level and cook for another 4 to 5 minutes, until the grains are soft and the water is completely absorbed. If you discover along the way that the ratio of water to rice is inaccurate, adjusting the heat during cooking will correct the problem: Turn the heat up a little if you have too much water, or turn it down for too little. Then dress the pilaf with browned butter (some Turks add a portion of the butter during cooking and add the rest of the butter at the end of cooking, which should last 15 to 20 minutes). Once all the butter is added, fluff the rice gently with a spoon.

Letting the pilaf sit awhile with the lid on before serving makes the grains separate from each other; rice that is a little moist, on the other hand, is also delicious and a couple of Ottoman recipes recommend cooking it this way. This does not mean overcooking, just that the rice has more moisture. Overcooked pilaf is mushy and can be improved by letting the steaming rice sit covered with a clean absorbent cloth. The taste, however, will never be the same as rice cooked with the proper ratio of water. Sometimes Turks deliberately produce a mushy pilaf called *lapa*, believing it to aid digestion.

Pilaf made using this method is light and has a heavenly aroma, and the grains do not stick together. Adding browned butter to the cooked rice makes it even more delicious. I like to use fragrant butter, preferably made from sheep's milk, for this step.

(ABOVE) A VARIETY OF SIEVES IN TAHTAKALE, NEAR THE EGYPTIAN BAZAAR.

The sautéing method: Restaurants and newer cooks generally skip soaking the rice in hot water. Instead, to prevent a mushy pilaf, they sauté washed rice in butter, an action known as *kavurma*, then add hot water or broth for cooking. This method is popular today, but presoaking the rice results in a far lighter pilaf.

WHEN THE *New York Times* food writer Melissa Clark arrived at my home in Istanbul, the bulgur pilaf I'd invited her to taste was still not cooked. I did that on purpose, as I wanted her to see the cooking firsthand. Melissa's introduction to bulgur pilaf was important to me; I believe we have to promote bulgur, which is relatively unknown outside of Anatolia, so that it can take its place in world cuisines. She asked how I knew when the bulgur was done, and I told her to look for the eyes that appear on the surface. "It's ready when it stares back at you," I said.

When she tasted the dish, which paired bulgur with pumpkin, she forgot almost entirely about everything else I had prepared. She loved the recipe but wanted to add her own creativity to the dish, so we went into the kitchen. I mentioned a recipe for chestnut bulgur pilaf that dates from the Ottoman period. The recipe below is what we came up with that day: a very unique bulgur pilaf that shows just how amenable this food is to different approaches.

Chestnut and Tangerine Bulgur Pilaf

15 to 20 fresh chestnuts, or whole canned chestnuts

1 tablespoon sunflower oil

4 tablespoons (55 g) unsalted butter

1 medium onion, chopped

1 ¾ cups (245 g) coarse bulgur

Salt

3 ½ cups (840 ml) chicken stock

½ cup (85 g) seedless raisins (Smyrna, if available)

3 teaspoons grated tangerine or orange zest

1 teaspoon mild red pepper flakes

1 teaspoon ground allspice

1 tablespoon minced purple basil (if fresh is not available use dried leaves, crushed between the palms of your hands)

Pinch of ground cinnamon or cassia (see page 17)

Serves 6

Preheat the oven to 400°F (205°C).

If using fresh chestnuts, score the skins, soak the chestnuts in cold water for 15 minutes, then drain and spread on a baking sheet. Bake for 10 minutes. Let cool for a few minutes, then peel off the shells and papery skins while they're still quite hot. (Roasting them makes them easy to peel.)

Heat the oil and 2 tablespoons of the butter in a pot, then add the onion and sauté until translucent. Add the bulgur, season with salt to taste, and sauté for 2 minutes. Add the stock, chestnuts, and raisins. Cook until the bulgur absorbs all the liquid and its surface has small indentations (or "eyes"), 15 to 20 minutes. Heat the remaining 2 tablespoons butter in a pan until aromatic, then add the tangerine or orange zest and red pepper flakes; sauté for about 30 seconds. Pour the seasoned butter mixture over the bulgur, sprinkle with the allspice, and stir well with a spoon so the bulgur fluffs up. Spoon into a serving dish, garnish with the basil and the cinnamon or cassia, and serve immediately.

IN THE WINTER, Turks vary plain pilaf by adding spices, raisins, almonds, pine nuts, and the like, while summer is the time for tomato pilaf. The sour taste of lemon reminds me of spring, so that's why I came up with this lemony rice dish. When I heard that the cooks of Crete add lemon juice to their rice, I decided to dress mine with lemon juice along with the rind. This pilaf tastes best when served immediately.

Lemony Pilaf

2 cups (400 g) medium-grain rice, soaked for 30 minutes in hot water with 1 tablespoon salt

Salt

About 2 cups (480 ml) chicken or vegetable stock

3 to 4 tablespoons (42 to 55 g) unsalted butter, cut into pea-size pieces

Grated zest of 1 lemon

Juice of ½ lemon

1 tablespoon whole black or green peppercorns, coarsely crushed with a mortar and pestle

Serves 6

Drain and rinse the rice. Combine the rice, salt to taste, and broth in a pot, making sure the stock covers the rice by no more than one finger-width. Cover tightly and cook over low heat for 15 to 20 minutes. When enough broth has been absorbed so that small holes appear in the rice's surface, add the butter and lemon zest. Let the butter melt, then add the lemon juice, stir, and serve with a sprinkle of peppercorns.

THIS IS a much-adored pilaf because of the extra dimension added by the orzo. It is served in most *esnaf lokantası* (modest eateries serving home-style lunches to tradesmen and other working people). Toasting the orzo before adding it to the rice gives the dish a more exciting appearance and a fuller flavor. It is a nice accompaniment to any grilled or stewed meat or poultry dish.

Pilaf with Orzo

½ cup (100 g) orzo

2 cups (400 g) medium-grain rice, soaked for 30 minutes in hot water with 1 tablespoon salt

Salt

About 2 cups (480 ml) beef or chicken stock

3 to 4 tablespoons (42 to 55 g) unsalted butter, cut into pea-size pieces

Serves 6

Lightly toast the orzo in a dry frying pan over medium heat until golden. Drain and rinse the rice. Put the rice, salt to taste, and broth in a pot, making sure the stock covers the rice by no more than one finger-width. Add the orzo, cover tightly, and cook over low heat for 25 to 30 minutes. When the rice is cooked, add the butter and let it melt into the rice. Let the pilaf sit for 5 minutes before inverting it onto a serving dish.

THIS IS yet another classic Turkish pilaf. No wedding banquet since Sultan Mehmet the Conqueror—no banquet, for that matter—was complete without this pilaf. Times are changing this custom, but street vendors still display this pilaf in big glass cases, and the chickpeas and flaky rice grains are an irresistible sight for the hungry. A delicious buttery aroma wafts from the pilaf, which is bursting with the flavor of homemade chicken stock. This dish is traditionally a meal in itself, especially if accompanied by a glass of lemonade, a salad, or a bowl of yogurt, or if followed by a bowl of compote. A sprinkling of freshly ground black pepper draws out the flavor. You can replace the chickpeas with black-eyed peas if you wish, and serve the pilaf with an egg for each guest; pilaf served with eggs on top is traditional.

White Pilaf with Chickpeas

2 cups (400 g) medium-grain rice, soaked for 30 minutes in hot water with 1 tablespoon salt

1 cup (200 g) cooked chickpeas

Salt

About 2⅓ cups (555 g) hot chicken or beef broth

4 to 5 tablespoons (55 to 70 g) unsalted butter

8 large eggs

Freshly ground black pepper

Ground cinnamon (optional)

Serves 8

Drain and rinse the rice. Put the rice and chickpeas in a saucepan, season with salt to taste, and add the broth, making sure that the broth covers the rice by no more than one finger-width. Cook for 5 minutes over high heat, then 5 minutes over medium heat. When tiny indentations appear on the rice's surface, reduce the heat to low and cook for 5 to 6 minutes. Remove from the heat.

While the rice cooks, heat the butter until melted and aromatic (see Note). Pour it gently over the cooked rice. Stir the rice well with a spoon to fluff.

Meanwhile, poach the eggs in boiling water for 3 to 4 minutes (see Notes). The yolks should be soft; they act as a sauce for the pilaf.

Spoon the chickpea pilaf onto a serving platter. Make eight indentations in the pilaf's surface with the back of a serving spoon and spoon an egg into each indentation. Sprinkle with pepper and cinnamon, if you like, and serve.

Note: Traditionally, butter is always heated until aromatic (but not browned) and then poured over the pilaf. If you wish, however, you can simply add dabs of butter to the rice and let them melt in, then stir and spread the butter evenly throughout the pilaf during fluffing.

THE UZBEKS are the largest Turkic ethnic group in Central Asia today. Ethnically, they are descendants of the Oğuz Turks, but have roots in the region that extend back to the ninth century. *Uz-* is a reference to Oğuz, and *bek* is the Turkish word for "beg," which eventually became *bey*, a courtesy word we use today at the end of a person's first name as people in the United States might use "Mister." Nowadays, this pilaf is cooked in many homes throughout Turkey. Because it is a wholesome, tasty dish and looks so festive, we cook it as a special dish for guests.

Uzbek Pilaf

4 medium onions, sliced into thin rings

3 tablespoons vegetable oil

3 tablespoons unsalted butter

2 pounds (910 g) beef or lamb, cut into cubes, with or without bone

4½ cups (1 L) hot water, or more as needed

3 carrots, cut into matchsticks

3 cups (600 g) medium-grain rice, soaked for 30 minutes in hot water with 1 tablespoon salt

3 whole heads garlic

1 tablespoon cumin seeds

Serves 6

In a large pot, sauté the onions in the oil and butter until translucent. Add the meat and sauté until nicely browned, then add 1 cup (240 ml) of the hot water and cook until the meat is tender. Add the carrots and sauté briefly, then drain the rice and add it to the pot; gently add the remaining 3½ cups (840 ml) hot water, pouring slowly down the edge of the pot so as not to disturb the rice mixture. (The water should cover the rice by one finger-width; if necessary, add more hot water.) Cover tightly and cook over low heat for 20 to 25 minutes, until the rice is almost tender, but not done. Uncover, bury the garlic in the rice, sprinkle with the cumin, re-cover, and steep for another 15 minutes over the lowest possible heat.

Remove the garlic and carefully invert the pilaf onto a serving platter. Place the garlic on a corner of the platter and serve.

Turkish Hospitality

Throughout their cultural history, Turks have imagined heroes who have carried people's hopes, fears, and desires through the ages. One of these heroes is Nasreddin Hodja, who cast a light on human foibles with his satirical approach to those considering themselves superior. Here's a story about Hodja that describes Turkish hospitality and those who might unfairly benefit from it. It also emphasizes the importance of stock in Turkish cooking.

A peasant brought Nasreddin Hodja a rabbit as a gift. To repay this kindness, Hodja treated the peasant to a meal of the cooked rabbit. The next day a person claiming to be a relative of the gift-giving peasant appeared at Hodja's doorstep, and Hodja invited him in for a meal. A couple days later another so-called relative visited, and Hodja reluctantly treated this person to a meal. Not many days later another peasant came by. Hodja asked him who he was. "I am a distant relative of the distant relative of the distant relative of the peasant who brought you a rabbit." Hodja invited him in, disappeared into the kitchen, and reappeared carrying a bowl of water. He placed the bowl in front of the peasant. "What is this?" asked the villager. Hodja answered, "This is the juice of the juice of the juice of the juice of the rabbit that the peasant brought me."

THIS DISH is a synthesis of Ottoman pilaf recipes that I found in historical cookbook manuscripts. One of my food-themed performances in cooperation with an art gallery, for an exhibition called "Neighbors," featured nearly thirty kinds of pilaf from around the world. This one scored the best.

Palace Pilaf with Lamb

. . . .

2 pounds (910 g) bone-in lamb, washed and cut into walnut-size pieces

1 medium onion, diced

1 (4- to 5-inch/10- to 12-cm) cassia stick (see page 17; optional)

1 tablespoon vegetable oil

1 cup (240 ml) hot water to cook meat, if necessary

3 cups (600 g) medium-grain rice, soaked for 30 minutes in hot water with 1 tablespoon salt

1 teaspoon ground allspice

½ cup (70 g) dried currants

1 cup (170 g) raisins

3 ¾ cups (900 ml) stock (preferably chicken)

Salt

FOR FINISHING

5 to 6 tablespoons (70 to 85 g) unsalted butter

1 cup (150 g) blanched almonds

½ cup (60 g) shelled unsalted pistachios

1 green lentil–size piece mastic (see page 16) and 2 teaspoons sugar, crushed with a mortar and pestle

¼ to ½ teaspoon whole black pepper-corns, crushed with a mortar and pestle (or ground in a mill)

¼ to ½ teaspoon ground cinnamon or cassia (see page 17)

Serves 6

In a tightly covered pot over high heat, cook the meat, onions, and cassia stick, if using, in the oil for 1 to 2 minutes, until steam forms inside the pot. Reduce the heat to very low and simmer until the meat is cooked by the steam, about 35 minutes. (If necessary, add the hot water and cook some more.) Drain and rinse the rice and add to the pot along with the allspice, currants, raisins, stock, and salt to taste. Cook for 5 minutes over high heat, then 5 minutes over medium, then 5 minutes over low. Remove and discard the cassia stick, if using.

To finish the dish, melt the butter in a skillet, lightly sauté the almonds and pistachios, and pour over the cooked rice. Sprinkle the rice with the mastic mixture and peppercorns, gently fluff it, and carefully invert the pilaf onto a serving platter. Sprinkle with ground cinnamon or cassia and serve.

"LIONS SLEEP WRAPPED IN CLOTHES" is a Turkish proverb meaning "judge a person by his essence, not by his clothes." Although it may have different names in other parts of Turkey, this pilaf from the province of Siirt in southeastern Turkey is served to couples on their wedding night, when they traditionally eat alone. Curtain (*Perde*) Pilaf has a special draping or covering, symbolizing that the private things shared by the couple should remain concealed from others. The ingredients also have symbolic meaning: rice symbolizes fertility, almonds a boy, pistachios a girl, raisins a sweet life, and black pepper the tragedies the couple must share. No other spices are added, and in days of old it was made with meat from a partridge, the symbol of peace and happiness. I have included a recipe for the dough covering for those who prefer to make this dish traditionally, but pre-made *yufka* or phyllo dough can also be used.

Curtain (*Perde*) Pilaf

FOR THE PILAF

3 medium onions, diced

1/2 cup (60 g) pine nuts

1 cup (150 g) blanched almonds or shelled pistachios

1 cup (2 sticks/225 g) unsalted butter

1 1/2 teaspoons salt

1 teaspoon black pepper

4 cups (960 ml) chicken stock

3 cups (600 g) medium-grain rice, soaked for 30 minutes in hot water with 1 tablespoon salt

1/3 cup (50 g) dried currants or seedless raisins

1 small chicken, cooked, deboned, and cut into bite-size pieces

FOR A TRADITIONAL DOUGH COVERING

1 large egg

1/3 cup (75 ml) olive oil

1/3 cup (75 ml) plain Greek yogurt

1 1/2 cups (170 g) all-purpose flour

FOR A LESS-TRADITIONAL COVERING

2 sheets *yufka* (or 4 sheets phyllo)

2 tablespoons olive oil

Serves 6

Sauté the onions, pine nuts, and almonds in the butter in a pot over medium heat. When the onions are translucent, add the salt and pepper. Sauté for 1 minute, then add the stock. When the stock begins to boil, add the rice. Cover tightly and cook for 5 minutes over high heat, then 5 minutes over medium heat, then 5 minutes over low heat. Remove from the heat, add the currants or raisins, and let cool for 1 to 2 hours.

To make a traditional dough covering, knead together the egg, oil, yogurt, and flour until smooth and uniform, cover, and let sit for 25 to 30 minutes. Roll out the dough into a large, thin circle. (The circle must fit a well-greased pan with enough extra that the ends of the dough can be folded up to completely cover the pilaf that will fill the pan. The traditional pan resembles a Turkish fez, but use whatever you have available!)

If you choose to use *yufka* or phyllo for the covering instead, completely line a well-greased pan with the pastry, allowing enough extra to cover the top of the pilaf once it's added to the pan. Phyllo is very thin, so use a double layer of sheets.

Preheat the oven to 350°F (175°C). Mix the chicken with the cooled rice mixture and then pack the chicken and rice pilaf into the dough-lined pan. Fold the sides of the dough over the pilaf, ensuring that the pilaf is completely covered by the dough; thin out the ends where the dough meets so it doesn't get too thick (or, if using *yufka*, wet the ends with water to seal). Bake for 20 to 25 minutes, or until the top is nicely browned. Serve hot.

VARIATION

It is also nice to make a dough or *yufka* casing for each individual serving. If using *yufka*, bring the ends of a square piece of *yufka* together and tie it with a string cut from *yufka*. If using dough, place a square of dough inside a ramekin that's larger than a muffin cup, sealing the dough at the bottom. It does not matter if the seal is pretty, because this is the side that will be on the serving plate.

IN SUMMER, this pilaf (without the shrimp) is very popular in the Aegean region, where gardens are literally invaded by tomatoes. It is a dish that makes the best use of red, juicy tomatoes, which grow to ultimate tastiness in the heat of the Aegean sun and in its fertile soil, and the olive oil that is a staple in the pantry there, in contrast to the eastern parts of Turkey where olives are a luxury. Serving this pilaf dressed with shrimp is my innovation.

This is a rustic regional pilaf with a consistency rather like that of risotto, soupy and a little creamy. This is achieved by retaining the starch from the rice, which is typically removed when making Turkish pilaf by soaking the rice in hot water before cooking (see page 140).

Aegean Juicy Tomato Pilaf with Shrimp

¾ cup (180 ml) plus 1 tablespoon extra-virgin olive oil

2 medium onions, diced

4 medium ripe tomatoes, peeled and diced

1 cup (240 g) medium-grain rice, washed

Salt

8 peeled and deveined large shrimp

3 large cloves garlic, crushed

2 tablespoons minced fresh mint

1 teaspoon freshly ground white or black pepper

Serves 6

Heat ¾ cup (180 ml) of the oil over medium heat in a pot large enough to cook the rice. Add the onions and sauté until they are transparent and just about to turn golden, 5 to 7 minutes. Add the tomatoes and cook until the tomatoes are almost half done but still juicy. Add the rice and salt to taste and stir for few seconds, then add 2½ cups (600 ml) cold water. Cover and cook over medium heat, checking occasionally to make sure the rice has not become dry. Add up to another ½ cup (120 ml) water in small amounts, as if cooking risotto. When the rice grains are al dente (the rice should still be moist), after 12 to 15 minutes, remove from the heat and uncover the pot to stop the cooking process.

In a pan, heat the remaining 1 tablespoon oil, add the shrimp, and fry over high heat, stirring, until they are cooked through but still juicy. Add the garlic and fry a minute more. Dish the pilaf out onto a serving platter, top with the shrimp, sprinkle with the mint and white pepper, and serve warm.

SEA BASS boasts a light flavor that has made it a favorite at important banquets, where it is either served cold, dressed with mayonnaise, or grilled, or in a soup at elegant dinners. And, in the palace, saffron rice was always an important dish. Therefore, it seemed only fitting to combine these traditions for a really impressive dish.

Sea Bass and Saffron Pilaf

Salt

3 tablespoons unsalted butter

3 cups (600 g) rice, soaked for 30 minutes in hot water with 1 tablespoon salt

2 tablespoons dried currants

2 pounds (910 g) sea bass fillets

Pinch of saffron threads, soaked in ¼ cup warm water

½ cup (75 g) blanched almonds, toasted and coarsely ground if desired

½ teaspoon ground cinnamon or cassia (see page 17)

Serves 6

Pour 3 cups (720 ml) water in a large pot, add some salt and the butter, and bring to a boil. Add the rice and currants, cover, and cook for 5 minutes over high heat, then 5 minutes over medium heat. Place the fish fillets on the rice, pour the saffron water over the fish, and cook, tightly covered, for another 3 to 4 minutes over medium heat, until the flesh of the fish is white and the rice is tender. Let sit for about 5 minutes before serving. Spoon the pilaf into a serving bowl and sprinkle with the almonds and cinnamon or cassia.

Fresh fava beans appear only in spring and for a very short time. Each year, it is traditional in every home to cook fava beans with olive oil at least once. This fava bean pilaf, which is Persian in origin, was cooked by Pervin Kaşo, who comes from a Persian family. Because basmati rice is the choice for Persian pilafs (and the rice selected by Pervin), I use it in this recipe.

Fava Bean Spring Pilaf

2 cups (370 g) basmati rice, soaked for 30 minutes in hot water and 1 tablespoon salt

18 ounces (500 g) fresh fava beans, sorted and peeled

1 ½ cups (360 ml) hot water

1 tablespoon olive oil

2 to 4 tablespoons (28 to 55 g) unsalted butter, cut into chickpea-size pieces

1 cup (20 g) fresh dill, minced

Black pepper (optional)

Serves 6

Drain and rinse the rice with plenty of water. Combine the rice and fava beans in a pot, add the hot water and oil, and cover. Cook for 6 to 7 minutes over medium heat, then 5 to 6 minutes over low heat. Arrange the butter on top of the rice. Cook, covered, over the lowest possible heat, for another 5 minutes. Add the dill, then slowly stir the rice to ensure that the melted butter is uniformly distributed. Fluff the pilaf gently with a spoon, sprinkle with pepper, if you choose, and serve.

THIS IS one of my favorite dishes that I acquired a taste for only a few years ago, after I tasted it in a small restaurant called Hünkar in the Fatih district in Istanbul. In the meantime, the chef-owner of this restaurant has opened three more restaurants and opened up a space for Turkish home cooking that not only brings this kind of food the recognition it deserves, but also inspires young chefs to specialize in Turkish cooking. The chef, Feridun Ügümü, is from Erzurum, but this dish is from the Black Sea region. This is always prepared with fresh anchovies, but if you wish, you may replace them with small fish of similar size, like small sardines.

Anchovy Pilaf (*Hamsili Pilav*)

3 tablespoons unsalted butter (see Notes), plus 2 tablespoons cut into pea-size pieces, plus more for greasing the pan

2 pounds (910 g) whole fresh anchovies, cleaned (see Notes), plus 15 cleaned and chopped fresh anchovies

2 large onions

2 tablespoons vegetable oil

2 ½ cups (500 g) medium-grain rice, soaked for 30 minutes in hot water with 1 tablespoon salt

1 large carrot, grated

½ cup (70 g) dried currants

2 tablespoons dried mint

½ teaspoon ground cinnamon or cassia (see page 17)

½ teaspoon ground allspice

¼ teaspoon black pepper

Salt

About 3 ½ cups (840 ml) fish or vegetable stock

Serves 8

Preheat the oven to 350°F (175°C) and grease an ovenproof baking dish with butter.

Arrange the whole anchovies back to back in the baking dish so they completely cover the bottom of the dish. Line the sides of the dish with more anchovies, letting them hang over the edge. (You will have some whole anchovies left over.)

Sauté the onions in the 3 tablespoons butter and the oil until translucent. Drain and rinse the rice. Add to the onions, along with the carrot, and sauté, stirring constantly. Add the currants, mint, cinnamon or cassia, allspice, pepper, and salt to taste. Add the stock and cook for 5 minutes over medium heat, then 5 minutes over low heat or until the stock is almost absorbed. (The rice should still be grainy and not quite cooked through.) Add the chopped anchovies and stir. Spoon all of the rice mixture over the whole anchovies in the baking dish, then flip the anchovies that are hanging over the sides of the dish over the rice. Arrange the reserved whole anchovies on top so that they cover the rice completely. Scatter the cubes of butter on top and bake for 10 to 15 minutes. Invert carefully onto a serving platter and serve.

Notes: While you can use different oils to make this dish, the traditional recipe calls for butter, which certainly gives a delicious taste.

To clean whole fresh anchovies, cut the head off and split the fish open so that it is like a butterfly. The bone will easily leave the flesh when you pull it away gently from the head to the tail.

TOMATO PILAF is a summertime classic. It is the Turkish equivalent of Italy's pasta with fresh tomato sauce, one might say. When cooked with ripe summer tomatoes, its flavor and consistency are wonderful, and it is addictive with a bowl of *cacik* (Cold Yogurt and Cucumber Soup; page 103). You must serve it immediately, however, or it will lose some of its mouthwatering moisture.

Tomato Pilaf

2 ½ cups (500 g) medium-grain rice, soaked for 30 minutes in plenty of hot water with 1 tablespoon salt

3 to 4 tablespoons (42 to 55 g) unsalted butter

4 tomatoes, peeled, seeded, and grated (3 cups/600 g; see Note, page 60)

1 ½ teaspoons salt

3 ½ cups (840 ml) hot water

Freshly ground black pepper for serving

Serves 6

Drain and rinse the rice. Combine the butter and tomatoes in a pot. Add the salt and cook over medium heat for 4 minutes. The tomatoes should be half-cooked and still juicy. Add the rice and the measured hot water, making sure that the tomato and water mixture covers the rice by one-and-a-half finger-widths. Cover and cook for 5 minutes over high heat, then 6 to 8 minutes over medium heat. Remove from the heat immediately. Gently stir once and serve immediately, sprinkled with lots of freshly ground pepper—the more the better! (Do not let the rice sit, as in other recipes, because it will lose its moisture; see Note.)

Note: This is the one and only pilaf that I do not leave over low heat to fluff; the slight stickiness the tomatoes impart makes it unique. I also do not use stock in this pilaf because it takes away from the freshness and aroma of the tomatoes.

THIS RECIPE from Bozca Island in the upper Aegean is for a Hıdırellez holiday meal. Hıdırellez is a special day when people ask the holy men Hızır and İlyas to grant their wishes. Hızır, who gives life to plants, and İlyas, protector of water and animals, meet during the night of the fifth of May and cross the seas and fields looking for people's wishes. These two characters eventually became one, called Hıdırellez. I remember writing the school grades I wanted on a mock report card and then throwing it into the sea for Hıdırellez to find. Women who want to have children put dolls or drawings of babies under trees for Hıdırellez. The holiday is celebrated on May 6 with picnics of cold food like hard-boiled eggs and stuffed vegetables eaten on kilim rugs spread over the spring grass. As this pilaf should be eaten hot, it would be served when the holiday is celebrated at home.

Meadow Pilaf

2 pounds (910 g) bone-in beef or lamb meat, cut into 1-inch (2.5-cm) cubes and bones reserved

2 medium onions, finely chopped

4 tablespoons (60 ml) olive oil

5 cups (1.2 L) hot water

1 ½ cups (300 g) rice, soaked for 30 minutes in hot water with 1 tablespoon salt

1 cup (140 g) coarse bulgur

Salt and black pepper

5 tablespoons (70 g) unsalted butter, cut into pea-size pieces

½ cup (10 g) minced green onions

½ cup (10 g) fresh dill, minced

½ cup (10 g) fresh parsley, minced

½ tablespoon dried mint

Serves 6

Put the meat, bones (they will add flavor to the broth), and onions in a pot and sauté in 3 tablespoons of the oil until the onions are translucent. Cover with the hot water and cook over low heat until the meat is done, about 1 hour. Remove the bones after cooking.

Preheat the oven to 350°F (175°C).

Transfer the cooked meat and 3 cups (720 ml) of the hot broth from the pot into another pot. Add the rice and bulgur and cook over medium heat for 8 to 10 minutes, then transfer the pilaf mixture to a roasting pan. Add an additional 1 cup (240 ml) hot broth and salt and pepper to taste. Scatter 4 tablespoons (55 g) of the butter on top of the rice, drizzle with the remaining 1 tablespoon oil, and cover loosely with foil. Bake until all the juices are absorbed, 17 to 20 minutes. Stir in the green onions, dill, parsley, and mint, and the remaining 1 tablespoon butter. Invert the pilaf onto a serving platter and serve (or serve directly from the oven dish).

MY INSPIRATION for this dish was Sicily's pasta with sardines. I replaced the pasta with bulgur for a Turkish twist on this dish. Wild fennel, which was used in the Ottoman palace for pickling, is a forgotten herb except in some areas of the Aegean, where lamb is cooked with it. If it's not available to you, you can substitute the chopped fronds of a fennel bulb or chopped dill.

Bulgur Pilaf with Wild Fennel and Sardines

2 medium or 1 large onion, chopped

3 tablespoons unsalted butter

2 tablespoons olive oil, plus more
    for frying

1 tomato, peeled, seeded, and diced,
    (optional)

2 cups (280 g) coarse bulgur

1 fresh hot pepper, chopped
    (or 1 dried)

1 packed cup (20 g) diced wild
    fennel (see above for substitu-
    tions)

4 to 5 canned sardines, oil drained

1 teaspoon salt

2 tablespoons all-purpose flour

2 pounds (910 g) fresh sardines,
    cleaned

Serves 6

Sauté the onion in the butter and oil until translucent. Add the tomato (if using), the bulgur, and the hot pepper and sauté for 2 to 3 minutes. Add 3⅓ cups (795 ml) water and cook, covered, over medium heat until "eyes" appear on the surface of the bulgur. (If the bulgur is still al dente, add another ½ cup/120 ml water and cook 1 or 2 minutes more. The bulgur should be cooked through.) Reduce the heat, stir in the fennel, and simmer for 2 to 3 minutes. Remove from the heat and fold in the canned sardines.

Heat ½ inch (12 mm) of oil in a frying pan over medium heat. Mix the salt and flour in a shallow dish. Coat the fresh sardines in the flour mixture and fry in the oil until both sides of the sardines are golden and the fish are cooked through, 4 to 5 minutes total, depending on the size of the sardines. Serve the bulgur pilaf on a platter, topped with the fried sardines.

Anatolian Gold: Bulgur

Bulgur, made from wheat, is one of humankind's oldest refined foods and is a testament to the ingenuity of Anatolian civilization. Turks have taken this simple food and devised seemingly countless ways to cook and enrich it. The Turkish saying "When traveling to Dimyat for rice, make sure you don't lose the bulgur that's at home" shows the important place of bulgur in Turkish life.

Bulgur is made from *Triticum durum*, a wheat so hard that it is almost impossible to grind into flour, and Anatolia's hot, dry climate is perfectly suitable to growing it. To make bulgur, the wheat is parboiled

and the individual grains are then cracked (shattered like glass, really) into tiny hard pieces. While this process is mostly done today in factories, many villages in Anatolia still produce their own bulgur using traditional methods.

After the wheat is harvested, it is partially cooked outdoors in a *kazan*, or copper cauldron, and then spread out in the sun to dry. Once dry, the wheat is then fed into the grinding stones (the traditional method) or the grinding machines (the more likely method these days). The wheat pieces are then tossed into the air so that some of the bran blows

AN OTTOMAN recipe in which rice was cooked with black-eyed peas was an inspiration for this dish. I substituted bulgur for the rice, since bulgur and black-eyed peas are rustic, regional ingredients, thus culturally a more fitting combination. Purple basil lends this dish an unusual rustic aroma. I have not encountered traditional recipes for dried or fresh black-eyed peas anywhere in Turkey but Muğla and the surrounding area. During the Seljuki period, a large number of immigrants from the Turcoman tribes (including my ancestors) migrated to Muğla and nearby areas like Gökova. I like to think that they brought this legume with them, which dries and keeps well and is used in many regional dishes.

Bulgur with Black-Eyed Peas and Purple Basil

1 medium onion, diced, plus 3 medium onions sliced into rings

½ cup (120 ml) plus 2 to 3 tablespoons olive oil

2 ½ cups (600 ml) hot water

1 cup (140 g) coarse bulgur

1 cup (75 g) cooked black-eyed peas

1 tablespoon hot red pepper flakes, preferably from Antep or Maraş

2 tablespoons unsalted butter, melted

1 cup (9 g) minced fresh purple basil or fresh tarragon (green basil is not a Turkish aromatic)

Serves 6 to 8

Sauté the diced onion in ½ cup (120 ml) of the oil in a pot until translucent. Add the hot water, bulgur, black-eyed peas, and red pepper flakes and cook until the bulgur has absorbed all the liquid, 12 to 15 minutes.

Meanwhile, in a skillet, caramelize the onion rings in the remaining 2 to 3 tablespoons oil over very low heat, about 10 minutes. Carefully pour the melted butter over the pilaf, sprinkle with the basil or tarragon, and stir with a spoon to fluff the pilaf. Spoon the pilaf onto a serving dish, top with the caramelized onions, and serve.

(continued)

away. Much of the bran remains, however, providing dietary fiber that makes bulgur a very nutritious food. In addition to fiber, durum wheat contains more protein than softer types of wheat. It is eaten both hot (as a pilaf) and cold, and is combined with practically any vegetables that come to mind. Bulgur is also one of the basic components of red lentil and meat kofta, an essential ingredient in the "uncooked" (*çiğ köfte*) meatballs so popular in southeast Turkey, and is used as a stuffing for dolma instead of rice. It also takes the place of rice in many regional soups, and bulgur salads are typically one of the offerings at Turkish teatime.

You will find three different sizes of bulgur in Turkey. One is ground fine for making bulgur kofta or the casing for kofta with ground meat filling; medium-grind bulgur is used for stuffings for dolma; and coarse-grind bulgur is used in bulgur pilafs.

MEAT AND POULTRY

Turkish meat dishes may be grouped under the headings kebab, kofta, *kavurma* (confit), *külbasti*, and *yahni*, and the meat used in all of these dishes is lamb, mutton, or beef. In some regions, however, kid is the only kind of meat consumed because the mountainous plateaus are not suited to herding lamb but are good for goat herding. The kid meat of Muğla (southwest Turkey) and its environs is considered especially tasty and is the only kind of meat eaten in this area. Of course, as for all kinds of meat, aromatic flora of this area make a difference in the taste of the meats. A unique aspect of Turkish meat dishes is that meat pieces the size of a small bird—called *kusbasi* (or "bird's head")—are cooked with vegetables, legumes, and even fruits. This tradition is not only healthy and delicious, but economical.

The meat eaten in Turkey is always halal and is killed according to Islamic rules. The animals for consumption are cut in the presence of an imam who has attained a certain level and can conduct religious ceremonies. He recites a short Koran verse while the animal is being killed with its head turned toward Mecca. The animal is killed by cutting off the head because there has to be blood coming out of the animal; otherwise it is not halal.

Turkish cuisine also includes a lot of poultry. We know from palace archives that once the Ottoman Empire was established, chicken was a valuable dish that was served on the tables of the sultans as early as the reign of Sultan Mehmet the Conqueror in the mid-fifteenth century. Nevertheless, chicken was raised and consumed in the eleventh century, when the Turks started settled life in Central Asia.

In Turkish cuisine, chicken, like meat, is cooked with vegetables; the traditional chicken and okra dish is the most prestigious and delicious. Chicken is usually cooked as a whole bird, and the broth is used for many purposes. In fact, one chicken delivers three different kinds of dishes (the bird itself, soup, and pilaf made delicious due to this freshly made broth). That is why, especially today, chicken is consumed more than red meat. In fact, chicken is the number one food at *muhallebi* shops, which are actually places that specialize in traditional desserts. Since their chicken breast pudding is made from the white meat of the chicken, the rest of the bird is used for chicken soup and rice.

Kebabs (keba): *Keba* was originally an Arabic term that meant "frying meat" and not "grilling meat," as it has come to mean today. Other cultures have borrowed the term to refer to grilled meat. But, in Turkish cuisine, *keba* has always referred to slow-cooked meat, no matter the technique used. Examples of *kebab* include *testi kebab*, where meat is cooked in a clay pot with a narrow neck; the ubiquitous *shish kebab*, pieces of meat on skewers called *sis* (shish); and *kuyu kebab*, which literally means "water-well kebab" (there is no water in the well; the name refers to a deep well-like hole specially dug for the purpose of cooking meat. The meat, usually a whole animal, is lowered into the hole and cooked for many hours, till the meat falls off the bones. The list may be lengthened with *sac kebab* (cooked on a metal sheet) and *tas kebab* (cooked under a pot on a metal tray). The variety of kebabs illustrates Turkish cuisine's never-ending creativity and adaptability in the kitchen. For every type of kebab, the meat is cut to fit the utensil it will be cooked with. Today kebabs grilled on skewers are a popular meze around the world; see pages 72 to 74 for recipes. They can also be served for dinner alongside a rice or bulgur pilaf.

Kofta (köfte): This term refers to ground meat, either lamb or beef or a mixture of the two, shaped into balls, ovals, or discs, and then grilled, fried, or cooked in a pot, according to the technique called for in the recipe. Certain spices, according to regional or personal preferences, and softened bread (or rice or bulgur) are usually added to the meat mixture. Because kofta are often served as part of a meze platter, in this book I've presented many recipes for kofta along with the other appetizers (see pages 71 to 79).

Külbasti: Originally, *külbasti* was a thin piece of lean lamb, cut from the leg and cooked very slowly over ashes. Today, *külbasti* is made from all kinds of meat and is prepared on a grill, even though the name, which literally means "on the ashes," signifies the original style of cook-

ing. According to Ottoman recipes, *külbasti* is made in such a way that the meat is first grilled and then steeped for a long time in a copper pot set on the ashes to soften the meat. I have come across this technique of cooking in the town of Tire, in the Aegean part of Turkey, where the Ottoman culture is very evident. The taste is completely different from that of meat that is only grilled or braised.

Yahni: This slow-cooked dish is always prepared in a single pot with big or small pieces of lamb, similar to what you would call a stew in the United States. Legumes or vegetables are usually added, and then it is generally named for this additional ingredient, for example, *bamyali* (okra) *yahni* or *nohutlu* (chickpea) *yahni*. Today's *yahnis* are always made with tomatoes and tomato paste; before the tomato arrived in the Old World, however, *yahni* was made without it.

Kavurma: *Kavurma*, one of the oldest cooking techniques, refers to frying usually small pieces of meat until they break down to create almost a confit. The meat may be used right away or kept in the rendered fat of sheep's tail and used later. Prepared *kavurma* is available in certain grocery stores in Turkey, but it is more difficult to find for sale in the United States. Any kind of meat cooked in butter, fat, or oil without added water is also known as *kavurma*, including the meat dish made for the first day of the Sacrifice Holiday when Muslims who can afford it sacrifice a sheep or even a cow and distribute pieces of it to those who cannot afford to eat meat regularly. *Kavurma* has also come to mean the frying of vegetables.

CONSIDERING THE large reach of the Ottoman Empire, it is not a surprise that Turkish cuisine features recipes from many far-flung places. Many dishes came out of the cultural interaction of the empire. This recipe has Georgian and Jewish roots. I love its simplicity, which is one aspect of Turkish cuisine. In that sense, Jewish and Turkish food traditions are very similar. Another version of this recipe was given to me by a lady from Azerbaijan, but instead of pomegranate she used tamarind. Since tamarind is not easily found, I got this version from my charming friend Anita Benadrete.

Chicken à la Georgian

2 large pomegranates, seeds removed and set aside

1 small onion, chopped

Juice of ½ to 1 lemon

1 medium chicken (3 to 4 pounds/ 1.4 to 1.8 kg)

1 tablespoon vegetable oil

Salt and black pepper

1 cup (240 ml) hot water

Serves 6

Preheat the oven to 400°F (205°C).

Mix the pomegranate seeds with the onion; if the pomegranate is not very sour, stir in the juice of ½ lemon. Pack the chicken cavity with the pomegranate mixture and fasten the ends of the skin closed with toothpicks. Mix together the juice of ½ lemon, the oil, and salt and pepper to taste and thoroughly massage into the chicken skin. Place the chicken, uncovered, in an ovenproof dish. Pour the hot water into the dish to prevent the chicken from drying out and roast for 30 minutes, sprinkling the chicken with the water in the baking dish throughout the cooking process. Reduce the oven temperature to 350°F (175°C) and bake for 1 hour 15 minutes more, continually basting the chicken with the cooking juices. If the skin is browning too quickly, cover lightly with foil. When the chicken is completely cooked (try moving a joint—it should almost fall off), remove all the filling, pass it through a sieve to remove the hard parts of the pomegranate seeds, pour it over the chicken, and serve. (If the chicken is cut into pieces before being served, it will absorb more of the tasty juices.)

IN MY childhood, chicks ran free in the yard, and I loved eating chicken to the bone—as a *yahni* (stew) or whatever way it was cooked. Our chickens' great taste came from their natural feeding; they always imparted a heavenly flavor to rice or soup made with chicken stock. This dolma, a special dish from Ula in southwestern Turkey, is always served to important guests, and my mother followed this tradition. When I saw it listed among the dishes served only to pashas at the circumcision banquets of Sultan Suleyman the Lawgiver in 1539, I realized it also had an important place among the dishes of the palace.

Chicken Dolma in a Clay Pot (*Tavuk Dolması*)

1 medium chicken (3 to 4 pounds/ 1.4 to 1.8 kg) with liver, heart, and giblets

4 tablespoons (55 g) unsalted butter

1 cup (200 g) medium-grain rice

Salt and black pepper

1 ½ packed cups (30 g) fresh parsley, minced, stems set aside

Juice of ½ lemon

1 tablespoon olive oil

2 fresh bay leaves

Mince the chicken innards and fry them in half the butter over high heat until browned and aromatic. Add the rice, sauté for 1 minute, and season with salt and pepper. Add the parsley and ¾ cup (180 ml) water. Cook, covered, over medium heat until the water is absorbed and the rice is nearly al dente. (If the rice is not done, add an additional 2 to 3 tablespoons water and continue cooking.) Let the rice cool for about 10 minutes.

Preheat the oven to 400°F (205°C). Mix together the lemon juice and oil and season with salt and pepper. Thoroughly baste the chicken with the lemon juice mixture, place half the remaining butter and a bay leaf under the skin of each breast, and spoon the rice stuffing into the chicken cavity. (Shake the chicken occasionally, holding it by the legs, so that the filling settles tightly.) Once completely filled, fasten the ends of the skin together with two or three toothpicks. Cover the bottom of a *güveç* (clay pot; see Note) with the reserved parsley stems and gently place the chicken on top. Tightly cover the pot with foil and bake for 30 minutes; reduce the oven temperature to 350°F (175°C) and cook for another 1½ hours. Turn off the oven and let the dish sit in the oven for at least 15 minutes. Serve the chicken in the clay pot, if you like.

Note: If a güveç *is not available, use any clay cooking pot. If it has a lid, all the better—the foil will be unnecessary.*

IN THE city of Urfa, in eastern Turkey, a dish made with chickpeas, chard, and pieces of lamb enriched with bulgur and kofta is known as *borani*. (The name also applies to the spinach dish on page 130.) An eggplant dish in ancient Persian cuisine was also referred to as *borani*, its name (*burani* in Persian) attributed to a charming Persian queen. Confusing nomenclature aside, one thing is for sure: *Borani* is supposed to be a special dish, and this version certainly is. (Here, I replaced the traditional bulgur kofta with pasta to make the recipe easier, although I've provided instructions for the kofta, opposite, so you can make them if you like.)

Meat and Swiss Chard *Borani* (*Etli Pazili Urfa Borani*)

1 pound (455 g) bone-in lamb shoulder or leg, meat cut into ½-inch (12-mm) cubes and bones reserved

1½ cups (300 g) chickpeas, soaked overnight

1 medium onion, chopped

4 tablespoons unsalted butter

1 tablespoon tomato paste

1 ripe tomato (if in season), peeled, seeded, and grated (see Note, page 60)

1 pound (455 g) Swiss chard, chopped

1 cup (100 g) pasta (preferably fettucini) or Bulgur Kofta (opposite)

1 tablespoon dried mint

½ cup (240 ml) plain Greek yogurt whisked with 1 clove garlic pounded with a pinch of salt in a mortar and pestle (optional)

Serves 6 to 8 as meze

Combine the meat, bones, and chickpeas in a large pot, add water to cover by at least 3 inches (7.5 cm), and bring to a boil, skimming off the foam with a slotted spoon when the water boils. Cook over medium heat until both the meat and chickpeas are soft, 50 to 60 minutes. (You should have at least 3 cups/720 ml stock left to use in the dish later.) Remove the bones after cooking.

In another large pot, sauté the onion in 2 tablespoons of the butter until translucent, then add the tomato paste and fresh tomato, if using. Mix well for 30 seconds or so, then add the meat and chickpeas, 3 cups (720 ml) of the reserved stock, and the Swiss chard. Cook for about 5 minutes, then add the pasta and cook until the pasta is al dente (see Note). (Alternatively, add the bulgur kofta instead of the pasta to the pot and cook for about 5 minutes.)

Brown the remaining 2 tablespoons butter in a pan, add the mint, and heat for about 30 seconds, stirring constantly. Pour over the *borani* and serve immediately, with a drizzle of garlic yogurt if you like.

Note: If you are not serving the borani *with pasta right away, cook the pasta for 4 to 5 minutes, and then remove from the heat. (This prevents the pasta, especially fettucini, from becoming too soft.) The dish has to be soupy enough to be eaten with a spoon. Add more stock if necessary.*

TO MAKE this *borani* more traditional, you can add these kofta instead of pasta.

Bulgur Kofta (*Bulgurlu Köfte*)

8 ounces (225 g) lean ground meat

½ cup (70 g) fine bulgur, soaked in ½ cup (120 ml) hot water for 15 minutes

1 teaspoon hot red pepper flakes, preferably isot (see page 18)

Salt

Serves 6

Knead together the meat, bulgur, and red pepper flakes, and season to taste with salt. Form into small (chickpea-size) balls.

THIS *YAHNI,* or meat stew, is an important dish, traditionally served at big banquets. Okra, a subtropical plant that grows well in the hotter areas of Turkey, has always been in my life. Even as a child, I appreciated this vegetable. Aegeans love okra and cook it with or without meat. I prefer okra *yahni* with meat or chicken. These have a fuller taste and are truly satisfying, whether served hot or cold, which is how the one prepared in olive oil is enjoyed. Usually people pair this stew with rice, but for me, a slice of bread is just as good.

Chicken may take the place of meat in many Turkish dishes, depending on what is handy. My mother's family raised chickens in their garden in the town of Ula and, whenever the family craved an okra *yahni,* she had her own source for the chicken. What a feast!

Okra Stew (*Bamyali Yahni*)

1 whole bone-in lamb shoulder (about 2 pounds/910 g), or 1 whole medium chicken, cut into 8 pieces

4 tablespoons (55 g) unsalted butter

3 tablespoons olive oil

3 medium onions, diced (about 2 cups/220 g)

1 heaping tablespoon tomato paste

3 ripe tomatoes, peeled, seeded, and chopped

5 cups (1.2 L) hot water, plus more as needed

2 pounds (910 g) okra, topped to create a cone shape

Salt

Juice of 2 lemons

Serves 6

Fry the meat in the butter and oil until browned on all sides. Add the onions and sauté until translucent. Add the tomato paste and mix with the meat and onions until aromatic. Add the tomatoes and cook until their juices are evaporated. Add the hot water. Simmer until the meat is thoroughly cooked, 50 to 60 minutes for the meat or free-range chicken. (There should still be some liquid in the pot to cook the okra; if not, add some more hot water, but not so much that the liquid covers the okra.) Add the okra, salt to taste, and the lemon juice. (Salt added too early will toughen the meat, so be sure to add it only after the meat is cooked.) Cook until the okra is tender, 25 to 30 minutes. The finished dish should have plenty of juice to mop up with bread. Serve, adding at least 2 tablespoons of the cooking liquid to each serving.

EVERY GOOD cook knows that baking in an earthenware dish gives the best results. The earthenware dish—*güveç* in Turkish cuisine—is also very pleasing to the eye; the nice black color it gets through long use is a special mark of warmth and family joy.

Lamb and Vegetable Casserole (*Sebzeli Kuzu Güveç*)

1 (2-pound/910-g) lamb shoulder with some fat, cut into 14 pieces (with bones)

2 long thin Japanese eggplants (10 inches/25 cm long), peeled in alternating stripes and cut into 1-inch (2.5-cm) thick slices

2 medium or large zucchini, cut into 1-inch (2.5-cm) thick slices

8 ounces (225 g) green beans, trimmed and cut into 1-inch pieces

8 ounces (225 g) okra, tops trimmed into a cone shape so they do not give off slime

2 to 3 cloves garlic, minced

Salt and black pepper

1 sprig fresh thyme

2 ripe tomatoes (if in season), peeled and diced, or 1 teaspoon tomato paste

1 tablespoon red pepper paste

3 to 4 tablespoons olive oil

Serves 6

Preheat the oven to 400°F (200°C).

In a large bowl, combine the lamb with the eggplants, zucchini, green beans, okra, and garlic and season with salt and pepper to taste. Add the thyme, tomatoes or tomato paste, red pepper paste, and oil and mix well. Transfer the mixture to an earthenware dish (a snug fit is best). Bake, covered, for 30 minutes, then reduce the oven temperature to 350°F (175°C) and cook for another 50 to 60 minutes, or until the vegetables are well cooked. (If the green beans are done, you may assume the rest are too.) Serve in the earthenware dish.

MARINATING MEAT in milk, and then basting the meat with cotton wool soaked in milk while grilling it over charcoal was a favored style of cooking in Ottoman times, and was rightly called *süt* (milk) *kebab*. Since first trying this Ottoman recipe, I have never grilled chops without using this technique. No matter how good the lamb is, the long soak in milk makes the taste even more delicate. Note that Turks never use knives for lamb chops, and they always eat the meat to the bone.

Lamb Chops Marinated in Milk
(*Pirzola, Sütlu Terbiyeli*)

18 (3-ounce/85-g) lamb chops
(3 chops per serving), pounded
(see Note)

2 cups (480 ml) cold milk, plus more
for brushing

Sea salt and black pepper

Serves 6

Soak the chops in the milk in the refrigerator for at least 2 hours and up to 6 hours. Drain and discard the milk.

Wrap the bare bones with foil (this makes it easier to eat the chops with your hands, which is the best way). Heat an outdoor grill to medium-high (see Notes), placing the grill grate at least 4 inches (10 cm) above the heat source (otherwise, the chops will burn). Grill the chops, continually brushing them with fresh milk, for 3 to 5 minutes per side (depending on the size and thickness of the chops). When the chops are golden on the outside and springy to the touch, sprinkle with salt and pepper to taste and serve immediately. (Take care not to overcook the chops, or the meat will be tough.)

Notes: This recipe is for chops prepared as they are in Turkey: The butcher pounds small chops with a special tool until they are ½ inch (12 mm) thick. For larger chops not pounded in the Turkish style, the grilling time should be increased.

If you have an indoor electric grill, the chops may be cooked on that as well.

EVEN BEFORE the tomato became a part of Turkish cuisine, Ottoman *yahni* dishes (meat stews) were classified as either white or red. Instead of getting their flavor and color from tomatoes as all *yahni* dishes do today, red *yahni* derived its color from caramelized onions as in the following stew recipe, which gets its sweetness and beautiful golden color from both caramelized onions and pekmez. Quince makes the dish lighter and more abundant (and prevents the diner from eating too much meat), while also adding a delicate aroma to the dish.

Lamb with Quince (*Ayvali Kuzu*)

2 ½ pounds (1.2 kg) bone-in lamb, preferably shoulder or shank (if shoulder, cut into 6 pieces)

5 medium onions, sliced

2 tablespoons unsalted butter

2 cups (480 ml) hot water

1 ½ pounds (680 g) quince (see sidebar, page 137), peeled and cut into thick wedges

6 to 8 apricots, whole or cut in half

½ orange, sliced into four rounds

½ cup (120 ml) pekmez (see page 20), plus more for serving

1 teaspoon ground cassia (see page 17)

Salt

Serves 6

Fry the meat and onions in 1 tablespoon of the butter until the onions are golden. Add the water, cover tightly, and cook over very low heat for about 1½ hours, until the meat is very tender.

In a separate pan, fry the quince in the remaining 1 tablespoon butter until golden, then add the quince, apricots, and orange to the meat along with the pekmez, cassia, and salt to taste. Cook for 10 to 15 minutes, until the quince is al dente. Arrange the meat and quince, apricots, and orange attractively on a serving dish, drizzle with a little more pekmez, and serve.

THIS IS a dish from the major towns of central Anatolia. It is very easy to prepare, but it makes a great impression at the table. It is thus understandable why it is an important dish, served at festivities like weddings or banquets. Surprisingly delicate, it is a good example of Turkish cuisine's grand yet not elaborate dishes.

Leg of Lamb with Eggplant (*Pehli*)

1 leg of lamb (keep the meat in one piece with its bone broken in several places to fit in the pot)

3 tablespoons vegetable oil for frying

1 sprig fresh thyme

1 dried bay leaf

10 whole black peppercorns, cracked with mortar and pestle

Hot water

4 pounds (1.8 kg) Italian eggplant, peeled at intervals and cut into 1-inch- (2.5-cm-) round thick slices

Salt

Olive oil for frying

1 medium onion, minced

7 or 8 long, thin mild green peppers, seeded and cut into ½-inch (12-mm) slices

5 or 6 ripe medium tomatoes, peeled and cut in small cubes

Serves 8

Fry the lamb on all sides in the vegetable oil, then transfer to a large pot. Add the thyme and bay leaf crushed into pieces, the peppercorns, and enough hot water to cover the leg halfway. Cook over medium heat, skimming the surface of any foam. When almost all the foam is gone, tightly cover the pot and cook until the lamb is very tender to the touch (2 to 3 hours, depending on the quality of the leg); reserve the cooking liquid. Soak the eggplant in salted water for about 30 minutes.

Preheat the oven to 375°F (190°C). Heat ½ inch (12 mm) of olive oil in a pan over medium heat. Squeeze the eggplant to get rid of excess water, pat dry with a towel, then carefully drop the eggplant into the hot oil; fry until golden, 4 to 5 minutes, turning them when necessary. Drain on paper towels. Add some of the frying oil to another pan and slowly sauté the onion until translucent. Add the peppers and fry quickly so that they are wilted but not browned. Remove from the heat and add the tomatoes; leave in the pan for 1 minute so all the vegetables are well integrated. (The tomatoes should not cook.)

Put the cooked leg of lamb in the middle of an oven dish with only a little space around it (otherwise, it will dry out). Arrange the fried eggplant around the leg and pour the onion, pepper, and tomato mixture over the leg. Add 1½ cups (360 ml) of the reserved cooking liquid. Bake, uncovered, basting the leg with liquid if the top gets dry. When the tomatoes are soft, after 35 to 40 minutes, turn the oven off, but keep the dish in the oven, covered with foil, until serving. Baste with the juices if the top gets dry. This dish may be served the day it is cooked, but it tastes even better the next day. (You may have to add a little stock when you reheat it, but keep it covered until the last few minutes.)

FILLET OF LAMB is the most prized part of the lamb, from a cultural perspective. (Mind you, it is also the best part!) It was the part served to the Khans and important guests in Central Asia for many centuries. Today prestigious restaurants in Turkey grill and serve fillet of lamb simply—and rightly so, as it is a tasty cut that needs little embellishment. If you can get fillet of lamb in the United States, by all means use it. But it can also be replaced in this recipe with fillet of beef, the most valuable part of the animal; see my variation below. This recipe was inspired by a French dish, which used pernod, a drink similar to but sweeter than raki.

Fillet of Lamb Sprinkled with Raki (*Kuzu Sırtı Cevirmesi, Rakili*)

1 tablespoon vegetable oil

1 tablespoon unsalted butter (clarified is best; it will not burn when fried)

3 lamb fillets (2½ pounds/1.2 kg)

1 tablespoon black peppercorns, cracked with a mortar and pestle

1 clove garlic, unpeeled, bruised

1 sprig fresh rosemary, or 2 sprigs fresh thyme

1 tablespoon fine sea salt

1 cup (240 ml) raki (see sidebar, page 24)

Serves 6

In a medium cast-iron frying pan, heat the oil and butter over high heat. Add the fillets and fry for 3 to 4 minutes with the pepper, garlic, rosemary, and salt. Reduce the heat to medium and fry for another 5 to 7 minutes, turning the fillets every minute or so to make make sure they brown evenly. (The fillets will take 10 to 12 minutes total for medium-rare; for well done, keep on the heat for another 3 minutes.) Heat the raki in a saucepan, pour over the fillets off the heat, ignite with a match, and let flame for a minute or until it dies down. Serve immediately, serving half a lamb fillet to each diner. (If you can immediately take the pan to the table, you can finish the dish there. It makes quite an impression!)

VARIATION

Fillet of Beef Sprinkled with Raki (*Kuzu ya da Sığır Sırtı Cevirmesi, Rakili*)

Preheat the oven to 400°F (205°C). Instead of 3 lamb fillets, use 1 beef fillet. Brown the whole fillet in a medium cast-iron frying pan over medium-high heat for 10 to 12 minutes, turning so all surfaces get a nice brown color. Transfer to an ovenproof dish, place it in the oven, and roast for 20 minutes for medium-rare, 25 minutes for medium, and 30 to 32 minutes for well-done. Remove from the oven, pour the raki all over the meat, ignite with a match, and serve while still in flame or when the flame is about to die. Wait for 5 minutes before cutting each serving to allow time for the juices to settle.

Lamb and Mutton: A Pastoral Legacy

Turkish tribes who made their living by raising animals slaughtered sheep only for festive days or in preparation for the long winter; meat was treasured whenever it was served. In contrast, the fact that 99,120 sheep were consumed in the Ottoman palace in the year 1669 to 1670 makes the claim of seventeenth-century French traveler Jean-Baptiste Tavernier that about 500 sheep were consumed in one day in the palace entirely believable. In the same year, 4 million sheep, 3 million lamb, and 200 cattle were consumed in the imperial city of Istanbul. Tavernier was also right in his observation that beef never entered the palace kitchens; it was, however, purchased by the palace to make *pastırma* (air-cured spicy beef) for the palace residents. Many dishes today are cooked with beef or veal, yet quite a few dishes still require lamb to give them a taste we can readily identify as Turkish.

The tremendous consumption of meat by the palace and in the city of Istanbul was fed by Turkmen (Turcoman) tribes in Anatolia and animal herders in the Balkans. In the Turkmen Ugulbeglu clan, one of the providers, there were 403 sheep per capita in 1540—a good example of the imbalance between raising and consumption among the pastoral tribes. Sheep raised by Turkmens included Karakoyun (black sheep), Akkoyun' (white sheep), Irik, and Yerli (meaning local sheep). Today, however, Kivircik and Karaman are the kinds of lamb that are raised in abundance. The Kivircik, with its miniature tail, is famous for its delicate taste, resulting from being fed the fragrant greens of Thrace. People who value an exceptional taste always cook with this variety, which has made the lamb of Turkey famous all around the world. The Karaman, with its fatty tail, not only takes a long time to cook, but also has a distinct, unpopular odor. Its long-cooking flesh has even inspired a proverb: "The mutton of Karaman shows its true character when it is too late."

Now, however, the mountainous Anatolian Peninsula has given way to goat herding, and kid has become a major meat source. These goats are herded by the *yörük*, who are a cultural extension of the Turkish nomads. They still produce similar nomadic products like goat cheese, strained yogurt, butter, and *çökelek* (whey cheese).

A TANDIR is a baked mud oven that was used in Central Asia, an important piece of cooking equipment that we share with Indian cuisine. The cooking techniques, however, differ. In Turkey, the meat is cooked in a closed oven over a fire, not directly in the fire as in India. In the recipe below, the dish is cooked over a burner, not in a tandir. Nevertheless, it is just as tasty. It is also proof of how delicious slow cooking can be, a method that Turkish cuisine excels at.

Pot Lamb Tandir
(*Tencerede Kuzu Tandiri*)

1 lamb shoulder

1 or 2 sprigs fresh oregano or thyme

1 or 2 fresh bay leaves, or ½ dried bay leaf (dried is much stronger than fresh)

6 cloves garlic, peel on, pierced with a knife (optional)

10 to 12 whole black peppercorns

Juice of ½ lemon

Salt

Serves 6

Break the bone in the lamb shoulder so it fits tightly in a small pot (see Note). Tuck the oregano or thyme, bay leaves, garlic, and peppercorns in the gaps and add the lemon juice and 3 to 4 tablespoons water. Tightly close the pot (place a weight on the lid if necessary). Cook over medium heat until the pot fills with steam, then reduce the heat to the lowest possible level and cook for 1½ hours. If any liquid remains, increase the heat to medium to evaporate it, and season the meat with salt at this point. Gently turn the lamb to brown on all sides. (Don't worry if the meat falls to pieces; this is the idea of a tandir.) Serve.

Note: If you open the lid too often, the juices will evaporate. Keep the heat at its lowest and you will have plenty of liquid in the pot. You can strain off the liquid and use it as a concentrated stock for pilaf or soup. After removing the liquid you can continue to brown the meat in what little juice is left in the pot.

CHEEKS ARE not cooked separately in traditional Turkish cuisine, but the best part of a lamb's head is the cheeks—and the same is true of the more widely available beef cheeks. This recipe is from Aydin Demir, once the head chef of Tuğra Restaurant, which was part of a luxury hotel that served only Turkish food. He is passionate about bringing more contemporary influences to Turkish food and has managed to do so without losing the essence of dishes like this one. Loquats, a delicate Asian fruit, give a tangy lightness to the dish, and when paired with beef cheeks they create a tasty stewlike dish. If you can't find loquats, try good ripe apricots or even sweet plums as a substitute. Traditionally, apricots and apples are cooked with meat in the regional cuisines of eastern Turkey.

Beef Cheeks with Loquat
(*Yeni Dunyali Yanak Yahnisi*)

2 pounds (910 g) beef cheeks

3 tablespoons olive oil

5 whole cloves garlic, peeled

1 pound whole shallots, peeled

1 carrot, peeled and chopped

2 celery sticks

1 cinnamon stick

3 green cardamom pods

1 tablespoon tomato paste

½ tablespoon all-purpose flour

1 fresh bay leaf (or ½ dried)

1 cup (240 ml) red wine

2 tablespoons unsalted butter

½ teaspoon black pepper

Salt

12 loquats, halved, seeds removed, or 12 good ripe apricots, halved and destoned, or 12 sturdy apples, peeled and chopped

Serves 6

Fry the meat in hot oil. When golden, add the following in this order: garlic, shallots, carrots, celery, cinnamon stick, and cardamom. Sauté 2 minutes, then add the tomato paste, sprinkle in the flour, and mix well so all the ingredients are coated with flour. Add the bay leaf and wine and enough water to cover the meat. Cook over low heat, skimming any foam from the surface with a slotted spoon. Once skimmed, turn the heat to very low and cook until the beef is very tender, about 1½ hours. Add the butter, pepper, and salt to taste and let sit for about 30 minutes. Remove and discard the cinnamon stick and bay leaf. Add the loquats, heat through, then serve.

THIS DISH is traditionally made in spring with lamb shanks. Like the lamb, the fresh herbs and lettuce are also fresh flavors that welcome the new season. It is a great dish for those who follow nature's rhythms in their cooking. If you can find good-quality lamb, I would use it instead of beef, though this recipe is one that's also wonderful with beef, which—more so than the lamb—really brings out the flavor of the romaine lettuce nicely.

Beef Shanks under a Lettuce Blanket (*Marullu Dana Kapama*)

6 beef or lamb shanks (not more than 1 ½ pounds/680 g), cut into 1 ½-inch (4-cm) pieces

1 medium onion, chopped

1 tablespoon olive oil

1 tablespoon unsalted butter

2 packed cups (40 g) fresh dill, minced

3 packed cups (60 g) fresh parsley, minced

1 packed cup (40 g) fresh mint, minced

4 to 5 green onions, cut into 2-inch (5-cm) pieces

2 tablespoons coarsely ground black pepper

Salt

12 to 14 romaine lettuce leaves, halved lengthwise

Serves 6

Put the meat in a large pot, add about 3 cups (720 ml) cold water (or enough to just barely rise above the meat), and bring to a boil (see Note). Skim off foam with a slotted spoon, tightly cover the pot, and continue to cook over very low heat (so the meat retains its tasty juices) for about 1 ½ hours.

Meanwhile, sauté the onion in the oil and butter until translucent. When the meat has cooked for about 1 ½ hours, stir in the dill, parsley, mint, green onions, sautéed onion, pepper, salt to taste, and romaine. (This dish should have some juice; if necessary, add ½ cup/120 ml water at this point.) Cook, tightly covered, over very low heat for 30 to 35 minutes more, or until the romaine is tender. Serve immediately or reheat and serve within a few hours.

Note: Before adding the water, you may also fry the meat in the butter and oil in which the onion will be fried. Then transfer it to the cooking pot and add 3 cups (720 ml) of hot water instead of cold. Bring to a boil and continue.

FISH AND SEAFOOD

I WILL EAT IT IF IT IS MY FATHER CAUGHT IN THE NET.
—TURKISH SAYING

Turks originally came from lands where there was no sea but there were lakes and rivers, and they had integrated fish from these fresh waters into their diet long before their empire spread to the wonderful coasts of the Mediterranean and the Aegean. Original Turkish names for freshwater fish include *sazan* (carp) and *turna* (pike). The tradition of consuming freshwater fish was so deeply engrained that fish from Lake Terkos near Istanbul was even brought to the palace during the reign of Sultan Mehmet the Conqueror. Indeed, Turkish mythology said that the world sat on a huge fish. Fish as a cultural object has many connotations: To dream about a fish means you will acquire a fortune; if a fortune-teller sees a fish in your coffee grounds, it means a financial windfall is coming your way.

Fish in Turkish cuisine is either fried or grilled. Since fish is almost always eaten fresh out of the water, these are surely the best methods. While bluefish is a favorite from the Bosphorus (see page 183), the popularity of anchovies from the Black Sea cannot be surpassed by another fish from this area (see page 185). Sardines, mostly eaten fried, are popular in the Marmara and Aegean area when in season, toward the end of summer and the beginning of fall, when they are oily. They are always cooked the day they are bought and brought home, either fried or wrapped in grape leaves and grilled (page 56). No fish can surpass the taste of mullet from the Aegean Sea, where they make their homes in the deepest, sandy areas. Gilded bream, red bream, and sea bass are farmed as elsewhere in the Aegean, but you still can find wild ones to buy. The bigger they are, the better tasting they will be. These fish are best grilled as soon as they come out of the sea, but it is traditional to serve the breams with an olive oil and lemon emulsion with minced parsley, as wild bream is not a fatty fish and needs this dressing.

The grouper category is also abundant around the Mediterrenean and other coasts of Turkey. You can easily find white grouper (*beyaz lagos*), which lives in sandy waters, and also the black grouper (*siyah lagos*, as it is called in Turkey) and brown rock grouper (*orfoz*), which both live deep at the bottom of the ocean in between rocks or in caves. Grouper is good cooked on skewers as shish kebab, alternating with pieces of fresh tomatoes, fresh bay leaves, and green peppers for a pretty presentation. They too require a lemon and olive oil emulsion. Since the grouper family has big bones, they are also good for cooking in a sauce used for *buğulama*, which is usually made with sea bass (page 182).

Shrimp (*karides*) are another favorite on the Turkish table, either just boiled and dressed with lemon and olive oil or cooked in small earthenware pots called *güveç*; meat and vegetables are cooked in bigger versions of

these pots. The best shrimp in Turkey come from Güllük Bay near Bodrum, where the water is very clean. These red-and-white-striped shrimp are crunchy and have an extraordinary taste. The small pink shrimps caught in and around Istanbul are good for making *göveç*.

It is a tradition that the father brings home the fish. Typically he buys it when passing by the town's fish market and brings it home fresh, where it is fried and served right away. Almost all towns and cities have their own fish markets where the residents buy their fish. In very small towns, when fresh fish is caught, it is announced by the municipality over loudspeakers so people can go and buy it before it gets older than a day. Local fish markets likely arose due to the *meyhane* culture, in which small fried or sautéed fish were a ubiquitous meze. As Istanbul became more cosmopolitan in the nineteenth century, fish markets were visited by increasing numbers of people, and it seems fish became a precious offering on the tables of the rich.

Sultan II Abdülhamit, the thirty-fourth sultan of the Ottoman Empire (1842–1918), was known for his appetite for the cheeks of bluefish. A plate containing only the cheeks would be specially prepared in the palace kitchens for him. Before his time, the thirtieth sultan, Sultan II Mehmet, had ordered a special kitchen unit exclusively for preparing fish. According to the archives of his time, the huge bonito called *torik*, red bream known as *mercan* (which means "coral," a reference to its color), sardines (*sardalya*), and sturgeon (*mersin balığı*) were all bought for the palace kitchens.

But fish was eaten by the Turkish people long before that. In the seventeenth century, the poverty of regular folks led them to consume fish instead of mutton, as the prices for mutton were extremely high. In his travelogue of the era, Evliya Çelebi describes how numerous fishermen would work together to catch groups of up to three hundred gigantic swordfish that had escaped from the huge waves of the Black Sea. They would install small, primitive huts called *dalyans* on top of tall logs near the sea coast and station themselves there to catch the fish.

The amazing abundance of fish in the straits of Istanbul is now remembered only in books. But in the sixteenth century, Pierre Gilles wrote that fishing was not that necessary because those who did not know how to fish could catch fish if they lowered a basket from their window into the sea. And Baron Durand de Fontmagne recounted in his memoir, *Istanbul after the Crimean War*, that there were bonitos as big as brown rock groupers (*orkinos*), and that the turbot in the Istanbul fish markets were the size of sea monsters. Luckily, we still can purchase a lot of good bonitos and turbots in Istanbul fish markets today.

The Balık Pazarı (fish market) at the pedestrian İstiklal Caddesi in Istanbul's Taksim Square and the fish market at Kumkapı are two of Istanbul's famous fish markets. They were established in the late nineteenth century to sell *meyhane* (small fish for meze), which was their specialty until the beginning of the twentieth century. In that era, they were probably owned by and served Istanbul's Christians, but today the clientele at these markets is mostly Muslims and tourists. I also have nostalgic feelings for the fish market in Sarıyer, which was established at about the same time, but if you visit Beşiktaş you should not miss its fish market, which is huge and has a special aura of belonging to the old Istanbul days.

I LIKE *çingene palamutu* (gypsy bonito), as they are small and are very tasty when grilled, but fried bonito in its *palamut* size is very popular. Since this dish is quick to make and not costly, it has become the favorite of both rich and poor. Adding the oil they are fried in will help the taste greatly, providing that the oil has not been burned.

Fried Bonito Steaks

⅓ cup (40 g) all-purpose flour

1 teaspoon salt

Olive oil for frying

6 bonito steaks, ½ inch (12 mm) thick, washed and dried

Red onions, cut in half and sliced into half-moons, for serving

Lemon wedges for serving

Serves 6

Mix the flour and salt in a resealable plastic bag large enough to hold one or more steaks. Heat ½ inch (12 mm) of oil in a frying pan over medium heat. Shake the steaks in the bag to coat them with the flour. Fry them in the oil for 2 minutes per side, taking care not to burn them (see Note). Transfer to a serving plate. When the oil is still hot but the residue has settled at the bottom of the pan, slowly pour it over the fish. Serve with onion rings and lemon wedges (as tradition requires).

Note: The oil will be fine if you keep adding a new piece of fish each time you take a couple pieces out and lowering the heat if necessary before the oil begins to smoke. If you leave the pan empty, the oil will burn in no time.

Bonito

Young bonito mate in the Bosphorus, migrate to the Black Sea in March and April, and pass through the Bosphorus again in July on their way to the Strait of Çanakkale. Popular wisdom holds that if bonito disappear from the Bosphorus Strait early, winter will come early. Pliny the Elder described their return: "Those bonito are coming down when they encounter the big white rock shining in deep waters at the narrowest point near Kalkhedon [today's Kadıköy, on the Asian side of Istanbul]. They get scared and turn to swim to Cape Byzantion [Seraglio or old Istanbul] and enter the Khrysokeras [the Gold Horn; *Halic* in Turkish; Arabic for 'inlet']."

The bonito are small in July, but toward mid-August they are c*ingene palamutu* (or gypsy bonito) size, and this is when their flesh is white and the tastiest. They reach *palamut* size, 8 to 10 inches (20 to 25 cm), in September. *Palamut* grow even larger and are then called *torik. Lakerda*, which is basically salted *torik*, is a delicacy. It is a taste legacy of non-Muslims, and the best was traditionally made by the Jewish community.

SEA BASS cooked in tomato sauce with butter is a classic, even though these are the only three ingredients everyone agrees on. This recipe is from a restaurant in Gökova, my ancestral home, that has been serving fish for forty years. What I like most is the chef's choice of fresh bay leaf; it gives a better aroma than the dried, which is too strong for the delicate sea bass.

Baked Sea Bass (*Levrek Buğulama*)

4 to 5 tablespoons (55 to 70 g) unsalted butter

1 tablespoon all-purpose flour

1 medium onion, cut in half and sliced into half-moons

1 medium carrot, sliced into rounds ¼ inch (6 mm) thick

2 medium tomatoes, peeled, seeded, and diced

3 fresh bay leaves

1 celery stalk

1 green bell pepper, cored, seeded, and sliced

10 to 12 whole black peppercorns

10 white button mushrooms (optional)

1 whole sea bass (about 5 pounds/2.3 kg)

2 tablespoons olive oil

1 lemon, peeled (including pith) and sliced

Serves 6

Preheat the oven to 375°F (190°C).

Melt the butter over low heat, add the flour, and cook, stirring well, for about 1 minute. Add 1 quart (960 ml) water, stir to create a smooth sauce, and remove from the heat.

In an ovenproof dish big enough to hold the sea bass, combine the onion, carrot, tomatoes, bay leaves, celery, bell pepper, peppercorns, and mushrooms, if using. Place the sea bass on top, pour the sauce over everything, and drizzle with the oil. Cover with foil and bake for 30 to 35 minutes, until the fish flesh has turned white near the bone and the bone separates from the flesh with the help of a knife. Add the lemon slices and bake for another 5 minutes. Let sit for a couple of minutes, then serve.

GRILLING OVER coals is undoubtedly the best method for preparing bluefish. Make sure the coals have some ash. Red coals will burn the fish, not cook it! You may use a gas grill if you like; just make sure the heat is on medium. This recipe is easily adapted to serve as many people as you like—simply multiply the ingredients accordingly.

Grilled Bluefish (*Lüfer Izgara*)

1 tablespoon all-purpose flour

½ teaspoon salt

1 whole bluefish or 2 *cinekop* (6-inch/15-cm bluefish) per person

1 fresh bay leaf per fish

Serves 1

Preheat a charcoal grill to medium. In a shallow bowl, toss together the flour and salt. Coat the fish with the flour mixture and shake off the excess. Place the fresh bay leaf in the slit where the innards were removed. Secure the fish to the grill rack and place on the grill 5 to 6 inches (12 to 15 cm) above the coals. Cook until the skin comes off on the grill rack, about 7 minutes (using tongs or a knife, lift up the fish to check). With tongs, turn the fish and cook until the other side is done, about 7 minutes (less time for smaller fish). Arrange on a platter and serve.

Bluefish

Bluefish from the Bosphorus, fattened by the cool undercurrents, are extraordinarily delicious. For Istanbul folks, "fish" means *lüfer* (bluefish). They are best eaten in the fall, and are most easily caught at night. The Bosphorus flickers with the lights of fishing boats during bluefish season. Some fishermen eat them right then and there, and such hedonism has been immortalized in books. Sultan Aziz, an enthusiastic bluefish fisherman, wrote about eating the cheeks of grilled bluefish. No one, especially those who love pure tastes, thinks of consuming it any way other than grilled.

Bluefish comes in many sizes. The 4-inch fish are called "bay leaf," those about 6 inches are çinekop, and those 7 inches long are *sari-kanat*. At 11 inches, it is a bluefish; bigger than this, it is a known as *kofana*. By September, the larger ones have migrated to the Bosphorus from the Black Sea. The smaller çinekop come last, in March. Because bluefish have no qualms about eating their young, the smaller ones come down after the big ones. Their taste is worth the wait.

THIS IS how any kind of small fried fish was served in my childhood home. I loved the garlicky taste the sauce gave to the fish. It surely is a heartwarming fish dish.

Fried Anchovies with Garlic

1 pound (455 g) anchovies

1 medium onion, chopped

2 tablespoons all-purpose flour

1 teaspoon salt

½ cup (120 ml) vegetable oil

11 cloves garlic, crushed in a garlic press

3 to 4 tablespoons white vinegar, preferably homemade (page 102) or fresh lemon juice

Serve 4 as meze (double to serve as a main course)

Toss the anchovies and onion together and let sit for 1 hour. Combine the flour and salt in a shallow dish. Heat the oil in a frying pan over medium heat. Coat three or four anchovies at a time with the flour mixture. Holding the fish by their tails, carefully place them in the hot oil, keeping them close together in the pan so that they stick together. When the sides of the fish start becoming golden, turn them over, keeping them close together. Transfer to a serving platter. Repeat with the remaining anchovies. Discard the onion.

To make the sauce, pour off all but 1 tablespoon of the oil in the pan. Put the garlic in the pan and fry until the garlic is aromatic. Add the vinegar or lemon juice, shake the pan quickly, and pour the sauce over the fried anchovies. Serve immediately.

THIS IS a quick dish but looks interestingly appetizing with its greens and cornmeal. It may also be presented as a fancy savory bread on the side, which is my preference for serving it.

Baked Anchovies with Greens

2 large eggs

½ cup (120 ml) vegetable oil, plus more for the pan

1 pound (455 g) whole fresh anchovies, deboned, if available; or salted or canned anchovies

3 leeks, thinly sliced

2 packed cups (450 g) thinly sliced Swiss chard (massage with your hands to bruise it)

½ packed cup (10 g) minced fresh dill

1 packed cup (20 g) minced fresh parsley

1 ½ cups (210 g) cornmeal

1 cup (130 g) all-purpose flour

½ teaspoon baking powder

Salt

1 teaspoon black pepper

Serves 6 to 8

Preheat the oven to 350°F (175°C). Oil an 11-inch (28-cm) square baking dish.

Lightly beat the eggs and oil in a large bowl, then add the anchovies, leeks, Swiss chard, dill, and parsley. In a separate bowl, combine the cornmeal, flour, baking powder, salt to taste, and the pepper. Pour both mixtures into the prepared dish. Bake for 30 minutes or until a toothpick inserted into the casserole comes out clean. Serve warm.

Turkish Anchovies (*Hamsi*)

Black Sea anchovies are called *hamsi* because they appear during Hamsin (Pentecost). In his seventeenth-century travel book, Evliya Çelebi (born in Kütahya, Anatolia, in 1611; died in Egypt in 1682) writes that forty different anchovy dishes are prepared in the Black Sea area. *Hamsi* literally means "fish" along the Black Sea's Turkish coastline, where anchovies are salted for the summer and thus available year-round. The secret of the Black Sea's unusually tasty anchovies is the counter-undercurrents of the Bosphorus that help the baby anchovies swim to the Black Sea during their growing season.

EGG DISHES

In the Ottoman era, the smell of eggs was considered so disagreeable that only the white of the egg was used to make noodles. There were, however, dishes such as eggs with caramelized onions, egg-laced pilaf, and boiled eggs and rice, which were served for lunch or dinner. There were even Ottoman egg dishes similar to omelettes; the word *omelette*, however, only began to be used in the nineteenth century due to French influences. Interestingly, the head of the palace pantry was selected according to the quality of the eggs with caramelized onions that he prepared for the sultan. This dish was served at the *iftar* dinner for the sultan during Ramadan and therefore was very important.

To this day, Turkish cooks don't fancy the smell of eggs on their own, but they do like to add vegetables, meat, and other ingredients to eggs to make egg-based dishes. Some, like *meneman* (similar to scrambled eggs), eggs fried with onions and ground meat, eggs with spinach, and *çılbır* (poached eggs with garlic yogurt sauce), are eaten at any time of day. Others are exclusively served for breakfast.

A food experience no Turk wants to miss, breakfast is actually quite a recent innovation in Turkish cuisine. Egg dishes are very popular at the breakfast table, including fried eggs with *sucuk* (spicy sausage) or *pastırma* (air-dried spicy beef). Eggs are not part of the breakfast table spread; instead they are prepared after everyone is seated around the table so they can be eaten fresh and hot.

THIS IS a great dish: It is hearty and very satisfying. Usually, in all regions, ground meat alone is used. The addition of parsley makes a sophisticated dish out of what would otherwise be an everyday one. The preparation for this recipe is almost exactly like Palace Eggs with (Almost) Caramelized Onions (page 188, and pictured with this dish on page 189), except this recipe uses sautéed meat instead of onions. Onions may be added to the meat: Dice them, sauté in a separate pan in a little oil, and add to the thoroughly cooked meat.

Eggs with Ground Meat and Parsley

10 ounces (280 g) mixed ground beef, veal, and lamb

2 tablespoons unsalted butter

2 packed cups (40 g) minced fresh parsley

Hot water

Salt and black pepper

6 large eggs

Serves 6

In a large frying pan, cook the meat in the butter over medium heat, breaking it up with a spatula, until it is cooked through. When the meat is just beginning to release its aroma and the ground meat pieces turn golden, add the parsley along with a sprinkle of 1 tablespoon hot water to help wilt the parsley. Season with salt and pepper and cook over low heat for 1 minute, taking care to fold the ingredients together to ensure even cooking. Make six indentations in the meat and parsley mixture (no need to change pans) and break the eggs into these "cups." To help ensure that the yolks cook as quickly as the whites of the eggs, drizzle the egg yolks with a few drops of hot water and cook for 2 minutes more (timing may be adjusted depending on how you like the eggs, but this dish is best when the yolks are still soft and somewhat runny). Serve immediately with a good sprinkle of pepper, or pass the pepper at the table (in Turkey, everyone usually seasons their own eggs).

THE NAME of this dish is not simply a whimsical invention of my own. In the Ottoman palace, the cook who held the position of head of the pantry (*kilerji başı*) was determined by the quality of one dish—eggs and onions—served to the sultan. The head supervised the pantry department, the third most important department in the royal palace. (This department was eliminated in the nineteenth century by Sultan Abdülmecid when he moved the palace from the older Topkapi complex to the newly constructed Dolmabahçe Palace.) Although this dish may appear to be quite simple, like all simple dishes it requires the utmost experience and attention. In presenting this dish, I am also commemorating our invaluable researcher Zarif Ongun, who provided us with this recipe.

Palace Eggs with (Almost) Caramelized Onions

6 medium onions, halved lengthwise and sliced into crescents

4 tablespoons unsalted butter

1 tablespoon sunflower oil

Salt

1 teaspoon sugar

1 teaspoon white vinegar, preferably homemade (page 102), mixed with 1 tablespoon water

¼ teaspoon black pepper

6 large eggs

3 teaspoons hot water

1¼ teaspoons ground cinnamon, cassia (see page 17), or black pepper

Snipped chives, for serving (optional)

Serves 6

Put the onions in a large frying pan with the butter and oil. Sprinkle with salt to taste and sauté over medium-low heat until the onions are translucent and just beginning to caramelize, stirring constantly with a wooden spoon. (The onions must not burn, but they must be soft and barely browned. You may need to add a spoonful of water now and then to achieve this.) Use a slotted spoon to transfer the onions to a tin-lined copper frying pan, if you have one. Sprinkle the onions with the sugar, vinegar, and pepper, and then use the back of the spoon to spread the mixture across the pan. With the spoon, make six indentations in the mixture in which to cook the eggs. Break the eggs into these "cups" and place the pan over medium heat. To ensure that the yolks cook as quickly as the whites, add ½ teaspoon hot water to each yolk. Reduce the heat to low and cook for another 1½ minutes. Remove from the heat and let the eggs sit, covered, for 2 minutes. (This will help ensure that the egg yolks are not too runny.) Uncover, sprinkle with the spice of your choice and snipped chives (if using), and serve immediately.

CLOCKWISE FROM LOWER LEFT: EGGS WITH GROUND MEAT AND PARSLEY (PAGE 107); PALACE EGGS WITH (ALMOST) CARAMELIZED ONIONS (ABOVE).

FEW TURKS know the interesting provenance of the rather strange name of this dish. *Çılbır* is an obsolete Turkish word meaning "tether and the rope connected to it." Perhaps the connection between the yolk of the egg to the egg white, a quite difficult one to break, was the inspiration for this name. *Çılbır* is often made when a quick meal has to be whipped up at the last minute (still, it is a dish people fall in love with). In some parts of the country, yogurt is the topping; in other parts it is the base. Some old recipes omit yogurt altogether and substitute onions lightly browned in butter. Be sure that the yogurt-garlic sauce is at room temperature; cold yogurt will cool the eggs and harden the butter.

Poached Eggs with Yogurt and Garlic Sauce (*Çılbır*)

1 pound (455 g) plain Greek yogurt, at room temperature

3 large cloves garlic, crushed with a mortar and pestle

3 to 4 tablespoons (42 to 55 g) unsalted butter

1 teaspoon mild red pepper flakes

2 tablespoons white vinegar, preferably homemade (page 102)

6 large eggs

Serves 6

Mix the yogurt and garlic.

Heat the butter in a frying pan until sizzling, then add the red pepper flakes. Remove from the heat and set aside.

Bring plenty of water to a boil in a deep frying pan, add the vinegar, and reduce to a simmer. Break the eggs one by one into a saucer and carefully slide each egg into the water without breaking the yolk; cook for 3 minutes (or longer if you like hard-poached eggs). With a slotted spoon, carefully transfer the eggs to individual plates. Top the eggs with the yogurt-garlic sauce and the hot butter with pepper flakes (you might need to give the butter another 30 seconds on the burner to heat through). Serve.

THIS IS A very simple dish to prepare at home (and the ingredients are all balanced for good nutrition). But somehow the best eggs and spinach are always found in the *esnaf lokantası* (the traditional restaurants where you can view all the dishes before making your selection). This is served directly from the pan, so prepare it in a "stove to table" dish.

Eggs and Spinach

2 medium onions, chopped

2 tablespoons unsalted butter

3 tablespoons olive oil

2 pounds (910 g) spinach leaves, washed, dried, and finely minced

Salt

Pinch of minced fresh parsley

6 large eggs

Black pepper

Serves 6

Sauté the onions in the butter and olive oil over medium heat until they turn golden. Add the spinach, salt to taste, and the parsley. Slowly fry until the spinach softens. (If the spinach is too dry, sprinkle with water to help soften it. Lowering the heat also helps because spinach will give off water during cooking.) Cover and cook for 5 to 7 minutes or until the liquid is evaporated. (Raise the heat if there is still a lot of water and the spinach is cooked.) Make six indentations in the spinach and break the eggs into these "cups." Continue cooking over low heat for 4 to 5 minutes. Spoon some of the spinach mixture over the egg whites to help cook them. Cover and cook for 5 minutes more. Top with black pepper or pass the pepper mill. Serve immediately.

MENEMEN IS a popular breakfast dish that can be eaten any time of the day. While some add onions, I prefer not to. I find that without them, the dish is lighter and better as a breakfast choice. My mother always told me to keep the eggs whole, but I like to scramble them. Either way is fine.

Scrambled Eggs with Tomatoes and Green Peppers (*Menemen*)

2 long green peppers (I like to combine one mild and one medium hot)

3 tablespoons unsalted butter or olive oil

2 tomatoes, peeled, seeded, and coarsely chopped

Salt

4 large eggs or 6 small eggs

Black pepper

1 tablespoon minced fresh parsley (optional)

Serves 4

In a frying pan, sauté the peppers in the butter or oil until almost soft. Add the tomatoes and salt to taste and cook for 2 to 3 minutes. (Do not cook the tomatoes so much that they stick to the bottom of the pan.) Break the eggs one by one into the pan and cook, slowly stirring. (Generally, 3 to 4 minutes is enough time for the eggs to be thoroughly cooked but not dried out.) Top with pepper to taste and the parsley, if using, and serve.

THE INTERESTING name of this regional egg salad first caught my attention, and then the taste did. When placed on green herbs, cut up hard-boiled eggs certainly look like daffodil flowers. This dish reminds me of the Caliphate era's Arab tradition of using yellow and white to enhance presentation. Some medieval Arab recipes suggest decorating dishes with egg slices to achieve this. This is a favorite picnic food in the southeastern city of Diyarbakır, where olive oil is not added. It is just as tasty to the Turkish palate without the oil.

Daffodil-Like Egg Salad (*Nergisleme*)

Hard-boiled large eggs (as many as desired; see Note), cooled, peeled, and diced

Green onions, minced

Fresh parsley, minced

1 or 2 fresh or dried hot red peppers, chopped

Sumac

Fresh dill (optional)

Virgin olive oil (optional)

Serves 1 egg per person

Toss together the eggs with enough green onions and parsley to equal the volume of the eggs, then add the peppers, season with sumac, sprinkle with dill (if using), and drizzle with just enough oil, if using, to coat the eggs. Serve at room temperature.

Note: Do not boil the eggs for more than 9 minutes; otherwise, the yolks will have a black ring.

BREAD AND SAVORY PASTRIES

Turkish tables are never complete without a basket of bread. But the bread inside the basket could be a different variety, depending on the region. The most-served ones are the loaf and the *pide*, a kind of flatbread. *Pide* owes its unique flavor not only to the rigor of the bakers, but also to the quality of the flour and the unique structure of *pide* ovens, the traditional wood-fired ovens in which the flatbread is baked. The bottom part of the *pide* oven is multilayered. The lowest level is made of cullet. Iron chips, excellent for retaining heat, are the next layer. Fine sand and salt constitute the third layer. The *karataş* or baker's stone is placed on top. These four- to six-inch-thick stones are scratched to create fine gouges, which act like the nails in a fakir's bed to evenly disperse heat over the whole surface of the stone and thus create appetizingly golden and crisp *pides.* The layered surface of the oven is covered all around with the same stone, a dome is made from firebrick, and

the firebrick is covered with red soil. Lastly, the dome is covered with concrete. To prevent cracking, the oven is not used for a whole day after it's first built. Almost all good kebab restaurants own a *pide fırın* (oven). Types of bread baked in *pide* ovens today include:

Kuppan: Puffy kebab bread. A blend of water, yogurt, and flour can be spread on top; however, the version flavored with egg and black cumin or sesame is currently in demand.

Lavash: This is also called "open bread." It is a flatbread used to wrap items like shish kebab, cheese, and so on and is baked by sprinkling only flour on top.

Tırnaklı: This is *pide* with indentations made with the fingertips. As with *kuppan*, a mix of water, yogurt, and flour is spread on the dough before baking. It is given an oval shape first, then using the pressure of the fingertips the indentations are made before the dough is put into the *pide* oven.

THE UNIQUE aroma of this bread has never left my memory. The huge prepared bread dough was formed into numerous loaves, round in shape and as big as palm leaves, then taken to the town's bakery on huge *sinis* (trays) covered lightly with a cloth. My aunt Saadet would make this under the direction of my grandmother with the assistance of the family's helpers a day or two before the Ramadan holiday. It was a ritual and never missed. There would be at least twenty or so round loaves. When they were brought back from the bakery, they would be covered with a blanket used only for this purpose. The day it was made, we would not eat this bread but instead wait for the first day of the holiday, when the elders would take their first breakfast after thirty days of fasting. Some of these loaves would have hard-boiled eggs stuck right in the middle of them to make the children of the family happy. At breakfast, loaves would be sliced and toasted on tongs or whatever was handy in the huge hearth of the living room, a place where extra guests sometimes slept. Fresh homemade butter would be spread on the warm slices, which in no time melted and created an unforgettable mixture of tastes and aromas.

Holiday Bread with Mastic
(*Sakızlı Ekmek*)

3 lentil-size pieces mastic
   (see page 16)

1 (2-inch/5-cm) cassia stick (see page 17), or 2 teaspoons freshly ground cloves

1 teaspoon salt

1 ½ tablespoons active dry yeast

3 cups (720 ml) nearly hot water

½ teaspoon sugar

2 ¼ pounds (1 kg) all-purpose flour

1 teaspoon vegetable oil

2 tablespoons white sesame seeds

Makes 3 loaves; serves 8 to 10

With a mortar and pestle or an electric spice grinder, finely grind together the mastic and cassia stick or cloves with the salt. Dissolve the yeast in 1 cup (240 ml) of the nearly hot water. Add the sugar and wait until it mixes in and the yeast foams. Put the flour in a large bowl, stir in the mastic mixture, and make a well in the center. Pour the yeasted water into the well, pull in some of the flour to combine, and then slowly add the remaining 2 cups (480 ml) of nearly hot water, gradually incorporating the rest of the flour, and then kneading to make a moderately stiff dough; roll the dough into a ball. (Alternatively, you can use the kneading program on a bread-making machine to mix the dough.) Lightly brush the top of the dough with some of the oil and cover with a clean cloth. Let sit in a warm place to rise until it doubles in the size, 2 to 3 hours depending on the temperature of the surroundings.

Knead the dough again and divide into three equal pieces. Roll each piece into a ball, put them on a large baking sheet, and press to flatten slightly. Brush the top of each with the remaining oil and let sit, covered with a cloth, until doubled in size, 1 to 2 hours.

Preheat the oven to 450°F (230°C) and put a bowl of water in the oven so the bread does not dry out while baking. Sprinkle the sesame seeds on the tops of the loaves and bake for 20 to 25 minutes, until the tops are brown. (If toasted the next day, the loaves taste and smell even better.)

ALTHOUGH *PIDE* is traditionally baked in special wood-fired ovens (see page 194), this recipe, which I developed with young *pide* master Nurullah Acar, came out almost as delicious from the kitchen oven as the *pide* sold in shops. This recipe will make six big flatbreads, each about twelve inches long and filled with an aromatic veal and tomato stuffing, but you can make smaller *pide* to serve as meze, if you prefer.

Oven-Baked Flatbread (*Pide*)

FOR THE DOUGH

½ ounce (14 g) fresh, wet yeast

2 teaspoons sugar

1 ½ cups (360 ml) warm water

4 to 5 cups (520 to 650 g) all-purpose flour, plus ½ tablespoon for shaping the dough

1 tablespoon salt

FOR THE STUFFING

2 medium onions, diced

2 tablespoons unsalted butter

1 pound (455 g) lean ground veal and lamb, minced together

2 medium tomatoes, peeled, chopped, and drained in a colander (2 cups/330 g)

4 long thin green peppers, minced (if 1 or 2 are hot, the stuffing will be tastier)

2 cups (40 g) fresh parsley, minced

Salt

½ teaspoon black pepper

FOR THE TOPPING

1 to 2 tablespoons unsalted butter, melted, or olive oil

Makes 6 large, stuffed flatbreads

Make the dough: Add the yeast and sugar to ½ cup (120 ml) of the warm water, stir, wait until it foams, then pour into a bowl. Stir in the remaining 1 cup (240 ml) warm water, then add the flour gradually, mixing to combine, and then the salt. (As the amount of flour absorbed by the water depends on the quality of the flour, add the last cup of flour very slowly and only as much as needed.) Mix until the dough is uniform and softer than an earlobe. Cover with a damp clean cloth and let sit at room temperature on a work surface (avoid marble, as this cool surface is not good for working with yeast doughs).

Make the stuffing: Sauté the onions in the butter in a large frying pan until translucent. Add two-thirds of the meat and fry in the butter, without letting it get too dry. Let cool. Add the remaining one-third meat, along with the tomatoes, peppers, parsley, salt to taste, and the black pepper, and stir with a spoon. (The reason for adding some uncooked meat is to affix the meat on the *pide*.)

Preheat the oven to 450°F (230°C).

Break off Ping Pong ball–size pieces of dough. Stretch each one to a diameter of 6 inches (15 cm), using your fingers and primarily pressing on the piece's outer edge to stretch it. (Thinning the outer edge prevents breaking from the center of the dough.) To stretch the middle, squeeze the center of the dough gently with one hand and pull 8 to 10 inches (20 to 25 cm) from the other side to make an oval. (By transferring the stretched dough from one hand to the other, you can stretch it in a very short time.) When the dough is 1/16 inch (2 mm) thick, spread some stuffing in the middle, leaving a ¾-inch (2-cm) space around the edges. Fold over the edges to create a rim all around the *pide*, leaving the stuffing completely uncovered. Repeat with the remaining dough and stuffing. Place the *pide* on a baking sheet and bake for 15 to 17 minutes, until there are brown spots on the flatbread. Brush the tops of the dough with butter or oil as soon as the *pide* are out of the oven and serve.

(OPPOSITE) *PIDE* WITH MEAT OR WITH HERBS AND GREENS (PAGE 198).

PIDE MADE with a stuffing of herbs, spinach, and chard is known as Pastry with Herbs. It is light, delicious, and flavored with dry cottage cheese.

Pastry with Herbs, *Pide*-Style

FOR THE STUFFING

1 ½ pounds (680 g) Swiss chard, spinach, stinging nettle (if seasonal), pigweed, mallow, or other edible greens, or a combination

1 cup (225 g) cottage cheese

3 green onions, minced (1 cup/120 g)

1 onion, minced (½ cup/60 g)

½ teaspoon salt

¼ teaspoon black pepper

½ teaspoon mild red pepper flakes

1 packed cup (20 g) minced fresh parsley

3 tablespoons olive oil

Black olives, for garnishing (optional)

1 recipe *pide* dough (see page 196)

1 to 2 tablespoons olive oil

Serves 6

Mix together all the stuffing ingredients.

Shape the *pide* dough, long and thin, as described in the recipe on page 196 but make the breads wider, about 5 inches (12 cm) in width. Top half of the rolled-out dough lengthwise with the filling, then fold the other half of the dough over the filling and lightly seal with your fingertips. (This helps ensure that the greens will cook well.) Garnish with black olives, if desired. Bake as described on page 196, for 15 to 17 minutes or until the top gets brown spots. Brush the top of the dough with olive oil as soon as it is out of the oven. Let sit, covered, at least 30 minutes, before serving.

Wheat: The Roots of Anatolian Cuisine

Wheat was cultivated in Anatolia by the Hittites, who lived in Central Anatolia, as early as 2000 B.C.E. They were neighbors of Mesopotamia, also known as the Fertile Crescent, which possessed ideal conditions for the cultivation of wheat and was one of the first areas where wheat was grown. As the peoples of these areas developed agriculture, the consumption of wheat increased and helped determine the course of their cuisine. Many of the wheat products consumed by the Hittites and other ancient civilizations remain staples of this area's cooking.

The simply structured einkorn wheat (*Triticum boeoticum*), the ancestor of all types of wheat, was first cultivated eleven thousand years ago at the foot of the Karacadag Mountains in Middle Anatolia in the upper part of the Fertile Crescent. When einkorn wheat was bred with wild grass (*Triticum speltoides*) two hybrids of wheat were obtained: emmer (*Triticum dicoccoides*) and durum (*Triticum durum*). The flour-rich kernel of emmer, grown in humid areas, is ideal for bread or pastry. The dough from this wheat is supple, making it easier to roll thin for *yufka* (similar to phyllo). Durum is perfectly suited to central Anatolia's hot and dry climate. Bulgur, a staple of this region's cuisine, is produced from durum wheat's hard and glassy kernel.

Turks arriving from Central Asia not only preserved Anatolia's natural diet, they created a unique cuisine by blending their culinary know-how with the benefits of the fertile land. The pliant bread dough made from emmer wheat led to different types of *yufka*, the Turks' staple. And hard wheat (also called yellow wheat because of its yellow strings) was the basis of many kinds of bulgur pilafs. The Turks also enriched Anatolian cuisine with numerous types of pastries, pastas, and dumplings.

THIS IS one of Turkish cuisine's most labor-intensive recipes. It is, however, also one of its most esteemed dishes. Thin sheets of homemade *yufka*, like homemade pasta but perhaps a little thinner, are first cooked in a pot of salted hot water then placed on a tray, alternately drizzled with melted butter and sprinkled with feta cheese between most of the layers, and then toasted over low heat until golden brown. Once you acquire the knack, it is not that difficult to prepare. For beginners, the main difficulty is removing the *yufka* from the boiling water without damaging them. Have no fear: The *yufka* may tear, but they are rather easy to patch—and the patch lines are not visible after the *börek* is cooked.

Water-Cooked Soft Inside, Crispy Outside *Börek* (*Su Böreği*)

....

FOR THE DOUGH

2 ¼ pounds (1 kg) all-purpose flour

3 large eggs

1 tablespoon salt, plus more as needed

7 to 8 tablespoons (100 to 115 g) unsalted butter, melted, plus more for the pan

⅓ cup (40 g) wheat starch for sprinkling

FOR THE FILLING

10 ½ ounces (300 g) feta cheese, flaked with a fork

1 packed cup (20 g) minced fresh parsley

Serves 12 to 15

Make the dough: Put the flour in a bowl, make a well in the middle, add the eggs, 2 cups (480 ml) water, and the salt and mix to combine. Knead thoroughly until the dough is the texture of an earlobe. Divide the dough equally into 8 balls. Flatten each ball a little, cover with a clean damp cloth, and let sit for 30 minutes. Bring a wide pot to a rolling boil with several pinches of salt in it.

Lightly grease a metal circular tray or sauté pan with butter, then roll out one piece of dough to form a round that's about 4 inches (10 cm) wider than the pan's diameter—the dough should be thin: 1/16 to ⅛ inch (2 to 3 mm) at most. Every so often, sprinkle it with wheat starch to prevent it from sticking. Carefully place the first sheet of dough on the greased circular tray (it's okay if the sheet hangs over the edges of the tray). Brush generously with some of the melted butter. Roll out the second piece of dough the same way, but drop this second one in the pot of boiling water. As soon as the dough softens, in 2 to 3 minutes, transfer to an upside-down colander. Rinse with cold water, dry as well as possible with a cloth, and place the boiled *yufka* on top of the buttered *yufka* on the tray. Butter the boiled *yufka*. Prepare the next two pieces of dough in the same way, buttering and stacking them on top of the others.

Make the filling: Mix the cheese and parsley together to make the filling and spread on the fourth piece of dough.

Boil and butter the next three pieces of dough as described above and add them to the tray. Those that are boiled will get larger due to cooking; to fit them in the tray they will need to be wrinkled a bit.

(continued)

Put the last sheet of dough on the top without boiling it. Fold the hanging edges of the sheet on the bottom over the top sheet to cover and put the tray on the stovetop over low heat. (Choose a large burner, or put the tray on two burners that are close to each other; the heat will spread more evenly that way.) Brush half of the remaining butter at intervals around the edges of the pastry and keep turning the tray in order to brown the *börek* evenly. (Using a spatula, occasionally lift the edges of the pastry to check the bottom.) When the bottom has browned thoroughly, invert the pastry onto another pan of the same size. Pour the remaining melted butter around the edges and brown the other side of the pastry in the same manner. When both the top and bottom are browned, let cool for 15 minutes. Cut into 2-inch (5-cm) squares and serve immediately. (They may be reheated in a pan over a burner the next day.)

AS THIS very tasty spinach-filled pastry is prepared with convenient ready-made *yufka* sheets, it is one of the pastries most frequently made at home. Still, every family has its own favorite recipe. This one, made with a softer pastry, is the one my family likes best.

Spinach *Börek* (*Ispanaklı Kol Böreği*)

4 sheets ready-made *yufka* or phyllo

FOR THE FILLING

2 pounds (910 g) spinach, washed and dried well, stems removed, leaves chopped

1 packed cup (20 g) minced fresh parsley (optional)

½ packed cup (10 g) minced fresh dill

3 to 4 green onions, finely chopped

1 large or medium onion, diced

1 ½ ounces (50 g) feta cheese, together with 3 ½ ounces (100 g) ricotta cheese, well mixed

3 to 4 tablespoons olive oil

FOR THE SPREAD

1 large egg, whipped

⅓ cup (75 ml) olive oil, plus 1 to 2 tablespoons for brushing

½ cup (120 ml) plain Greek yogurt

About ½ cup (120 ml) milk

Serves 8

Preheat the oven to 350°F (175°C). Lightly oil a baking sheet. Cut the sheets of *yufka* or phyllo in half down the middle and stack them one on top of the other.

Make the filling: Place the spinach in a bowl and add the parsley (if using), dill, green onions, regular onion, cheese mix, and oil and mix thoroughly.

Make the spread: Beat together the egg, oil, and yogurt and then beat in the milk gradually to create a thick mixture (you may not use all the milk).

Place one piece of dough in front of you, with the long cut edge nearest to you. Lightly brush on the yogurt spread to cover the *yufka*, and then place a row of the spinach filling along the long cut edge. Roll up the dough away from you, enclosing the filling inside. Transfer the roll to the prepared baking sheet, carefully bending the roll if it is too long to fit on the tray. Repeat with the remaining sheets of dough, yogurt spread, and spinach filling. When all eight pastry rolls are on the baking sheet, brush them with 1 to 2 tablespoons oil. Bake for 30 to 35 minutes, until the tops are lightly browned. Let cool a little, and then cut into 3-inch (7.5-cm) pieces. Arrange the pieces of *börek* on a serving platter at different angles so they do not crush each other.

I TRIED this recipe from whirling dervish Sheikh Ali Eşref Dede's nineteenth-century cooking booklet because it was comprehensible and easy, and I'm glad I did so because it's excellent. (Modesty is highly valued in Turkish culture, but it is also said, "Don't be too modest; they might believe you.") This pastry's flavor takes us back to the Ottoman era, but everyone who tried my rendition agreed that it has a contemporary taste as well.

Onion *Börek* (*Soğan Böreği*)

FOR THE FILLING

8 large onions, diced

2 tablespoons corn oil

4 tablespoons (55 g) unsalted butter

4 or 5 large eggs, beaten

Salt

1 ½ teaspoons ground cinnamon

1 teaspoon ground coriander

2 teaspoons coarsely ground black pepper

FOR THE DOUGH

4 sheets ready-made *yufka* or phyllo

FOR ROLLING

4 tablespoons (60 ml) olive oil whisked with 2 to 3 tablespoons water to emulsify

All-purpose flour, for sprinkling

VARIATION

FOR THE FILLING

3 onions, minced

4 tablespoons (55 g) unsalted butter

2 tablespoons corn oil

1 ½ teaspoons salt

10 ½ ounces (300 g) ground beef

2 ½ teaspoons freshly ground coriander

1 ½ teaspoons freshly ground black pepper

1 cup (20 g) minced fresh parsley

Serves 8

Make the filling: Put the onions in a large pan or pot with the oil, butter, and ½ cup (120 ml) water and cook over medium heat until translucent, about 10 minutes. Remove from the heat and add the eggs; stir and cook until the eggs are half cooked but still partially runny. Season with salt to taste, add the cinnamon, coriander, and pepper, mix well, and let cool.

Preheat the oven to 375°F (190°C).

Cut the *yufka* or phyllo sheets in half down the middle and spread in a semicircle on a work surface. Place one piece in front of you with the long cut edge nearest to you, dot with the oil-water emulsion, and sprinkle lightly with flour. Arrange the other half so they are superimposed. Place 4 to 5 tablespoons (about 250 g) of the onion mixture along the long cut edge of the second sheet of dough. Place the onion mixture all along this cut edge and roll up halfway, enclosing the stuffing inside. Dot the rest with the oil-water emulsion, lightly sprinkle with flour, and finish rolling. The edge will seal because of the emulsion. Transfer the roll to a greased baking sheet, carefully bending the roll if it is too long to fit on the tray. Brush the top with the leftover emulsion. Bake for 15 minutes, then lower the oven temperature to 350°F (180°C) and bake for 15 minutes longer. Let cool a little, then slice and serve.

VARIATION

Onion Rolled *Börek* with Meat

Make the filling: Fry the onions in the butter and oil with a sprinkle of water and the salt, add the ground beef, and sauté until the beef is cooked through. Remove from the heat. Add the coriander, pepper, and parsley and mix well. Let the filling cool, then roll and bake.

EVERYONE WILL be happy to eat these puffy pastries, which boast golden brown, lacelike home-made *yufka*. Whether you serve them for breakfast or as meze with a drink, your guests will gobble them up reflexively, as if in a dream state. In the past, these pastries were fried and served as soon as they were prepared. However, I realized they can be assembled and kept in the freezer for a few days, and I usually take advantage of that fact.

Puffed Cheese *Börek* (*Puf Börek*)

FOR THE DOUGH

1 pound (455 g) all-purpose flour, plus more flour and some cornstarch for sprinkling

½ teaspoon salt

2 large egg yolks, lightly beaten

1 tablespoon plain Greek yogurt

⅓ cup (75 ml) light olive oil

½ teaspoon fresh lemon juice or white vinegar

½ cup (120 ml) milk

2 tablespoons unsalted butter, melted

FOR THE FILLING

7 ounces (200 g) feta cheese

1 packed cup (20 g) minced fresh parsley

Olive oil for frying

Make the dough: In a large bowl, mix together the flour, salt, and egg yolks, then stir in the yogurt and oil. Add the lemon juice, milk, and ½ cup (120 ml) water, mixing until a slightly stiff dough forms. Divide the dough equally into 10 balls. Flatten them out to 5 inches (12 cm) in diameter, each time brushing some butter on each piece of flattened dough, and stack them on top of one another. Roll out the first 5 balls, one by one, to dessert-plate size; the dough should be just ¹⁄₁₀ inch (3 mm) thick. (Let the second stack wait until you are finished with the first one; otherwise the rolled out dough will dry and become unworkable.) Sprinkle the dough with some flour mixed with cornstarch each time you roll it out so the dough doesn't stick to the rolling pin.

Make the filling: Crumble the cheese finely and stir in the parsley. Place 1-tablespoon dollops of filling around half of the circumference of each round of dough, at 4- to 5-inch (10- to 12-cm) intervals, about 2 inches (5 cm) from the edge of the dough. Fold the edges of the dough over to cover the filling, and then, using a cookie cutter, cut the filled dough into half-moon shapes. (The *yufka* pieces left over after cutting the half moons may be saved and used again when there is enough to form another ball after softening it by kneading it with buttered hands.) Repeat this process until no *yufka* dough remains that can be cut to form a half-moon-shaped *börek*. Place the *börek* on a cloth-covered tray, and cover them with another cloth. Prepare the remaining 5 balls of *yufka* the same way. Fry the *börek* immediately or refrigerate on a covered plate for 1 to 2 hours, or freeze on a platter wrapped in foil for 2 to 3 days.

When you're ready to fry the *börek*, heat ¾ inch (2 cm) oil in a deep frying pan over medium heat. Working in small batches, as this fries very quickly, slide in the *börek*. Shake the pan frequently as the oil heats up and spoon some of the hot oil on the pastries. (This will make the pastries even puffier.) Fry the pastries for about 1 minute per side (monitor the heat level so that the hot oil does not burn the pastries) and serve. Draining is not necessary because they will not absorb oil.

street food vendors and restaurants are as prevalent in Turkey today as they were during the Ottoman Empire. You may chance upon a delicious ram's head delicacy in a village when you least expect it, served modestly yet with care in a quaint country roadside setting. In fact, almost every town in Turkey has its own special food. Kütahya (in the Aegean region) is known for its poppy seed buns, Afyonkarahisar (also in the Aegean region) for its cream candy (*kaymaklı lokum*), Bursa for its chestnut candy, Izmit for its hair-thin halva (*pismaniye*), and Gaziantep for its baklava. There are Izmir's little figs (served fresh in the summer and dried in the winter), Datça's (near Muğla in the Aegean region) almonds, and Mardin's (in eastern Turkey) and Çorum's (in northern central Anatolia) roasted chickpeas. In central Anatolia, there is Kayseri's *pastırma* and Tokat's spicy cumin paste, which is spread on bread for breakfast or used in stuffings. Eastern Turkey has Erzincan's Tulum cheese encased in goat skin. All of these regional delicacies contribute to a rich and varied food culture.

The ready-cooked food sold in the bazaars takes your imagination to faraway places. For kebabs, the Gaziantep, Urfa, and Adana (southeastern Turkey) varieties are all so good that it is hard to choose a favorite. Close to noon, as if the Ramadan cannons have been fired, Istanbul's streets come alive: Meat is finely sliced from vertical spits (the *doner kebab*); wood paddles are slid into open ovens to bring out traditional Turkish "pizzas"—*lahmacun* and *pide* topped with meat, cheese, or vegetables—that completely overwhelm the invading aromas of western pizza shops.

The stalls selling grilled lamb intestines (*kokorech*) are something altogether different. At noon, the finely chopped *kokorech* is placed in a large wok (or *sach*, literally "a thin sheet of round metal") and stir-ried with tomatoes, fresh greens, and hot red pepper flakes. When cooked, it is stuffed into half a loaf of bread and enjoyed as a takeaway. Savory pancakes

traveler Evliya Çelebi, are now the most popular fast food in Turkey. On offer are fillings of cheese, meat, potato, and even *tarhana* (page 118). "Generous ladle restaurants" (*esnaf lokantası*) serve home-cooked food to customers, mostly shopkeepers and tradesmen who live in distant areas of the city and cannot go home for lunch. They provide quick and satisfying meals, with delicious and colorful dishes like *karnıyarık* (eggplant boats, page 128), a variety of dolma, *Beans à la Turka* (page 131), and spinach *borani* (page 130) arrayed in rows behind the counter. Most of these restaurants do not serve alcohol.

For those in a great hurry, street vendors sell baked goods such as Turkish bagels (*simit*), Turkish croissants (*açma*), and sweet Turkish pretzels (*catal*). There are also carts that feature semolina cake (*sham tatlısı*), cut into four rectangles and glistening with honey-colored syrup. Other carts sell chickpea pilaf, the snow-white rice displayed behind glass and looking fit for a palace feast. The aromatic smoke from street sellers' *cızbız köftes* will make you change your direction, especially close to the areas when and where there is a football match, a favorite sport for all Turkish people.

In the summer, sherbet sellers wear traditional costumes to sell the delicacies still made from secret recipes with ingredients like tamarind, cranberries, and sour cherries. The sherbet sellers serve the thirsty from shiny pitchers secured to their backs, pouring the sherbet into cups that dangle from their waists. The hot summer months are also the time for Maraş ice cream. Thickened with *sahlep* and flavored with mastic, this popular ice cream is sometimes eaten between slices of bread. Winter is the time for a hot, warming cup of *sahlep* (milk and orchid root starch) sprinkled with cinnamon. Any season is the time for *börek*, flaky pastries with savory fillings. Sarıyer in northwest Istanbul is especially noted for the varieties of puffy, golden *börek* displayed in its shop windows, a delicious invitation to all who pass

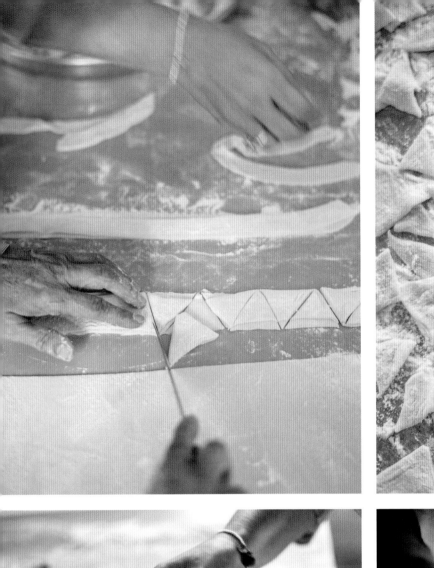

THIS SAVORY pastry is an everyday dish that can be made whenever *mantı* (page 219) or *erişte* (page 217) would be served. It can be dried and kept for a week or even more in a covered glass jar. It is a handy product to have on hand, and can be served with this garlicky butter and yogurt topping, with or without the ground beef, whenever you need a quick meal. If preparing the dough seems too involved, you can substitute ready-made pasta; fresh pappardelle or any kind of flat pasta with some texture would be a good choice. In this case, cook the pasta according to the package directions, then follow the rest of the instructions in the recipe.

Tartar Pastry with or without Meat (*Tatar Böreği*)

FOR THE DOUGH

10 ½ ounces (500 g) all-purpose flour, plus more for dusting

2 teaspoons salt

FOR THE TOPPING

10 ½ ounces (300 g) ground beef (optional)

3 to 4 tablespoons unsalted butter

1 ½ cups (360 ml) plain Greek yogurt, at room temperature

2 or 3 cloves garlic, crushed with a mortar and pestle

Salt and black pepper

7 or 8 fresh mint leaves, torn lengthwise by hand

Serves 6

Make the dough: Put the flour and salt in a bowl, make an indentation in the middle of the flour, add 1 cup (240 ml) water, and mix well. Knead for at least 5 minutes, adding more water if needed. (The dough becomes stiffer as you knead because of the gluten.) Roll into a ball and let sit for 10 minutes to relax (this is a must!). Dust a tabletop or cutting board with flour and roll out the dough with a rolling pin until just $\frac{1}{16}$ to $\frac{1}{8}$ inch (2 to 3 mm) thick with a diameter of about 22 inches (55 cm). Cut the dough into strips ¾ inch (2 cm) wide, then cut the strips crosswise on a diagonal to get triangles. (For beginners, or if a surface of that size is not available, make two dough balls and roll each one separately, making sure you get the same thickness.)

Make the topping: Sauté the meat, if using, in a frying pan with 1 to 2 tablespoons of the butter until cooked through. Beat the yogurt and garlic together to make a sauce (it should not be too runny) and season with salt to taste. Bring a large pot of water to a full boil, add the dough triangles, and cook for 5 to 6 minutes, or until soft. Drain and transfer to another pot. Melt 1 to 2 tablespoons of the butter in a small pot, toss with the dough, and cook over very low heat, uncovered, for 3 to 4 minutes. Pour the yogurt sauce onto a serving platter, place the dough pieces on top, spread the meat, if using, over the dough, garnish with the mint, season with pepper, and serve.

THIS IS another favorite pastry that's stuffed with tomato, string cheese, and *pastırma*, an air-dried beef in a spicy casing. It can be replaced with any spicy salami, if *pastırma* is not available—I could not leave this recipe out, as it is a ubiquitous dish that everyone loves.

Amulet-Shaped *Pastırma* Pies (*Pastırmalı Muska Börek*)

1 sheet ready-made *yufka* or phyllo

3 ½ ounces (100 g) *pastırma*, thinly sliced then chopped

½ packed cup (10 g) minced fresh parsley

½ cup (20 g) chopped string cheese

1 medium tomato, peeled, diced, and drained in a colander

Vegetable or corn oil for frying

Serves 6 as meze

Fill a shallow container with water; you'll use this to seal the ends of the dough strips. Cut the sheet of *yufka* or phyllo into strips 2 inches (5 cm) wide. Cut the longest strips in half (each strip should be about 8 inches/ 20 cm long).

Prepare the filling by mixing together the *pastırma*, parsley, cheese, and tomato. Place 1 tablespoon of filling at one end of a strip. Fold one corner of the dough over the filling to form a triangle that encloses it. Continue folding the triangle, like a flag, taking care that the stuffing stays enclosed in the dough. Seal the loose end of the strip with a dab of the water. Repeat with the remaining strips of dough and the filling (you should have about 12 amulets). Fry in plenty of oil until golden, about 1 minute on each side. Serve hot.

MARMARINA DOUBTLESS came to Turkish cuisine from the country's Greek community; its name is one clue, and its similarity to the round cheese pies Greeks make is another. I like it because it's easy to make. Zucchini paired with feta takes the place of the spinach typically used in the filling.

Tossed *Marmarina*

....

FOR THE FILLING

4 to 5 zucchini (about 2 pounds/
   910 g)

½ teaspoon salt

2 large eggs

1 large onion, diced

1 packed cup (20 g) minced fresh
   parsley

1 packed cup (20 g) minced fresh dill

2 ½ ounces (70 g) feta cheese,
   grated or finely crumbled

5 to 6 tablespoons (75 to 90 ml)
   olive oil

¾ teaspoon black pepper

2 sheets *yufka* (see page 50)

3 to 4 tablespoons olive oil whisked
   with 2 tablespoons water to
   emulsify

All-purpose flour, for sprinkling

Serves 6

Make the filling: Coarsely grate the zucchini into a bowl and toss with the salt. Let sit for 15 minutes, then squeeze the zucchini to remove excess moisture (use cheesecloth if necessary). Beat the eggs. In a large bowl, combine the zucchini, eggs, onion, parsley, dill, and cheese with the oil and pepper.

Preheat the oven to 350°F (175°C). Grease the bottom and sides of a 13-by-9-inch (33-by-23-cm) baking dish.

Add the filling to the prepared dish and spread in an even layer. Lay one sheet of *yufka* on top of the filling, creasing it to fit over the filling. Thoroughly brush the *yufka*, including the creases, with the olive oil–water emulsion and sprinkle it very lightly with flour. Add the second sheet of *yufka*, creasing it in the same way and brushing with the rest of the oil emulsion. Bake for 20 to 25 minutes, until the top is browned. Cut into squares, transfer to a platter, and serve.

FOR THEIR nutritional value and flavor, lentils deserve to be used more often in Turkish cuisine. Happily, using lentils as a filling has become popular recently. This lentil-based filling is inspired by a *börek* I had at a restaurant, but the zucchini is my addition. This makes a tasty meze or a luncheon dish, especially for those who do not eat meat. The name *muska* ("amulet") comes from its shape. It was an ancient shaman ritual to wrap rice and nigella seeds in a black cloth and sew it in the shape of an amulet. This was given to children or anyone in need of good luck, a tradition that continues today.

Lentil and Zucchini Amulets
(*Muska Börek, Mercimekli-Kabaklı*)

3 tablespoons olive oil

2 medium onions, minced

1 teaspoon salt

2 zucchini (about 7 inches/17 cm long), grated, salted, and squeezed dry after 30 minutes

1 cup (190 g) lentils, soaked for 2 hours in lukewarm water and cooked until al dente

1 tablespoon dried tarragon, crushed between your palms

Black pepper

3 sheets ready-made *yufka* or phyllo

¼ cup (60 ml) vegetable or corn oil whisked with 2 to 3 tablespoons water to emulsify

All-purpose flour for sprinkling

Serves 6 as meze

Heat the olive oil in a frying pan and sauté the onions with the salt until translucent. Add the grated and squeezed zucchini and sauté for 2 minutes, then stir in the lentils, tarragon, and pepper to taste.

Preheat the oven to 350°F (175°C).

Cut the *yufka* or phyllo into strips 2 inches (5 cm) wide, then cut the longest strips in half. Place 1 tablespoon of the stuffing at one end of a strip. Fold one corner of the dough over the filling to form a triangle that encloses it. Dot the rest of the strip with the oil-water emulsion and sprinkle lightly with flour, then continue folding the triangle, like a flag, taking care that the stuffing stays enclosed in the dough. Seal the loose end of the strip with a dab of the oil mixture or dip the end in water. Repeat with the remaining strips of dough and filling. Place the amulets on a baking sheet, brush with the oil mixture, and bake for 25 to 30 minutes, until the tops are brown. Arrange on a platter and serve.

PASTA AND DUMPLINGS

*E*rişte, or Turkish pasta, is perhaps the most important staple in all of Anatolia, where plenty is kept in every pantry for use at any time. In early fall, old bedsheets are spread out on which to dry the hand-cut *erişte*. We know from Mahmut from Kaşgar's dictionary that *erişte* was an important part of the diet of Asian Turks in his time, the eleventh century. According to this dictionary, *Divanü Lügat it-Türk*, they used rolling pins specially made for rolling out *erişte*. The dough is made with flour, eggs, water, and salt. *Erişte yufka* is about ¼ inch (6 mm) thick and is cut into strips about ¼ inch (6 mm) wide and dried. It is generally eaten with cheese sprinkled on top or sautéed ground meat, but what gives it a heavenly taste is the generous amount of butter used in every recipe. Here I share a unique recipe for an *erişte* that was was made at the palace. The common *erişte* may be substituted with your pasta of choice, but the recipe opposite may be a revelation. It was for me. Even if you cook the noodles longer than necessary, they will retain their structure and not get sticky. I've also provided a recipe for dried *erişte* you can easily make at home.

I TRIED this old recipe purely out of curiosity, and it works surprisingly well. The recipe called for three hundred eggs. As I did not have to feed a palace, I used only three egg whites for my trial run—and still I ended up with a lot of pasta. As it can be kept for a long time, there is no harm in preparing large quantities. Store the pasta in a soft, breathable fabric bag; in Turkey, we use calico bags.

Ottoman Pasta (*Erişte*)

6 large egg whites

About 3 cups (385 g) all-purpose flour, plus more for dusting

½ teaspoon salt

Serves 6

Put the egg whites in a bowl. Gradually add the flour and salt, kneading with your hands until you have a slightly stiff dough (you may not use all the flour, or you might need to add a little more, a tablespoon at a time). Divide the dough into three balls. With a rolling pin, roll them out to 1 inch (2.5 cm) thick. Cut into strips 2 inches (5 cm) wide. Stack on top of each other with flour dusted in between. With a knife, cut crosswise into pieces no more than ⅛ inch (3 mm) wide, place on a cloth, and let dry for 5 to 6 hours. When dry, put the pasta strips in a cloth bag and tie it shut. You can keep them in the bag for about a month in a dry kitchen cabinet.

I LIKE to serve this as a dinner party entrée since roe is not an everyday dish but served at special occasions. I prefer to sauce it with butter rather than olive oil, as the butter blends better with the other ingredients and also makes the dish more impressive. It can also be made with fresh homemade pasta (page 217) instead of the dried pasta. Use the large holes of the grater to grate the botargo.

Ottoman Pasta (*Erişte*) with Botargo

¼ teaspoon salt

3 cups (300 g) Ottoman Pasta (*Erişte*) (above)

2 tablespoons unsalted butter or olive oil

Salt

¾ cup (20 g) grated botargo, preferably gray mullet roe

½ packed cup (5 g) finely minced fresh parsley

Freshly ground white or black pepper

Serves 6

Bring 2 quarts (2 L) water to a boil and add the salt. Add the pasta and cook until soft, 8 to 10 minutes. (The egg white *erişte* will never be sticky, so they must be well cooked. They will still be chewy even when soft.) Drain in a colander. Transfer to a bowl and add the butter and salt to taste. Toss, top with the botargo, parsley, and pepper to taste, and serve.

CIRCASSIAN SMOKED cheese has an unusual taste. Smoking gives it body, yet it is not that strong and deserves to be used more frequently. If you can't locate this authentic cheese, you can substitute smoked mozzarella.

Ottoman Pasta (*Erişte*) with Circassian Smoked Cheese

1 tablespoon salt

3 cups (300 g) Ottoman Pasta (*Erişte*) (page 215) or Homemade Pasta (*Erişte*) (opposite)

3 ½ ounces (100 g) Circassian smoked cheese, grated

3 tablespoons unsalted butter, heated until sizzling

Freshly ground black pepper

Serves 6

Bring 2 quarts (2 L) water to a boil and add the salt. Add the pasta and cook until soft, 8 to 10 minutes. (The egg white *erişte* will never be sticky, so they must be well cooked. They will still be chewy even when soft.) Drain in a colander, then divide among deep serving bowls (deep bowls will help it retain its heat). Top with the cheese, then the sizzling butter. Serve immediately, passing the pepper mill alongside.

THIS IS a common and very tasty dish. It will save your life if you do not have much time to cook. Make sure you have a *hoşaf* (page 232) or salad to serve alongside. No worries if you do not have time to prepare homemade *erişte*: You can always just use a thin, flat Italian pasta.

Homemade Pasta (*Erişte*) with White Cheese

1 teaspoon salt

2 large eggs

2 pounds (910 g) all-purpose flour, plus more for dusting

1 tablespoon salt, plus more to taste (optional)

3 tablespoons unsalted butter

3 ½ ounces (100 g) feta cheese, flaked with a fork

½ cup (15 g) flaked walnuts (flake walnuts using a knife)

Serves 6

Mix ¼ cup (60 ml) water, the salt, and eggs, then gradually add the flour and knead with your hands, as the amount may be too small for a mixer. When you have a stiff dough, knead for 5 minutes more, then let sit for 10 minutes, covered with a cloth. Divide the dough into two balls and cover one with a wet cloth. Roll out the other with a rolling pin on a floured wooden surface until ¼ inch (6 mm) thick. Cut into strips 2 inches (5 cm) wide, dust with flour, and then cut into pieces ¼ inch (6 mm) wide. Let dry on a clean cloth for 1 or 2 days, or in a low oven for 6 to 8 hours or until dry, then store in a cloth bag for up to 2 months.

Boil 3 cups of the dried pasta for 7 to 8 minutes in salted water. Drain in a colander and rinse briefly with cold water. Transfer to a pot. Add the butter, then the cheese and cook, tossing, for 4 to 5 minutes. Sprinkle with salt to taste if the cheese is not salty enough. Transfer to a platter, sprinkle with the walnuts, and serve.

IT IS said that these dumplings are a gift to our cuisine from the Chinese, from the Chinese *mantou* to *mantı*, but they have always been in Turkish cuisine in a range of incarnations: *Tutmach* and tartar pastry are two of the oldest varieties. "Dumplings with yogurt" are mentioned in Sultan Mehmet the Conqueror's kitchen books, a very important source that records the oldest palace dishes. We'll never know if these dumplings were available without yogurt, but the main feature of Ottoman dumplings is the melted butter and yogurt with garlic poured on it. If cheese is used instead of meat, the dumpling is called *piruhi*. This recipe is the one we make at our house. Each household has its own dumpling recipe and makes *mantı* in a different shape. We chose the simplest, believing that taste comes not from shape but from the ingredients and how it is made. Also this shape yields a thinner and more delicate dumpling along the sealing edge.

Turkish Dumplings (*Mantı*)

....

FOR THE DOUGH

21 ounces (1 kg) all-purpose flour, plus more if needed

3 large eggs

1 ½ tablespoons salt, plus 1 table-spoon for the cooking water

FOR THE STUFFING

2 pounds (910 g) ground lamb, veal, or a mixture

1 big onion, grated (excess moisture squeezed out)

1 teaspoon black pepper

1 teaspoon salt

All-purpose flour for dusting

FOR TOPPING AND SERVING

1 ½ cups (360 ml) plain Greek yogurt

2 to 3 large cloves garlic, crushed with a mortar and pestle (if you must use a garlic press, add a pinch of salt to the yogurt)

3 to 4 tablespoons unsalted butter, melted

1 tablespoon mild red pepper flakes

1 tablespoon dried mint (optional)

Serves 8 as a main dish

Make the dough: Put the flour in a large bowl, make a well in the center, break the eggs into it, add the 1½ tablespoons salt, and mix by hand. Add 1¼ cups (300 ml) water and knead until the flour is absorbed. Add 1¼ cups (300 ml) more water and knead until you have a slightly stiff dough. (If it is too soft or too stiff, add water or flour accordingly.) Make a ball, which will be a little stiff, cover with a clean cloth, and let the dough sit for 10 minutes, until it is as soft as an earlobe, then divide the dough into four pieces. Cover three pieces with dry cheesecloth (since *mantı* dough is softer than bread dough, it has to be covered with a dry cloth), and roll the fourth piece with a rolling pin into a very thin circular sheet, 16½ to 17½ inches (42 to 44.5 cm) in diameter and about 1 mm thick (this is to say that the dough practically has no thickness at all and looks like it would easily tear, but it will still be elastic enough to allow cutting and shaping). Cut lengthwise into strips 1 inch (2.5 cm) wide (you may get strips in slightly different lengths because the dough is circular, which is fine). Then cut these strips into 1-inch (2.5-cm) squares. An efficient way to cut the squares is to pull the dough into an accordion formation by cutting the dough lengthwise into 1-inch (2.5-cm) strips, then putting the strips on top of each other and cutting at 1-inch (2.5-cm) intervals so that you get squares of pastry (this also helps keep the dough from drying out).

Make the stuffing: Combine all the ingredients together and knead well to blend. Put a chickpea-size portion of stuffing in the middle of each square. Fold the squares in half to form triangles and pinch the edges to seal with your fingers. Arrange them on a flour-dusted surface and dust with flour occasionally to prevent them from sticking while you cook the dumplings in batches. (You can cook immediately or transfer them to a double-layer

(continued)

of resealable plastic bags and freeze for up to 10 days. Do not thaw before cooking.)

Bring 6 cups water and the 1 tablespoon salt to a boil in a large pot, sift the excess flour from the dumplings with a fine-mesh sieve, and slowly lower them into the pot. (If they are frozen, sift in any case.) Cook for 8 to 9 minutes after the water returns to a full boil; they are done 5 to 6 minutes after they rise to the surface. (Frozen dumplings may need 12 to 15 minutes.) It is important to add them to the boiling water immediately. If you let them sit they get sticky and will be inedible.

Make the topping: Meanwhile, mix together the yogurt and garlic. When the dumplings are done, use a slotted spoon to transfer them to individual serving plates. Add 2 tablespoons yogurt topping to each serving. Reheat the butter to reach the browned butter state, remove from the heat, add the red pepper flakes and mint, if using, and drizzle the seasoned butter over the dumplings. Serve.

SHOPPING AT A *BAKKAL* (GROCERY STORE) AT ÇIÇEK PASAJI NEAR İSTIKLAL CADDESI IN ISTANBUL.

Shopping at Turkish Bazaars and Markets

Istanbul is a capital of food, and the center of Istanbul's gastronomy remains the Egyptian Spice Bazaar (Mısır Çarşısı), in Eminönü near the historical Galata Bridge, which assails visitors with its heady blend of colors and fragrances. Spices and homemade foods from Anatolia are waiting here to be experienced, offering full pleasure to all the senses. It is easy to observe that food is the center of the lives of Turkish people as one takes a walk around the city. There are vegetable shops (called *manav*), bakeries, and stores called *bakkal,* groceries that will carry all manner of items, from daily bread to nuts, soda pop, milk, and cheese. However, for the best fresh vegetables and a wide variety of milk products, one goes to the bazaars that set up once a week on the same day in the same place. This is very important in small towns as *manavs* or *bakkals* sell very limited foodstuffs that are usually packaged goods, whereas in bazaars one can find specialty foods brought from nearby towns and villages. As there are weekly bazaars that are set up on different days in different sections of larger cities, people will visit one if they miss the day of the other.

In Istanbul, aside from Mısır Çarşışı there are certain places that are called bazaars but are actually permanent shops, namely Beşiktaş Pazarı, in the area called Beşiktaş; Balık Pazarı in the area called Taksim, on the pedestrian street İstiklal Caddesi; and Kadıköy Pazarı on the Asian side. All these *pazars* (meaning "permanent markets") carry a huge variety of fresh meat, fish, cheeses, fresh fruits and vegetables, dried fruits and vegetables, dried spiced meat, *pastırma,* and *sucuk* (spicy sausages, an important component of the ready-to-eat-food culture of Turkey). Kadıköy Pazarı carries a lot of Anatolian handmade specialties and also has a nostalgic coffee shop where they will grind coffee roasted according to your preference.

Of course there are the famous fish markets like Beşiktaş Pazarı, Sarıyer Pazarı, and Kumkapı Balık Pazarı, but in many districts—like Ortaköy, and along the coast of Yeniköy—there are fish mongers where one can stop the car and choose a freshly caught fish. To buy dried fish to make çiroz and fish eggs for *tarama* (page 30) however, one has to visit the Balık Pazarı in Taksim.

Near the Egyptian Spice Bazaar is Kurukahveci Mehmet Efendi, at one time the largest supplier of Turkish coffee in Istanbul. Passing by its very popular shop on Tahmis ("coffee roasting") Street, visitors are enticed by the aroma of freshly roasted, ground beans—it fills the senses so you feel as if you have just enjoyed a cup of unsweetened Turkish coffee. The visitor interested in food finds much to see here, wandering the narrow streets from the Spice Market to Tahtakale ("wood castle"), where an endless variety of kitchen utensils, pots and pans, wooden spoons, rolling pins, and oven paddles are sold. At the end of such a stimulating day, the visitor heads home carrying a load of fresh, appetizing food.

CIRCASSIANS WHO immigrated to Turkey have made important contributions to Turkish cuisine, especially with their pastries and cheeses. The Circassian pastry known as *fiçin* looks like Turkish dumplings, but it is bigger, so two pieces are usually enough for a single serving. *Halishka* is another Circassian pasta dish: These large square noodles look exotic on the plate. They are usually topped with grated *kesh* (Circassian dry curd cheese), but if *kesh* is not available, dry cottage cheese mixed with some strong grated cheese like pecorino can be used. I've included a variation that incorporates chard into the dough, and the delicious taste and smell of the melted butter drizzled over the top leaves nothing to be desired.

Circassian Pasta (*Halishka*)

FOR THE DOUGH

About 1 pound (455 g) all-purpose flour, plus more for dusting

1 large egg

1 teaspoon salt plus ½ teaspoon for cooking

FOR THE TOPPING

6 tablespoons (85 g) unsalted butter

1 cup (225 g) cottage cheese, dried for about 15 minutes in a 320°F (160°C) oven (take care not to overdry), or 1 ½ cups (180 g) grated or finely crumbled feta cheese

2 tablespoons slivered walnuts (optional)

Serves 6

Make the dough: Put the flour in a large bowl, make a well in the center, and add the egg, salt, and ½ cup (120 ml) water. Mix well and add ½ cup (120 ml) more water and knead. The dough should be slightly stiff. (The dough will soften as it sits, so judge accordingly.) Let the dough sit for 10 minutes. Form into a ball and roll out into a sheet that's between 1/16 and 1/8 inch (2 and 3 mm) thick. Cut into 2½-inch (6-cm) squares and place on a lightly floured cloth. When all the dough is cut, cover the pieces with parchment paper and let sit for 1 to 2 hours.

When it is almost time to eat, boil plenty of water in a wide pot and add ½ teaspoon salt. As soon as the water comes to a boil, add the dough squares and cook for 8 to 10 minutes.

Make the topping: Meanwhile, heat the butter until aromatic and warm serving plates, if possible (in a low-temperature oven, for example). With a slotted spoon, transfer the pasta to the plates. Sprinkle with the cheese and walnuts, if using, on top, pour the butter over the pasta, and serve.

VARIATION

For those who would like a more flavorful *halishka*, here's one with chard: Sauté 1 diced onion in 2 tablespoons vegetable oil until translucent, then add 5 packed cups (1.1 kg) chopped chard leaves (stems discarded) and sauté until wilted. To soften the chard, add ½ cup (120 ml) water at a time. When the water completely evaporates and the chard is soft to your liking (if not, add a little more water), it is ready. Season with salt and pepper and place the chard on serving plates. Place the pasta on top, sprinkle with the cheese mix (cottage cheese mixed with pecorino), and serve.

THIS IS a favorite dish of everyone, young and old. Now that Italian pasta is very popular in Turkey, this baked macaroni is not being cooked as often as it used to be, but the simple restaurants called *esnaf lokantası* that serve only at lunchtime still cook the old favorites like this. This recipe is from a chef named Tahsin Kutlu who is from Erzurum, and, as young as he is, he understands and cooks the classic dishes very well. We cooked it together. (In Turkey, special long, thick tubelike macaroni is sold for this dish, but Italian pastas like manicotti, mostaccioli, or tubini will do.)

Macaroni in the Oven (*Fırın Makarna*)

1 package (17 ounces/500 g) manicotti, mostaccioli, or tubini

1 teaspoon salt, plus more for cooking

3 to 4 tablespoons (42 to 55 g) unsalted butter

¼ cup (60 ml) corn oil

½ cup plus 2 tablespoons (70 g) all-purpose flour

2 cups (480 ml) whole milk

1 ½ cups (360 ml) hot water

1 ½ teaspoons black pepper

Pinch of grated nutmeg

1 ½ cups (180 g) crumbled feta cheese

2 tablespoons minced fresh parsley

1 ½ cups (180 g) grated kashkaval or percorino cheese

Serves 6

Preheat the oven to 350°F (175°C).

Cook the pasta in plenty of salted water, drain, and run cold water over it to stop the cooking and keep it from getting too soft. The texture should be a little more done than al dente but not mushy.

Heat the butter with the oil in a pot. When melted, add the flour and mix well, then add the milk and hot water, mixing well. When the mixture comes to a boil, remove from the heat right away. Stir in the salt, pepper, and nutmeg. Add the cooked pasta, feta, and parsley and mix well with a big wooden spoon. Spread the macaroni mixture evenly in a baking dish. Sprinkle with the kashkaval cheese and bake for 35 to 40 minutes, until the top of the casserole has brown spots. Let sit for 10 minutes before serving. Cut into squares and serve.

Note: Boiled chicken pieces may be added to the sauce and baked along with the macaroni; 2 to 3 cups (480 to 720 ml) of chicken meat will be plenty. In that case, you may replace the nutmeg with 1 tablespoon dried tarragon, crushed between your palms.

DESSERTS, TURKISH TEA & COFFEE

"WHAT IS SWEETER THAN HONEY? SUGAR!"
(TURKISH PROVERB)

The Turks are well-known for their collective sweet tooth, and the evidence is everywhere. There are sweets shops where only sweet pastries are served. People stop by at any hour of the day to enjoy a few squares of baklava or other pastries, rolled or shaped like a rose or a nest. The treats are usually accompanied by a glass of lemonade or tea, depending on how cold or hot the weather is. There is no town without a sweet shop like this. Even shops along the highways offer good choices of these kinds of sweets for those who are traveling and would like to get an energy boost or satisfy their sweet tooth. And mind you, they all taste good. Also there are special shops that sell *muhallebi*, or "milk desserts," including chicken breast pudding (a very special dessert actually made with the breast meat of a freshly killed chicken), water *muhallebi*, and rice pudding. But nowadays these shops have also started carrying pastries like baklava and the like to offer a wider variety of choices.

It would be wrong not to think that the Turks' love of sweets started with their conversion to Islam. Islam forbade wine to its adherents and in return offered them sweet sherbet (here I'm referring to the drinks like lemonade, not the frozen ice cream–like sweet). Ironically, wine and sherbet are both made from fruit juices; wine, however, is fermented, while sherbet retains the taste of fruit sweetened with sugar. Sherbet thus became an important drink in the Ottoman Empire as early as the sixteenth century. At festive or auspicious gatherings where food was served, these fruit sherbets were offered only to men of importance, like wine once was in the West. (Less important people were served only water.) Eventually, the variety of sherbets was creatively expanded to include a luxurious assortment of flavors—such as rose, violet, licorice, and tamarind—that were being imported to the East, and eventually the religious meaning and importance of sherbet was left behind.

Islam's defense of sweet tastes most likely paved the way for the creation of many of the Turkish sweets and desserts enjoyed to this day. The Ottoman Empire's strength, at its height in the sixteenth century, facilitated the acquisition of great amounts of sugar, which was considered a precious commodity in Europe until the eighteenth century. Sugar was used because of this abundance and the delicate flavor it gave to desserts, and not because of the digestive qualities Arabs supposed it had. As early as the fifteenth century, there were numerous kinds of jams made with sugar instead of honey and these were offered to people of importance at festivities.

Popular Turkish sweets may be categorized as sweet pastries, milk desserts, *halvas* (made of butter and flour or starch or rice flour), and *hoşafs* (fresh fruit in sherbet). These do not include the many regional specialties such as *pişmaniye* from the Izmit area (a *halva* composed of hair-thin strips) or the famous sweet *kaymak* (clotted cream) of Afyonkarahisar. Palatial *lokum* (Turkish delight) won Turkey an international reputation for master candy

making. This rich world of sweets has earned the Ramadan holiday the name *Şeker Bayramı* ("Sugar Holiday"), a time when the offering of all kinds of sweets is unlimited.

TURKISH TEA AND TREATS

Given the contemporary popularity of tea drinking in Turkey, one would think the love of Turkish tea was an ongoing, centuries-old phenomenon, but that rendition of the story is not entirely accurate. Tea was first used by Central Asian Turkish tribes around the seventh century as a symbol of friendship and accord. In the ritual, the person whose friendship was sought was offered tea, and he drank it to reciprocate the sentiment. However, this tradition eventually disappeared among Muslim Turks, most likely because tea drinking became associated with Buddhists, who drank tea as part of their religious rituals.

By the nineteenth century, however, tea became popular again as Turks began to appreciate the drink for its medicinal properties. At that time, it was served mostly in wealthier homes and only after meals to aid digestion. Today, of course, it is served and drunk at almost every hour of the day. Even children are served a tea cooled and diluted with cold water known as pasha tea, a tepid tea drunk in the homes of the rich to aid digestion.

Tea is not only an essential part of socializing, but also an unrivaled staple at breakfast too. For Turks, the most important gathering around the table is breakfast, but this custom is actually quite a recent innovation in Turkish cuisine. The popularity of breakfast parallels tea's reappearance in Turkish culture in the late nineteenth century. Of course, the Turks' genius at making pastries that go very well with a glass of tea certainly helped make teatime gatherings for the ladies popular too. So, along with instructions for making a perfect cup of Turkish tea, below I've included recipes for pastries and other sweets that pair nicely with tea, at breakfast or any time of day.

USING SEMOLINA in desserts gives them a grainy texture. It also prevents mushiness, which is not too pleasant to the palate. This is a dessert for those who love cakelike treats. It is light and makes a perfect post-dinner finale. Serve with a dollop of *kaymak* or clotted cream, if desired.

Semolina Cake in Syrup (*Revani*)

FOR THE CAKE

¾ cup (115 g) semolina flour

⅓ cup (45 g) blanched and ground almonds (optional)

3 tablespoons all-purpose flour, plus more for the pan

5 large eggs, separated

½ cup (100 g) sugar

2 tablespoons grated lemon zest

Pinch of salt

Butter, for greasing

5 or 6 dried apricots, quartered (whole blanched almonds may replace the apricots for extra crunch)

FOR THE SYRUP

1 pound (455 g) sugar

Juice of ½ lemon (about 2 tablespoons)

Serves 8 to 10

Preheat the oven to 350°F (175°C).

Make the cake: Mix the semolina and the almonds (if using) with the flour. In a large bowl, beat the egg yolks with the sugar and lemon zest until light. In a separate bowl, beat the egg whites with the salt until stiff. Fold the flour mixture into the egg yolk mixture, and then fold in the egg whites. Grease a 12-inch (30- to 31-cm) round cake pan, dust with flour, and pour in the batter. Arrange the apricots on top. Bake for 30 minutes, or until the top of the cake is golden.

While the cake is baking, make the syrup: Boil 4 cups (960 ml) water with the sugar and lemon juice for about 10 minutes, until the syrup loses its runniness and is near the consistency of olive oil. When the cake is done, turn the oven off, and pour the hot syrup into the pan in the oven. Keep the oven door closed until all the syrup is absorbed, about 20 minutes. Let the cake cool completely before serving.

The Skillful Bakers of Kayseri

The baking skills of Anatolian women have led to customs that demonstrate this prowess. Until quite recently, men of the Kayseri province in central Turkey used to visit each other's homes late at night, and with little notice the host's wife was expected to prepare savory pastry, *mantı* or *piruhi* dumplings, and baklava for the visitors. Even today, preparing savory pastry, sweetened shredded wheat, or baklava under time constraints is a matter of pride for housewives in this part of Anatolia. As long as there are three eggs available—one for pastry, one for dumplings (tray dumplings, *piruhu*, spring dumplings, "open lips," and so on), and the third for sweetened shredded wheat—anything is possible! All guests are welcome at these rich and meticulously prepared dining tables, thanks to the wheat of Anatolia and the dexterity of Anatolian women.

KÜNEFE IS a dessert pastry made out of extra-long, vermicelli-like threads, filled with a special salt-less cheese, and dressed with syrup and a variety of nuts. (Minus the cheese, this dessert is known as *kadayıf*.) The popularity of *künefe* spans a geography much larger than just Turkey (in this case mostly southeastern Turkey). Looking at a map of the Ottoman Empire at its peak, it is easy to understand how many dishes besides this delicious dessert have been exported or imported far beyond their areas of origin. The easy preparation of this sweet pastry helps feed its acclaim. You will need six *künefe* dishes, typically made of brass with simple wide rims that makes for a pretty presentation (these can be ordered online), or six 2-inch (5-cm) round cake pans. Traditionally, the pastry is cooked on gas burners on the stovetop, but to cook six portions at the same time I devised this simple oven method.

Syrup-Soaked Cheese Pastry (*Künefe*)

1 pound (455 g) fresh wet *kadayıf* (see Notes)

10 tablespoons (140 g) unsalted butter, melted

8 ounces (225 g) fresh, saltless cheese, such as ricotta, divided into 6 pieces

FOR THE SYRUP

1 pound (455 g) sugar

2 tablespoons fresh lemon juice

3 tablespoons freshly ground pistachios

Serves 6

Spread the *kadayıf* on a baking sheet and sprinkle with the melted butter. Using your hands, rub the butter all over portions of the *kadayıf* (the threads are so thin that rubbing them between your fingers will butter entire portions). Divide the *kadayıf* into six equal portions, then divide each portion into two pieces. Spread one piece on the bottom of each *künefe* dish or 2-inch (5-cm) cake pan. Divide the cheese among the pans, and then place a second piece of *kadayıf* on top of each, making sure the cheese is well covered. Place the dishes on top of each other, so they press on the one below (placing any kind of weight, such as a pot, on the last one is a good idea). Refrigerate for 1 to 2 hours.

While the pastries are chilling, prepare the syrup: Boil the sugar and 3½ cups (840 ml) water, stirring until the sugar dissolves. Add the lemon juice and boil for 10 to 12 minutes more. When the syrup is the consistency of olive oil, remove from the heat and let cool.

When ready to bake, place an oven rack in the top third of the oven (to take advantage of the upper heating element) and preheat the oven to 400°F (205°C).

Place the pans on the highest oven rack and bake for 3 to 4 minutes. When the tops are golden, take the *künefe* out of the oven, carefully invert them onto a baking sheet, removing the pans, and bake 3 to 4 minutes, or until both sides turn golden. Return the *künefe* to their pans or remove to heated serving plates. Spoon about 3 tablespoons of the syrup onto each *künefe*,

(continued)

sprinkle with the ground pistachios, and serve immediately. The *künefe* is best when it is eaten quite warm or the cheese will harden (see Notes).

  Notes: Wet kadayıf *may be purchased at select Middle Eastern shops.* Kadayıf *is also sold dry, ready to be immersed in syrup. Do not confuse the two.*

Serving künefe *in their special baking dishes enables you to serve them hot. Transferring them to another serving dish will cool them down. The* künefe *dishes also boast wide frames, which allow space for you to pour on the syrup.*

THE KITCHEN archives of Fatih Sultan Mehmet indicate that *kadayıf* dressed with a milk syrup was served to him in the fifteenth century. As simple as it is, this is still very popular and a favorite among the sweet pastries.

Kadayıf in Milk Syrup (*Sütlü Kadayıf*)

8 ounces (225 g) fresh wet *kadayıf* (see Notes above)

4 tablespoons (55 g) unsalted butter, melted

1 cup (100 g) walnuts, chopped

Ground cinnamon

FOR THE SYRUP

3 cups (720 ml) milk

1 ½ cups (800 g) sugar

3 tablespoons natural rose water (see page 18)

Serves 6

Preheat the oven to 350°F (175°C).

Spread the *kadayıf* on a baking sheet and sprinkle with the melted butter. Using your hands, butter portions of the *kadayıf* threads by rubbing them with your fingers. Divide the *kadayıf* into six equal portions. Spread a portion in your palm. Put 1 tablespoon of the walnuts in the center. Cover the walnuts with the *kadayıf*, creating a ball. Repeat with the other portions. Place them in muffin cups or ramekins. Bake for 30 to 35 minutes, until they are golden.

Meanwhile, prepare the syrup (see Note): Boil the milk and sugar for 7 to 8 minutes (the syrup should be thin, but not too watery). Let cool to lukewarm then stir in the rose water. When the pastries are done, dish them into a deep pan. Pour the warm syrup over the balls. Refrigerate for at least 1 hour. Transfer to serving plates and top each with a generous sprinkle of cinnamon.

  Note: It might be safer, timing wise, to prepare the syrup ahead of time and reheat it to lukewarm before pouring it over the kadayıf *balls.*

THIS DELICATE dessert is made from milk, pomegranate seeds, rose water, and a special pastry known as *güllaç* leaves made from flour and cornstarch. As weightless as clouds and as fragile as the thinnest crystal, this sweet, once prepared only for the sultan's important banquets, has become the symbolic dessert of Ramadan.

Like other popular Turkish desserts, namely baklava and *kadayıf*, when it comes to preparing Palace Delight, the hardest part of the work is done by masters, who still produce the *güllaç* leaves by hand. A descendant of Saffet Abdullah, the famous fifth *güllaç* maker, reveals the secret to perfect *güllaç*: "The reason one will feel each leaf on the palate depends on the ratio of flour to starch. If the texture of the leaf cannot be felt by the palate, then it is no different than jelly!" I also learned from them that the shiny part of the leaf has to look at you when piling them to make this dessert. That is another reason you will feel the leaves on your tongue.

Palace Delight (*Güllaç*)

10 ½ cups (2.5 L) milk

1 ¾ pounds (795 g) sugar

1/3 cup (75 ml) natural rose water (see page 18)

10 dry *güllaç* leaves (see Note)

1 ½ cups (135 g) blanched slivered almonds

Pomegranate seeds

Serves 10 to 12

Bring the milk and the sugar to the boiling point, then stir in the rose water. (Keep this mixture hot during preparation.) Pour 1 cup of the milk syrup into an 11-inch (28-cm) square pan. Take one *güllaç* leaf, break it into two equal pieces (so they can be easily layered in the pan), lay them in the pan shiny sides up (to keep the leaves from sticking), and spread them flat. Pour about 2 cups (480 ml) of the milk syrup over the leaf, and sprinkle with some almond slivers. Continue this process until all the leaves are immersed in hot milk syrup in the pan. Add the rest of the milk syrup. (If the milk syrup cools during preparation, reheat it.) Refrigerate the assembled *güllaç* until cold. Cut into squares. Sprinkle with almond slivers and pomegranate seeds, spoon some extra milk over the squares, and serve.

Note: Güllaç *leaves or sheets are sold in large, round, vacuum-sealed packages and they can be kept for a long time since they are bone dry. If you don't have easy access to dry* güllaç, *you can find it at Middle Eastern markets or on websites selling Turkish ingredients.*

THIS PUDDING is the result of nomadic wisdom. It is difficult to believe that the milk becomes a pudding without boiling it when figs are added, but it does. Before commercial yeasts appeared, the stomachs of sheep, and likewise figs, were used to ferment milk. Although this dessert is the product of ancient know-how, it is very much in line with the precepts of modern cooking, which is always in search of simple but sophisticated tastes. You will need a candy thermometer to prepare this dish.

Uncooked Fig and Milk Pudding with Mahlep (*Teleme İncir Tatlısı*)

4 ½ cups (1 L) cow's or sheep's milk

2 fresh bay leaves

1 teaspoon ground mahlep (see page 17)

4 cups (600 grams) dried figs (see Note), cut into quarters, the insides scraped out as much as possible and reserved

Serves 6

In a large pot, bring the milk and bay leaves almost to the boiling point, then remove from the heat. Dissolve the mahlep in a little bit of the hot milk, then add the mixture to the pot. Insert a candy thermometer. When the temperature reaches 98 to 100°F (37 to 38°C), add the fig seeds that have been scraped out, along with the peels. (This temperature is a little hotter than lukewarm, but barely hot to the touch. If the figs are added when the milk is very hot, the milk will separate. If it is too cool, the milk will ferment.) Stir with a wooden spoon to incorporate as much of the fig seeds as possible, then pass the mixture through a sieve with small enough holes to strain out the seeds; discard the fig peels after pressing them with a spoon so as to get as much flesh as possible through the strainer. With a ladle, transfer the pudding into tiny bowls or pudding glasses and cover them with muslin (it will absorb any wetness rising from the steam) for about 1 hour, until completely cool. Chill the pudding in the refrigerator for 2 to 3 hours and serve cold.

Note: The world-famous Turkish figs that grow around the Aydın area near İzmir and ancient Smyrna in the Aegean region are the only figs used for drying in Turkey. Known regionally as bardacık, *they are as sweet as honey and develop an even sweeter taste once they are dried. If the figs that you are using for this pudding are not especially sweet, add some sugar to taste when the milk is still very hot so that the sugar will dissolve quickly. Separating the fig seeds from the rest of the fig saves time in the strainer and helps ensure that the pudding benefits as much as possible from the yeastlike qualities of the figs.*

Hoşaflar: Fresh or Dried Fruit in Sherbet

HOŞAFS WERE the sweet served most often in the Ottoman palace. Made from fresh seasonal fruit, these delicate, juicy compotes were served only to important guests. *Hoşafs* made from dried fruits were for everyone. They were cooled with the snow brought from the Olympos Mountain in Bursa. On one occasion, Sultan Suleyman the Lawgiver was invited by Ibrahim Pasha and his wife (the sultan's sister) to dine in their luxurious home in what is today called Ibrahim Pasha Palace. When the sultan was served *hoşaf* and it appeared to have no ice, he remarked on its absence. The pasha replied that the serving bowls were *made* of ice. *Hoşaf's* sweet and refreshing flavor is a wonderful accompaniment to savory dishes, especially pilafs and simple pasta with cheese and, of course, *böreks* with any kind of filling.

Orange *Hoşaf*

6 ounces (175 g) sugar

Juice of 1 orange

3 medium oranges, peeled and thinly sliced or diced (according to preference)

Serves 6   Boil 4 cups (960 ml) water with the sugar until the sugar dissolves, add the orange juice, and boil for a few seconds more. Remove from the heat and let cool; when it is lukewarm, add the orange. Refrigerate until cold, then serve.

Pear *Hoşaf*

6 ounces (175 g) sugar

4 whole cloves

1 tablespoon fresh lemon juice

3 pears with soft flesh, Bartlett if available

Serves 6   Put the sugar, cloves, lemon juice, and pears in a deep pan. Bring 4 cups (960 ml) water to a boil and pour over the pear mixture. Cook the pears for 1 minute over medium heat (if you are using hard-fleshed pears, cook them for 8 to 10 minutes). Remove from the heat and cover tightly. Let cool to lukewarm. Refrigerate until cold, then serve.

Fresh Sour Cherry *Hoşaf (Vişne Hoşafı)*

2 pounds (910 g) unpitted whole sour cherries

½ pound (230 g) sugar

Serves 6   Divide the cherries into two groups: harder and softer. Press the softer cherries in a colander to squeeze out their juice, then rinse with ½ cup (120 ml) water to make sure no juice remains. Transfer the cherry juice to a pot, add the sugar, bring to a boil, then immediately remove from heat. Stir well to ensure that the sugar is dissolved, then add the harder cherries and 4 cups (960 ml) water. Chill in the refrigerator until ready to serve. Serve cold with ice cubes. If the *hoşaf* is too sweet, add more cold water or ice.

Both dry and fresh fruit have long been revered in Turkey, and today across the country fresh fruit is always displayed like colorful jewels in grocery stalls. In fact, each street in Turkey seems to have a small shop specializing in the sale of various nuts and dried fruits called *kuruyemişci*. People buy small quantities, appreciating the fruits and nuts as a delicacy, and consume them at their freshest. This love of fruit probably dates back to the Turks of Central Asia. In both Asia and Anatolia, serving apples expressed a person's desire to marry. Many young girls still give a young man they fancy an apple as a token of their feelings. Turkmen who live today around Edremit (on the Aegean Sea) continue an ancestral tradition of leaving fruit on the graves of loved ones on special days. Today's custom of serving guests fresh or dried fruit at any time of the day is an extension of this ancient fruit-loving culture. And the essential mezes to accompany raki are fresh cantaloupe and feta cheese (*beyaz peynir* in Turkish), a custom that reflects the long-held love of cantaloupe by the Turks.

THE NAME of this milk dessert, *kazan,* literally means "bottom of the cauldron." It is delicious and very much a favorite. It seems its origins go back to the period when Mahmut from Kaşgar wrote his Turkish-to-Arabic dictionary, *Divanü Lügat-it Türk,* in the eleventh century. One of the words listed in this invaluable source is *kez,* which is defined as the burnt milk that sticks to the bottom of the pot. Authentic versions are prepared by special dessert makers using *sübye,* a handcrafted ingredient made by soaking and grinding a type of rice with water. All *muhallebi* (milk desserts) sold in Turkish stores that serve traditional desserts are made with *sübye.* This homemade version skips this special ingredient; nevertheless, it is tasty.

"Burnt" *Muhallebi* (*Kazandibi*)

½ cup plus 2 tablespoons (75 g) cornstarch

½ cup plus 1 tablespoon (70 g) all-purpose flour

2 quarts plus 2½ cups (2.5 L) milk

1½ cups (300 g) sugar

5 to 6 drops essence of vanilla

1 chickpea-size piece of mastic (see page 16) and 1 teaspoon sugar, ground with a mortar and pestle

Serves 10 to 12

Dissolve the cornstarch and flour in 1½ cups (360 ml) cold water. In a large saucepan, boil the milk with the sugar until the sugar dissolves. Stir in the cornstarch and flour mixture. Cook for about 15 minutes, stirring, until it thickens and comes to a boil; boil for 30 seconds, then remove from the heat. Tilt a 14-by-11-inch (36-by-28-cm) or similar-sized flameproof metal baking pan over a medium-hot burner and ladle in a small amount of the milk mixture. Repeat several times, until the bottom of the pan is covered by the milk. Straighten the pan and hold it horizontally over the heat to burn the mixture. (To get an evenly burned milky bottom, occasionally tilt the pan back and forth.) Set the baking pan aside.

Add the vanilla and the mastic mixture to the milk mixture in the saucepan, bring to a boil, then pour it over the burned pudding in the baking pan. Refrigerate for at least 6 hours. Cut into squares and, with a spatula, invert the squares onto individual serving plates, burned bottoms up.

LEMON SHERBET used to be ubiquitous but nowadays it is a delicacy; people have not been making this delicious tangy cooling dessert very frequently. Whereas all other sherbets get their name by adding the word *sherbet* at the end, this one acquired one special name, *limonata*. Could it be that when it was served to non-Turkish people, they thought it was called "lemonade," hence its modern name *limonata*? Mind you, there are special *limonata* glasses—about 4½ inches (11 cm) tall, with about a 2¾-inch (6.5-cm) diameter—but you can use small parfait glasses if you like. The *limonata* glasses are a good size, though, as each serving will be satisfying but not too much. You can add more cold water to make the *limonata* less sweet. To serve, you can garnish with a leaf of fresh mint, which will give it a twist.

Lemon Sherbet (*Limonata*)

5 to 7 lemons

2 ½ cups (500 g) sugar

Mint leaves, for serving (optional)

Serves 12

The day before serving, grate the lemons to remove the zest (you should have about 5 tablespoons zest). Add the zest to the sugar with the juice of ½ lemon, and knead well. The next day, squeeze the lemons (you'll need about 1 cup lemon juice) and add the juice to the sugar and zest. Give this mixture a good rub with your hands to combine. Add 12 cups (2.8 L) cold water, stirring to make sure the sugar dissolves. Strain the mixture through cheesecloth. Refrigerate in a glass pitcher for at least 3 hours, or until the *limonata* is cold. Serve cold, with mint leaves, if desired, pouring carefully from the pitcher into twelve *limonata* glasses (or small parfait glasses).

CLOCKWISE FROM LEFT: *LIMONATA*, SOUMAC SHERBET, AND ROSE SHERBET.

THIS RECIPE is the creation of Atılay Beyoğlu, owner of the famous Atılay Balık Restaurant in Bodrum, the renowned resort town in the south of the Aegean where celebrities like Kate Moss and Beyoncé come for vacation. I loved these sweet cigars at first bite. And they are so easy to make: You just roll the tahini *halva* in the *yufka* and fry. (My version is a little more elaborate.) Chef Beyoğlu serves it with ice cream, which is a very good idea.

Sweet Tahini Cigars

½ sheet *yufka* or 1 sheet of phyllo

5 ounces (140 g) tahini halva (available at Middle Eastern grocers), cut into 12 pieces

3 ½ ounces (100 g) fresh, unsalted cheese, such as ricotta or marscapone, divided into 12 portions

¼ cup (30 g) shelled unsalted pistachios

Corn oil for frying

3 tablespoons confectioners' sugar

1 tablespoon ground cinnamon

Serves 6

Fold the *yufka* or phyllo in half six times, then cut the *yufka* to create twelve wedges (or divide the phyllo sheet into 12 equal pieces). On each section, place a piece of halva and a portion of the cheese at the wide end of the triangle. Sprinkle the pistachios on top. To roll, first secure each horizontal end by overlapping one side of the dough on the halva-cheese filling, then roll up each wedge, but not too tightly. Dip the ends in water to seal them. (Water will make the dough stick together, so the filling will not spill out during frying.)

In a frying pan, heat 1 inch (2.5 cm) of oil until medium hot. Fry the cigars for 3 to 4 minutes, until golden, and drain on paper towels. Sprinkle with the confectioners' sugar and cinnamon and serve immediately.

"ANYONE CAN BANG A DRUM, BUT NOT EVERYONE CAN KEEP TIME WITH THE TUNE."
(Turkish proverb)

EVERYONE IN Turkey makes *halva*, but to give it the right texture requires expertise and patience because no *halva* forgives inattention and impatience. An important food culturally, twenty-six kinds of *halva* are documented in an Ottoman-era manuscript of cookery. It is one sweet always served at celebrations, after funerals, and at religious gatherings like *Mevlüt* (a religious poem about the Prophet Mohammed recited by a beautifully voiced man or woman to celebrate an occasion or commemorate a deceased person of the family). Its aroma while being made is heavenly—one could make it just for the smell—and that's one reason why some must always be sent over to the neighbors when it's done.

Semolina *Halva* with Orange
(*Portakallı İrmik Helvası*)

1 cup (200 g) sugar

½ cup (120 ml) milk

Juice of 1 orange

4 tablespoons (55 g) unsalted butter

2 tablespoons vegetable oil

1 pound (455 g) semolina flour (the finest grind available)

½ cup (60 g) pine nuts

Grated zest of 1 orange

Ground cinnamon

Serves 8 to 10

In a pot, combine 2½ cups (600 ml) water with ¾ cup (150 g) of the sugar and heat until the sugar dissolves. Let cool, then stir in the milk and orange juice.

Heat the butter and oil in a deep pot. As soon as the butter melts, add the semolina and mix well. Cook over medium heat for about 15 minutes, stirring constantly with a wooden spoon, then add the pine nuts. Cook for 10 to 15 minutes, stirring constantly, to toast the semolina (see Note). When the semolina is golden, reduce the heat to very low and add the cooled syrup and the orange zest. Cover the pot and cook for 5 to 6 minutes, until all the liquid is absorbed. (Heating the pot longer than this will burn the bottom of the *halva*.) Sprinkle with the remaining ¼ cup (50 g) sugar, fold the sugar in quickly, and fluff the cooked *halva*. Let the *halva* sit, covered, for 15 minutes, and then serve sprinkled with cinnamon.

Note: The time required for toasting the semolina depends on the heat level, which should never be near high; otherwise, the semolina will get burned, not toasted. Turkish pots have round bottoms, so they are ideal for mixing halva. *If you are a fan of Turkish cuisine, it would be wise to acquire a pot with a round bottom. Many Turkish dishes cook better in such a pot, especially dolma, pilafs, and* halva.

AŞURE (from the Arabic *ashura*) is a special dish made on the tenth day of the Hijri (Islamic) year's first month, Muharram. Since there is no mention of this dish in earlier documents, it must be a late Ottoman period dish, most likely derived from a similar dish called *ekşi aş*, meaning "tangy food," cooked at the time of Sultan Fatih Mehmet, the Conqueror (fifteenth century). *Ekşi aş* was also one of the dishes served to guests at the circumcision banquets given for Şehzade Bayezid and Şehzade Cihangir, sons of Sultan Suleyman the Lawgiver in the sixteenth century. I was served a similar dish in the eastern city of Bayburt. It had all the ingredients—raisins, figs, and sweet plums—mentioned in the documents. This one was made with naturally sour rose hips juice so it was not sweet. It is most likely that this dish has picked up other ingredients like chickpeas and white beans along its journey through Central Asia. The *aşure* made by the Ottoman bourgeoisie was strained according to Dede Eşref's nineteenth-century manuscript.

Since the origin of *aşure* is not clear, it has become commonly known as Noah's Pudding among non-Turkish people. But it is a symbolic dish for Alevi Muslims, who make *aşure* on the tenth day of Muharram, the first month of the Hijri year, to commemorate the tragic killing of Prophet Muhammed's grandson Hüsseyin. The *aşure* made by the Alevis has twelve ingredients to honor the twelve imams who, according to their belief, were divinely inspired. Sunnis, who make up the larger Muslim population in Turkey, do not apply such sacred meaning to the dish, but while the *muhallebi* houses carry *aşure* year round, the whole month of Muharram remains the traditional time for making *aşure*. It has become a way of telling people at least once a year that you are thinking of them. *Aşure* is made in large amounts and is sent to relatives and neighbors and friends the day it is made, its top decorated with nuts and pomegranate seeds.

Turkish Delight (Lokum)

Known around the world, this sugar-based confection is typically presented in small pale pink or green squares that are generously coated in confectioners' sugar. Chopped dates, pistachios, or hazelnuts may be added to Turkish delight, although traditional varieties are typically flavored simply with rose water, mastic, or citrus. The perfect *lokum*, which can be produced expertly only after long years of apprenticeship, should be soft enough to chew effortlessly yet should not stick to the teeth. It should not tickle the throat, but instead should soothe it. This is one reason why in Ottoman times it was called *rahatü-l-hulkum*, which means "throat-soothing."

Tradititionally *lokum*, preferably flavored with mastic, was served to important guests and during religious holidays. In part because of this ritual, and also the master craftsmanship required to make the confection, *lokum* became a highly regarded delicacy that rightly earned the name "Turkish delight." In due course, and largely because of *lokum*, Turkish candymaking became famous worldwide.

Aşure

2½ cups (500 g) hulled wheat berries, washed

FOR THE SHERBET

3½ to 5 cups (750 g to 1 kg) sugar

½ cup (975 g) blanched almonds

½ cup (120 g) precooked white beans

½ cup (120 g) cooked chickpeas

4 or 5 dried apricots, cut into small pieces

3 or 4 dried figs, cut into small pieces

Rind of ½ orange, cut into tiny pieces and boiled for few minutes so that they are not too bitter

2 or 3 fresh bay leaves, if available (do not use dried leaves)

¼ cup (60 ml) natural rose water (see page 18)

TO DECORATE THE TOP

Pomegranate seeds

Walnuts

Sesame seeds

Ground cinnamon (optional)

Serves 14 to 16

Let the washed wheat berries soak in a large pot with plenty of water for at least 3 to 4 hours or overnight. Drain and cover with fresh water. Cook on low heat until the berries open up and have given up all their starch. (They should be overcooked.)

Combine the sugar with 3 quarts (2.8 L) water in a large pot. Bring to a boil over medium heat and cook for 5 minutes. Add the cooked wheat berries, the almonds, beans, chickpeas, orange peel, and bay leaves, if using. Cook the *aşure* over medium heat until it reaches the consistency of olive oil. Add the rose water and let cook 1 minute more. Spoon the dried apricots and figs into a large serving bowl and pour the *aşure* over them. When cool, decorate as you like with the pomegranate seeds, walnuts, sesame seeds, and cinnamon.

Note: Aşure is a communal dish that is meant to be shared with a large group. You may adapt the fruits and nuts as you like; I like to add cooked chestnuts when they're in season.

QUINCE IS beloved in Turkish cuisine. It adds a unique taste to both savory and sweet dishes, like these quince halves baked in syrup, and this versatility has been discovered in many of the country's regions. A good ripe quince is also popular paired with a drink of raki. Not all quinces are soft enough to be eaten raw, however. *Ekmek ayvasi* (literally "bread quince") is a favorite raw, as it is soft. *Limon ayvasi* (literally "lemon quince") is harder, so it is preferred for making jam. This dessert is usually served with *kaymak* (clotted cream), which adds a delicate richness to their taste.

Upside-Down Quince Domes

3 large quinces (each big enough for two people) or 6 small ones

Juice of ½ lemon, plus more for the quince water

2 tart apples, such as Granny Smith, peeled and cut into ½-inch (12-mm) cubes

6 whole cloves

1 pound (455 g) sugar

Serves 6

Preheat the oven to 350°F (175°C).

Peel, halve, and core the large quinces, reserving the removed seeds. (If using small quince, peel and core them as if they will be filled but do not empty them.) Place the quince in plenty of water with lemon juice to avoid browning if you are not using them immediately. Spread the apple cubes in a large baking pan and add the reserved quince seeds and the cloves. Add the quince halves, cored sides up (or whole quince can be placed with the cored hole on top). Mix 1½ cups (360 ml) water with the lemon juice and pour over the quinces. Sprinkle the quinces with the sugar, reserving about 3 tablespoons to sprinkle on later. Bake for 20 minutes, then turn the quince halves dome side up, sprinkle with the reserved 3 tablespoons sugar, and bake for 15 minutes, until the quince are cooked through. (If the halves start to burn on top, cover loosely with foil.) Let cool and serve.

(OPPOSITE) A VARIETY OF TURKISH CANDIES AND *LOKUM*.

portakal draje
55.00 tl/kg.

fındık draje
55.00 tl/kg.

badem draje
55.00 tl/kg.

a.fıstık draje
65.00 tl/kg.

kahve draje
55.00 tl/kg.

badem şekeri
40.00 tl/kg.

jöle
36.00 tl/kg.

THE ROSE is considered a mystical flower in Turkish culture, and even more so in Islamic lore. It is said that the skin of the Prophet Mohammed smelled of roses. Okka roses, which bloom only briefly during the month of May, are the variety used for jam making in Turkey. Their petals are light pink with a violet tone and burst very thickly from the middle of these rather small roses. The petals impart a sweet fragrance to the jam, which can be enjoyed year round in these preserves. You may use whatever variety of rose is available to you, so long as the plants are organic and have not been sprayed with any fertilizer or chemicals, but remember not all roses will give away a scent. It is the mystical scent that makes this jam special.

Rose Petal Jam (*Gül Reçeli*)

10 cups (16 g) trimmed edible (unsprayed) fresh rose petals (see Note)

3 pounds 5 ounces (1.5 kg) sugar

8 to 10 tablespoons (120 to 150 ml) fresh lemon juice

Makes 2.65 pints (1300 ml)

Cut away the white part of the petals close to the center of the flower (they would give a bitter taste to the jam). Put the petals in a colander and rinse very gently to remove any fine dirt. Spread the petals out on a cloth in the shade to dry, then knead the petals with ½ cup (100 g) of the sugar.

Fill a large pot to no more than two-thirds of its capacity with 2 quarts (2 L) water and the remaining sugar. (Choosing the appropriate-size pot saves you from a mess when the jam comes to a boil.) Bring to a boil and continue boiling until the sugar syrup reaches the texture of olive oil when drizzled from a spoon, about 40 minutes, not stirring at all. Add the kneaded petals and cook over medium heat until the texture is a little thicker than olive oil; drops should form at the edge of a wooden spoon. At this point, stir in the lemon juice. This will dilute the jam a little, so cook for 3 to 5 minutes more over medium heat, or until the jam reaches its previous consistency—a little thicker than olive oil. (Take care that the sugar does not caramelize, as this will detract from the aroma and taste of the roses.) Let the jam cool in the pot, then transfer to clean jars of your choice. Cover tightly and store in a cool place, or you can refrigerate the jam. This thickens the jam a little but it loosens up once it is returned to room temperature.

Note: If possible, collect the rose petals directly from an organic rosebush by securing the whole blossom in your palm and gently pulling; the petals will come off cleanly, almost in a stack. Depending on the type of rose, one flower can yield 1 to 2 cups of petals. This method saves a lot of time, as it will make it easier to trim off the white parts of the petals near the stem. With kitchen scissors, cut off the white parts of the petals and discard. If you are not lucky enough to have your own rose garden, look for unsprayed roses at farmers' markets. You may also find dried rose petals in some Latin groceries; online sources tend to be very expensive.

(OPPOSITE) CLOCKWISE FROM TOP LEFT: ROSE PETAL JAM, PEACH JAM, BERGAMOT JAM, AND UNRIPENED WALNUT JAM IN THEIR SOFT PEELS.

TO MAKE Turkish tea, one needs a *çaydanlık*, a pot for boiling water with a big opening for the *demlik*, a much smaller pot where the Turkish tea leaves or orthodox tea (finely crushed leaves) are put for brewing. I have a lot of Turkish tea–loving friends in Italy and the United States who have asked me to send them these two pots along with Turkish tea leaves. No doubt it is a good investment. People love tea offered in tulip-shaped glasses. The transparent red color of Turkish tea warms the heart, while its heat warms minds and souls. It also helps get rid of toxins and aids digestion. It will keep you awake, so you might not want to drink it at night, but it is perfect for mornings. You can purchase Turkish tea and tea-making equipment at Middle Eastern grocers or online.

Turkish Tea

1 quart (960 ml) cold good-quality water

5 to 6 tablespoons (28 to 30 g) Turkish tea leaves or your favorite loose black tea, preferably orthodox

Serves 6 to 8 (two tea glasses per person)

Put 2 cups (480 ml) of the cold water in the *çaydanlık* and the tea leaves in the *demlik*. (Pouring about 3 tablespoons cold water over the tea will hasten the brewing process.) Place the *çaydanlık* on a burner and place the *demlik* on top. When the water boils, pour half of it into the *demlik*. Add about 2 more cups (480 ml) cold water to the *çaydanlık*, and place the *çaydanlık* over medium heat to allow the tea time to steep. When the water boils, pour the tea from the *demlik* through a tea strainer into a tea glass, filling one-fifth of the glass. Fill to four-fifths with boiling water from the *çaydanlık*, leaving the top fifth empty for hands to hold the glass without getting burned. For another round of tea, replace the hot water poured from the *çaydanlık*, then refill the tea glasses. The tea may be drunk for about 40 minutes before getting bitter.

Note: If you'd like to have more than one round of tea, keep the water level in the çaydalık *by adding more water each time you pour a glass.*

A *KURABIYE* is a cookielike pastry that is dome-shaped rather than flat. Etymologically, the name can be traced back to an Arabic term for dome-shaped objects. I like to think that it is connected, nevertheless; *kurabiyes* have a special buttery taste, a crumbly texture, and a festive aura. This is one of the oldest recipes for cookies, and they continue to be made for religious holidays and other important days. In the Ottoman palace kitchens, they were covered with gold leaf, and that fashion continues in the homes of the wealthy even today. My grandmother made the best dome cookies, usually for the Ramadan holiday *(Sheker Bayrami)*. She did it all by hand, and it took her ages of hand-whisking until the butter was as white as snow. I have just enough patience to make these cookies with an electric mixer.

Dome Cookies *(Kurabiye)*

1 pound (4 sticks/455 g) unsalted butter, clarified (see Note)

1⅓ cups (171 g) confectioners' sugar

3 cups (385 g) plus 2 tablespoons all-purpose flour

30 to 32 whole blanched almonds

Makes about 30 cookies

Melt the butter over very low heat until it is melted, but not too runny. Add 1 cup (180 g) of the confectioners' sugar and beat with a mixer for at least 10 minutes, until the butter is white. Add the flour in batches and mix until all the flour is incorporated and a smooth dough forms. (The dough should not stick to your hands.)

Preheat the oven to 350°F (175°C). Take walnut-size pieces of dough, roll them between the palms of your hands into dome-shaped balls, and place on ungreased cookie sheets. If the dough begins to stick, flour your hands and continue. Place an almond on top of each cookie and bake for 20 minutes, or until golden. Let cool on the pans, then generously sprinkle with the remaining ⅓ cup (40 g) confectioners' sugar.

Note: To clarify butter, put the butter in a deep pot and cook over medium heat until it begins to foam. Lower the heat and continue to cook until the foam dies and particles appear on the bottom of the pot. Finish the process when the butter is still golden and has not turned to brown. Watch carefully through the entire process, as butter will quickly burn. (You may clarify a large amount and later use it for pilafs, as it keeps well.)

Two Special Turkish Drinks

AYRAN: No one can miss the sight of a milk-colored glass of *ayran* served at restaurants, cafés, or even at tea gardens. This is a traditional drink that developed from the requirements of nomadic living, making use of everything one had.

Ayran is a by-product of yogurt and is gathered, not purposefully made, when butter is churned from yogurt. During the process of churning, the butter collects on top and the fat-free liquid that collects in the bottom is *ayran*. This is a delectable, healthy, tangy drink that satisfies the thirst and is a favored companion to kebabs, *pide*, and sandwiches. Since churning your own butter is a chore not performed anymore in urban living, finding authentic *ayran* is like finding a gem by chance on the street. There are, however, people like Seref Usta at Kadın Pazarı in Istanbul, who serve it in authentic metal bowls with special deep, round-shaped metal spoons. Nowadays, though, *ayran* is usually drunk from a glass and made by mixing natural yogurt with water. The consistency will be to personal liking but usually salt is added, most likely to make up for the tang missing from yogurt today.

BOZA: A NOURISHING FERMENTED BEVERAGE

A popular fermented beverage traditionally drunk during the cold winter months, *boza* is prepared from grains such as maize, barley, or wheat that are made into dough and then left to ferment. This sour dough is stored in a cool place and the alcohol level is kept under check. *Boza* made in Turkey has an alcohol content of less than 1 percent. *Boza* made in Caucasia, however, can have an alcohol content of between 4 and 6 percent. As it is a fermented drink, it keeps its distinct taste without spoiling. *Boza* is stored and sold in marble or metal containers in order to maintain a constant temperature. Because it contains vitamins A, B^1, B^2, and C, it is widely accepted as a drink that nourishes the body.

Boza was initially made by Central Asian Turks in the tenth century. Its golden age was in the early Ottoman era, when *boza* making became one of the principal urban trades. The reach of the Ottoman Empire carried the tradition of making and drinking *boza* into European countries such as Albania, Bulgaria, and Serbia, where it was very popular.

Boza was drunk freely everywhere until the sixteenth century, but making the so-called Tartar *boza*, which was laced with opium, incurred the wrath of the authorities. Sultan Selim II (1524–1574) prohibited Tartar *boza*. During the Ottoman era, each and every craft and trade had a master overseer. The *boza* makers' master, a man named Sarı ("blond") Saltuk, was also a man revered among Christians for his piousness and spiritual leadership of the Turkmen and Bektashi Alaouites sects.

One of Turkey's most popular *bozas* is Vefa *Boza*, made by a company founded in 1876 by Hacı Sadık Bey. He created the first *boza* brand by trademarking his recipe. Still successful today, Vefa uses the same recipe formulated by the company nearly two centuries ago. The taste created by Hacı Sadık Bey was especially favored by the sultans, who appreciated that it was slightly sweeter than the thin and sour *boza* commonly made by the Armenians at that time. The Ottoman palace preferred white *boza*, which was made from rice. We understand that thicker *boza* was more valued; in the words of Evliya Çelebi, "thick enough to wrap and carry in a handkerchief." It is traditional to sprinkle cinnamon on top of *boza*, and some people like to add a handful of roasted chickpeas (*leblebi*) to the top of their sour drink. *Boza* may be drunk at all hours of the day, morning till midnight—if not later. The Vefa *Boza*, a popular *boza* shop in Istanbul, is full of people of all ages at all hours.

AÇMA, TOGETHER with *simit* and *çatal,* are pastries sold throughout the streets of Istanbul at any time of the day. *Açma* is the croissant of Turkish cuisine; its history goes back to the Turks of Central Asia. Experienced bakers work their magic to produce pastries that are as light as cotton candy. I had to include a recipe for it and tasted many *açmas* to find the best. I finally decided to work with a master at his humble bakery. Here is the result.

Açma

....

Scant 8 cups (1 kg) good bread flour, plus more as needed

2¼ cups (540 ml) water—or 1¼ cups (300 ml) water mixed with 1 cup (240 ml) milk—that is hot, but not too hot, to the touch

2 ounces (60 g) fresh, wet yeast

Heaping 3¾ cups (100 g) Confectioners' sugar

4 tablespoons corn oil

1 heaping teaspoon mahlep (see page 17)

1 tablespoon salt

4 tablespoons (50 g) butter, softened

1 egg yolk, beaten

1 tablespoon nigella seeds

Makes 12 to 14 pieces of açma

Place the flour in a bowl and make a well in the middle. Pour in half of the water or water-and-milk mixture; add the yeast and sugar to the liquid, mixing well with your hands. Add the oil, mahlep, and salt to the liquid and mix well. Pull in the flour and start kneading. Add the rest of the water gradually to make a very soft dough. (The dough is very sticky, so you should keep a dish of extra flour to the side to dip your hands in while working.)

Tip the dough out onto a floured wooden surface, cover with a light cloth, and let it stand in an area away from drafts for 30 to 40 minutes, or until doubled in size. Roll the raised dough out to no more than 1 inch (2.5 cm) thickness. Spread the softened butter over the entire surface and fold the dough in two, buttered side in.

Divide the dough into 20 pieces and roll each piece into a stick, 1 inch (2.5 cm) in diameter and 5 inches (12 cm) long. Make a bracelet-size hoop from each, pressing the ends together tightly. Brush generously with egg yolk and let stand at least 1 hour or until doubled in size.

Preheat the oven to 425°F (220°C). Sprinkle the tops of the *açma* with the nigella seeds and bake for 20 to 25 minutes, until golden brown.

KATMER IS a favorite traditional pastry. It is rustic and can accompany jams and honey. The addition of walnuts and sugar make it crunchy and more exciting.

Layered *Yufka* (*Katmer*)

½ ounce (15 g) fresh, wet yeast

1 teaspoon sugar, plus 5 tablespoons (60 g) for sprinkling

⅓ cup (75 g) nearly hot water

2 cups (255 g) plus 1 tablespoon all-purpose flour, plus more if needed

1 teaspoon salt

¼ cup (100 g) unsalted butter, melted

4 tablespoons (60 ml) tahini

Serves 6 to 8

Dissolve the yeast and 1 teaspoon of the sugar in the nearly hot water and wait until it foams. Put the flour in a bowl, make a well in the center, and add the salt and the yeast mixture. Knead until the dough is uniform and feels softer than an earlobe but leaves the hands clean. If the dough sticks to your hands, gradually add a little more flour, or add 2 to 4 tablespoons more water if the dough is too stiff. (Each type of flour has a different absorption rate.) Cover the bowl with a clean cloth and let sit in a warm place until the dough rises by one-third, about 45 minutes (the exact rising time will depend on the temperature of your surroundings).

Flour a work surface and roll out the dough with a rolling pin to form a circle with a 20-inch (50-cm) diameter. Generously brush the dough's surface with the butter and tahini, then evenly sprinkle with the remaining 5 tablespoons (60 g) sugar. Make a hole, 2 inches (5 cm) in diameter, in the middle of the dough. With your hands, beginning at the hole and working out to the circumference, roll the dough until you have a circle about 22 inches (55 cm) in diameter.

Cut the circle into four equal pieces and, without lifting the dough from the table, roll each piece into a round. With the rolling pin, roll each round into a disc 4 to 5 inches (10 to 12 cm) in diameter.

Cook the pastries in a pan over medium to low heat without oil or butter, 3 minutes per side, or until brown spots appear all over both sides. Serve hot or warm.

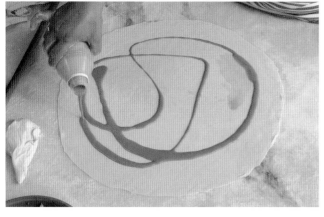

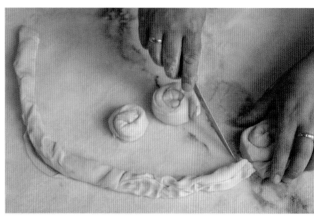

I ENCOUNTERED a recipe for this pastry in a manuscript of Ottoman recipes. Coincidentally, I found a similar regional recipe from southeastern Turkey called *şıllık,* a Turkish term used for women who dress too fancily. Perhaps the fanciness of this dessert inspired folks to give it this regional name instead of the name used in the palace. In the traditional recipe, the dough of this crêpelike pastry is made with yeast. I decided to replace the dough with crêpe batter instead since crêpes are now popular on Turkish tables. Ottoman Turks were one of the first peoples to experience globalization in their food culture; consider this another small contribution.

Crêpes with Tahini and Pekmez (*Petule*)

5 tablespoons (75 ml) tahini

1 tablespoon sugar

6 to 7 tablespoons (90 to 105 ml) pekmez (see page 18)

12 crêpes (recipe follows)

½ cup (55 g) walnut pieces

1 teaspoon ground cinnamon

1 tablespoon sugar (optional)

Serves 8

Mix together the tahini, sugar, and pekmez and brush onto the crêpes. Roll each crêpe tightly, then cut into 1-inch (2.5-cm) square pieces. In an ovenproof serving dish, arrange the cut crêpe squares snugly next to one another, with the cut ends facing up. (This looks pretty and is suggested in the Ottoman recipe.) Sprinkle with the walnut pieces. Cover with foil and bake for 12 to 15 minutes, until they are warm (1 minute more or less will not make a difference). Serve warm with a sprinkle of cinnamon and sugar, if using. (Sugar particles will enhance the texture.)

Crêpes

4 large eggs

2 ½ cups (600 ml) milk, plus more if needed

2 cups (255 g) all-purpose flour

4 tablespoons (55 g) unsalted butter, melted

½ teaspoon salt

Serves 8

Mix the eggs in a food processor or blender, gradually adding 1 cup (240 ml) of the milk. Mix in 1 cup (130 g) of the flour. Alternating, add the remaining 1½ cups (360 ml) milk and 1 cup (130 g) flour. (This method creates a smoother, more uniform batter.) Mix in the melted butter and salt. Preheat a crêpe pan or a skillet no more than 8 inches (22 cm) in diameter until hot, remove it from the heat, and slowly pour about ¼ cup (60 ml) of batter to cover the bottom of the pan very thinly. Tilt the pan back and forth to spread it evenly. (If you are using a crepe maker, it is domed, so its shape will help to disperse the batter.) Once bubbles appear on the dough, carefully flip the crepe using a flexible spatula. Cook the other side for about 30 seconds, then slide it onto a plate. Make sure you have two plates to stack them up; otherwise the hot crepes will stick to each other. (Thinner crepes yield the best results, so try to make the crepes as thin as possible. To thin the batter, add a little milk.) Repeat with the rest of the batter, using ¼ cup (60 ml) of the batter to make each crepe.

THIS SWEET yeast bread used to be made in the homes of Istanbul's Christian population at Eastertime, as its name *Paskalya* suggests (*Paskalya* means Easter in Turkish). It eventually became a specialty of Turkish bakeries that is popular among Muslims and Christians alike. The mastic used in this precious legacy of the Ottoman Christians is a reflection of the empire's means and the palace's cuisine. *Paskalya çöreği* is a type of *çörek* (sweet breads eaten on their own as snacks) that can now be found at bakeries throughout the year, not just during Easter.

Easter Sweet Bread (*Paskalya Çöreği*)

2 ounces (55 g) fresh, wet yeast

1 teaspoon sugar

6 tablespoons (90 ml) nearly hot water

6 ¾ cups (880 g) all-purpose flour

1½ teaspoons mahlep (see page 17)

1 chickpea-size piece of mastic (see page 16) ground with a mortar and pestle with 1 teaspoon sugar

5 large eggs, at room temperature

Pinch of salt

1½ cups (300 g) sugar

1 cup (2 sticks/455 g) unsalted butter

1 large egg yolk for brushing

Serves 6 to 8

Dissolve the yeast and the 1 teaspoon sugar in the hot water and wait until it foams. Add to 1½ cups (200 g) of the flour and knead until smooth. Cover the dough with a clean cloth and let sit in a warm area until the dough doubles in size, about 45 minutes. Add the remaining 5¼ cups (680 g) flour, the mahlep, and mastic and knead until smooth.

With a mixer, beat the whole eggs with the salt, the 1½ cups (300 g) sugar, and butter until the mixture whitens, then add to the dough. Knead for 3 to 4 minutes, until the dough is elastic. Let sit, covered, in a warm area until it doubles in size, 45 minutes to 1 hour.

Knead gently so that the dough falls. Divide the dough equally into six pieces, then divide each into three portions to create eighteen in all. Roll each section into a 6-inch (15-cm) length and braid three of them together to create six braids in all. Let sit, covered, on a baking sheet in a warm area until they double in size, about 1 to 2 hours, and then brush with the egg yolk.

Preheat the oven to 400°F (210°C).

Bake for about 30 minutes, or until golden. Served warm or at room temperature. This bread keeps well if covered.

Turkish coffee is made in a special pot called a cezve with a wide bottom, narrower neck, a long handle, and a spout and served in miniature teacups, known as *finjans*, which are narrow at the bottom and wider at the top. The cups are always made of porcelain and they hold ¼ cup coffee at most. A copper cezve yields the best results. There are different sizes of cezve available, manufactured according to the number of *finjan* of coffee you plan to make. For the best results, choose the correct size. The heat level is also key: Good coffee is made over very low heat. This gives the water time to really absorb the flavor and aroma of the ground beans. (In the old days, coffee was always made over a charcoal fire.) Today's Turkish coffeemakers, on the other hand, are programmed to make a delicious Turkish coffee.

To make a successful cup, Turkish coffee must be made from a special finely ground coffee. Everyone in the household used to take turns grinding this coffee in hand grinders. Nowadays everyone buys their coffee from special coffee sellers already ground. These purveyors roast the beans and will grind them on request or sell the beans already ground in sealed packages. Coffee for espresso or drip machines will not work for making Turkish coffee.

During the Ottoman Empire's reign, coffee was made from mocha beans brought from the port of Mocha in Yemen. But today, as elsewhere, it is mostly made from Arabica beans, usually from Brazil or Colombia, although recently, certain coffee-selling shops have started carrying the more delicate-tasting mocha beans. Why one *finjan* of coffee differs from another depends most of all on the roast of the beans. Some people like a very dark roast, while others prefer a medium or light roast.

Turkish coffee is referred to as "with foam" or "without foam," but there are also four main tastes that designate the amount of sugar desired (see "How Much Sugar Do You Fancy?" below). Foaminess is achieved by pouring the foam from the cezve into the *finjan* when the coffee is about to boil (this also

adding the rest of the coffee, close to the edge of the *finjan*, right when it boils. The proverb "A *finjan* of bitter coffee has a memory of forty years" stems from the time when coffee was a precious commodity and was served in the most elaborate way, honoring those who were served. In the homes of government members and the rich, there would be a fancily uniformed coffee master who was followed by two helpers. The coffee was offered with special ceremony, poured from silver ewers into the finest china *finjans* enclosed in silver holders *(zarfs)*. (The sultan's *finjans* were inlayed with precious gems.) In rural areas, the *agas*, who owned a lot of land and were almost the sultans of their area, would periodically have coffee boiled in cauldrons to offer to all the people far and near. Coffee at this period was made by boiling it for hours, in the Arabic style, so that it became almost bitter (thus the proverb). It was such an event that many people from neighboring areas would travel on horseback to attend.

HOW MUCH SUGAR DO YOU FANCY?

Here's how to order a *finjan* of Turkish coffee with the amount of sugar you desire.

SADE: No sugar

AZ ŞEKERLI: ½ to 1 teaspoon sugar

ORTA: 1 to 1½ teaspoons sugar

ŞEKERLI: 1½ to 2 teaspoons sugar

When making Turkish coffee, the cold water is measured, the sugar (if any) and the coffee are added, the two (or three) ingredients are mixed well and then heated, and the cooking is finished as you stand over the pot. When the coffee foams, and looks like it's about to run over, it must be pulled away from the heat source immediately. For those who like foam, you gently pour this foam into the *finjan* and let the rest of the coffee mixture come to a boil once again. To fill more than one *finjan* in a single batch, the foam is divided among the *finjans*. Dividing holds true for the rest of the contents of coffee and residue. For those who like coffee without foam, the coffee has to be boiled for at least a minute as you pull the pot back and forth and stir.

Since Turkish coffee is drunk slowly like wine, there is always time for the residue to sink down to the bottom of the *finjan*. At home, coffee is served on a small tray along with a small glass of water. The water is customarily drunk first so that you get full satisfaction out of the coffee. The coffee residue is left in the bottom of the cup. This led to the practice of fortune reading based on the residue left in *finjans*. After several minutes, when the bottom of the *finjan* is cold, the fortune-teller will take it in her hands and tell you what she sees in the cup.

Coffee has long been an important offering in Turkey. It gained special importance in the seventeenth century, when it began to be enjoyed not just in coffee shops but at home. It was offered to guests of importance along with Turkish delight. And drinking a *finjan* of coffee at about eleven o'clock, or mid-morning, which is called *kuÐluk vakti*, became a tradition that is followed even today. The *finjans* during the Ottoman period were held in special outer cups made of gold or silver inlaid with precious gems. Many of these wares may be viewed today at Topkapi Palace. To witness the pomp and circumstance surrounding what today is a part of daily life is an interesting experience.

Today coffee is drunk at *kuşluk* or any time of the day, and when two people get together, whether at home or outside, they will have a *finjan* of coffee. One can order a cup of coffee in any café or restaurant. They will always ask you whether you'd like sugar or not, but if you'd like your cup with foam or no foam, you must request it.

THIS COFFEE drink may rightly be called indigenous to Turkey because it is made with Turkish-grind coffee, which is very finely ground—almost as fine as cocoa powder. It is served like tea in Turkish tea glasses, not in the *finjans* described above. These tulip-shaped glasses make hot tea or coffee with milk easy to hold. I love to drink it before going to bed. I find that the little bit of coffee does not keep me awake, and the hot milk is very soothing and makes me ready for sleep. This recipe makes enough coffee to fill one Turkish tea glass. In order to make it, you will need a special copper coffee pot called a *cezve* (see details above). These can be purchased online for a modest price, as can the tea glasses. (Alternatively, I've provided instructions for making this drink in a diminuitive saucepan, but the *cezve* will yield the best results.)

Turkish Coffee with Milk

1 small tea glass of milk (⅓ cup/75 ml)

½ heaping teaspoon Turkish coffee

Sugar (optional)

Put the milk in a *cezve* or in a small pan used for heating milk. Add the coffee and, if desired, sugar to taste. Cook over medium heat, stirring constantly. When the milk rises up, pour into a tea glass and serve.

Acknowledgments

This book is the result of the support, spirit, and efforts of my maternal grandmother, a memorable *"Hanım ağa"* of Ula and a top-level chef; my beautiful mother, a perfectionist in her cooking; my father, who taught me to enjoy new foods at any time (like botarga for breakfast); my entire extended family, who always rejoiced in food and making each *sofra*—a table spread with food is always called a *sofra*, a word making it special—a spontaneous degustation session; and many other people. I am obliged to mention some who have empowered me with their support.

I would like to express my deepest thanks to Halise Akıncı for sharing recipes accumulated over her ninety-three-year life; Sultan Yalçın, who passed on the old family recipes; Döndü Dazkırılı for being a most helpful assistant in the kitchen; Zeynep Taymas, who provided special props for the photo session; award-winning film director Yüksel Aksu, for sharing invaluable information of the last of the Turcoman tribes; Sarikecililer in Anatolia, a nomadic group who have kept alive the unique culture of nomadic Turkish tribes; Vedat Başaran, Turkey's gastronomy leader, for sharing his invaluable archives; my lovely friend Anita Benadrete for her delicious Georgian chicken recipe; Ruti Levi for the recipe for the best *tarama* I have ever tasted; Guiletta Şavul for sending me the Jewish recipes from İzmir; Aspasia Israfil, who helped me understand the ingredients found in the United States that could be substituted in Turkish dishes; chefs Şirvan Payasli (master of authentic Gaziantep kebabs), Feridun Ügümü, Tahsin Kurtlu, and Aydin Demir, who have successfully promoted Turkish food for many years through their passionate, professional cooking; Civan Er and Emre Sen for sharing recipes created with their passion for a futuristic Turkish cuisine; and last but not least chef Carlo Bernardini, for interpreting Turkish dishes through his expertise of Venetian cooking. My most heartful thanks go to Gürsel Göncü, for sharing his research on Turkish fish culture in the period of Ottoman Empire for this book. Special thanks to Galip Yorgancıoğlu for sharing his knowledge on Turkish wine.

Many grateful thanks go to my ever-so-true friend Filiz Hösüköğlu for answering in detail my never-ending questions about one of most important culinary centers of Turkey, Gaziantep. I am forever indebted to the late Dun Gifford, the founder of Oldways Foundation, one of the first people to show confidence in my cooking and Turkish cuisine, and Sara Bear-Sinnot for her support of my works. Thanks also to esteemed American writers Deborah Dunn, Melissa Clark, and Paula Wolfert, who have helped my book come alive with their enthusiasm at my dinner table and their unflagging support of Turkish cuisine abroad, and encouraged me by giving space to my food in their articles or books; London chefs Samuel and Samantha Clark, whose admiration for Turkish food helped me create new tastes; esteemed writer Barrie Kerper, for publishing my musings on the subtleties of Turkish cooking in her book *Istanbul: The Collected Traveler*; and last but not least, Dana Cowin, editor of *Food & Wine* magazine, who featured my recipes and thus made it possible for Turkish cuisine to gain worldwide recognition long before it was recognized by other publications.

I thoroughly enjoyed working with my photographers Helen Cathcart and Bekir İşcen, and without doubt their beautiful photographs give a wonderful dimension to my book. I am grateful to Kari Stuart for supporting me all the way and finding me the best publisher, and also Lauren Zelin who, after spending her honeymoon in Ula cooking with me, introduced me to Kari Stuart. Thank you to my team at Abrams, Camaren Subhiyah, Holly Dolce, Sally Knapp, and True Sims, and to Kimberly Glyder for her beautiful design. My ever-grateful thanks to my editor Marisa Bulzone for her sensitivity and precision over the text and recipes, and of course esteemed cooking expert and author Anya von Bremzen, an expert in Turkish cuisine through years of unending interest in Turkish dishes, who not only helped to present the recipes in this book, but also so kindly and generously provided the foreword, which has brought tears to my eyes. *Engin Akın*

Sources

THE MAJORITY of the ingredients for the recipes in this book can be found at your local farmers' market, in supermarkets, and in the various ethnic and Middle Eastern grocery stores across the United States and Europe. Here are some sources for the best quality spices and other foods that may be difficult to find in your neighborhood.

Alteya Organics
(312) 528-9161
(877) 425-8392
www.alteya.com

Amazon Grocery
www.amazon.com

Aphrodite Greek Imports
5886 Leesburg Pike
Falls Church, VA 22041
(703) 931-5055

Arabica Food & Spice
Company
Arch 257 Grosvenor Court
Grosvenor Terrace
London SE5 0NP UK
+44 (0) 20 7708 5577
www.arabicafoodandspice.
com
*online ordering and other
retail locations throughout
the UK and Europe*

Asadur's Market
5536 Randolph Road
Rockville, MD 20852
(301) 770-5558

Best Turkish Food
165 Prairie Lake Road,
Suite G
East Dundee, IL 60118
(866) 969-3663
www.bestturkishfood.com

Dayna's Market
26300 Ford Road,
Suite 239
Dearborn Heights, MI
48127
(313) 999-1980
www.daynasmarket.com

Formaggio Kitchen
244 Huron Avenue
Cambridge, MA 02138
(888) 212-3224
www.formaggiokitchen.com
*good source of specialty
peppers like Maraş and
Urfa, and dried herbs and
spices like Tuscan fennel
pollen*

igourmet.com
508 Delaware Avenue
West Pittston, PA 18643
(877) 446-8763
www.igourmet.com
*molasses, shelled pistachios,
and so on*

Kalamala
15900 Blythe Street
Van Nuys, CA 91406
(855) 525-2625
www.kalamala.com
*online Middle Eastern
grocery*

Kalustyan's
123 Lexington Avenue
New York, NY 10016
(800) 352-3451
www.kalustyans.com

Mediterranean Bakery (and
Store)
3362 Chamblee-Tucker
Road
Atlanta, GA 30341
(770) 220-0706
www.mediterranean-bakery.
com

Melissa's/World Variety
Produce
PO Box 514599
Los Angeles, CA 90051
(800) 588-0151
www.melissas.com

Penzeys Spices
12001 W Capitol Drive
Wauwatosa, WI 53222
(800) 741-7787
www.penzeys.com

Sahadi's
187 Atlantic Avenue
Brooklyn, NY 11201
(718) 624-4550
www.sahadis.com

Sepette
British Columbia, Canada
Toll-free (855) 370-3044
www.sepette.ca/en/
*Canadian online retailer;
importer of Mediterranean
foods, including spices
and prepared foods, and
kitchenware such as Turkish
coffee sets*

Shamra
2650 University Blvd.
Wheaton, MD 20902
(301) 942-9726
www.shamra.com

The Spice House
1941 Central Street
Evanston, IL 60201
(847) 328-3711
www.thespicehouse.com

Tulumba
129 15th Street
Brooklyn, NY 11215
(718) 369-8904
(866) 855-8622
www.tulumba.com

World Spice Merchants
1509 Western Avenue
Seattle, WA 98101
(206) 682-7274
www.worldspice.com

Zamouri Spices
1250 N. Winchester Blvd.
Olathe, KS 66061
(913) 829-5988
www.zamourispices.com

Index

ENGIN AKIN lives in Istanbul, Turkey, and is author of the Turkish cookbooks *Çadırdan Saraya Osmanlı Türk Mutfağı* and *Turkish Greek Cuisine*. A global ambassador for Turkish cuisine who has been featured in publications throughout the world, she has written and hosted *Taste Chats (Tat Muhabbetleri)*, a food program on Turkey's Open Radio *(Açık Radyo)*, for the last ten years. She also writes the Gourmet column for Turkey's *Vatan* newspaper. Akin enjoys hosting foreign guests and preparing Turkish food for them at her family home in Ula, where she also teaches Turkish cooking.